Justification by Faith

Justification by Faith

by
John MacArthur, Jr.

MOODY PRESS
CHICAGO

Moody Press Edition, 1985
Original title: *Justified by Faith*

All Scripture quotations, unless otherwise noted, are from the *New Scofield Reference Bible*, King James Version, © 1967 by Oxford Univeristy Press, Inc. Reprinted by permission.

Library of Congress Cataloging in Publication Data

MacArthur, John F.
    Justification by faith.

    (John MacArthur's Bible studies)
    "Romans 3:20-4:25"—Cover.
    Previously published as: Justified by faith.
1984.
    Includes index.
    1. Bible. N.T. Romans III, 20-IV, 25—Criticism, interpretation, etc. 2. Salvation—Biblical teaching.
3. Justification—Biblical teaching. I. Title.
II. Series: MacArthur, John F. Bible studies.
BS2665.2.M2 1986   227'.107   85-29808
ISBN 0-8024-5120-9 (pbk.)

2 3 4 5 6 7 Printing/EP/Year 91 90 89 88 87 86

Printed in the United States of America

Contents

CHAPTER   PAGE

1. False Elements Added to Salvation   7
   Tape GC 45-28—Rom. 3:20-31

2. How to Be Right with God—Part 1   24
   Tape GC 45-29—Rom. 3:21-22*a*

3. How to Be Right with God—Part 2   40
   Tape GC 45-30—Rom. 3:21-25*a*

4. How Christ Died for God—Part 1   55
   Tape GC 45-31—Rom. 3:25-26

5. How Christ Died for God—Part 2   70
   Tape GC 45-32—Rom. 3:27-28

6. How Christ Died for God—Part 3   96
   Tape GC 45-33—Rom. 3:29-31

7. Abraham—Justified by Faith—Part 1   112
   Tape GC 45-34—Rom. 4:1-3

8. Abraham—Justified by Faith—Part 2   125
   Tape GC 45-35—Rom. 4:3

9. Abraham—Justified by Faith—Part 3   139
   Tape GC 45-36—Rom. 4:4-8

10. Abraham—Justified by Grace—Part 1   155
    Tape GC 45-37—Rom. 4:9-12

11. Abraham—Justified by Grace—Part 2   170
    Tape GC 45-38—Rom. 4:13-17

12. Salvation by Divine Power—Not Human Effort   183
    Tape GC 45-39—Rom. 4:18-25

    Scripture Index   198

These Bible studies are taken from messages delivered by Pastor-Teacher John MacArthur, Jr., at Grace Community Church in Panorama City, California. The recorded messages themselves may be purchased as a series or individually. Please request the current price list by writing to:

WORD OF GRACE COMMUNICATIONS
P.O. Box 4000
Panorama City, CA 91412

Or call the following toll-free number:
1-800-55-GRACE

1
False Elements Added to Salvation

Outline

Introduction
A. A Foundational Survey
  1. Salvation is apart from the law
  2. Grace establishes the law
B. The Forbidden Separation
  1. Salvation from lordship
    a) An artificial dichotomy
    b) An affirmation of dominion
      (1) John 20:28
      (2) Romans 10:9
      (3) Acts 2:36
      (4) 1 Corinthians 12:3
  2. Faith from obedience
    a) The teaching of the grace of God
      (1) James S. Stewart
      (2) John Calvin
      (3) C. J. Spurgeon
    b) The theology of the grace of God
    c) The transformation by the grace of God
      (1) Dead in sin
      (2) Saved by grace
      (3) Created for good works

Lesson
I. The Manifestation of Gracious Salvation
  A. The Content of Salvation
    1. The positional reality
    2. The practical reality
  B. The Completeness of Salvation
II. The False Effort of Human Religion
  A. Philosophy
    1. The strategy of philosophy
    2. The source of philosophy
    a) The tradition of men
    b) The rudiments of the world
  B. Ritualism

1. The true circumcision
2. The triumph of the cross
C. Legalism
   1. The imposition of the Judaizers
   2. The identification of the standards
      a) Food or drink
      b) Days of the week
D. Mysticism
   1. The recognition of mysticism
      a) The center of heresy
      b) The claim of higher knowledge
         (1) Delighting in humility
         (2) Worshiping angels
         (3) Taking a stand on visions
   2. The result of mysticism
E. Asceticism
   1. The perversion of self-denial
   2. The preoccupation of self-worship

Introduction

A. A Foundational Survey

Salvation is the heart of the Roman epistle. By way of a survey, I want us to look at Romans 3:20-31 in order to lay a foundation for our study.

1. Salvation is apart from the law

I believe that we see the transition in Paul's thinking in verse 20 rather than in verse 21. Paul says, "Therefore, by the deeds of the law there shall no flesh be justified in his sight." No one is redeemed or made just—declared righteous before God— through some effort of law keeping by the flesh or by his own humanness. Verse 20 continues, "For by the law is the knowledge of sin. But now the righteousness of God apart from the law is manifested" (vv. 20*b*-21*a*). Salvation is not a matter of maintaining some religious law in the flesh, but righteousness (or salvation) is apart from the law. Verse 21 continues, "Being witnessed by the law and the prophets." That means that it is revealed in Scripture. Verse 22 says, "Even the righteousness of God which is by faith of Jesus Christ unto all and upon all them that believe; for there is no difference. For all have sinned, and come short of the glory of God, being justified freely by his grace through the redemption that is in Christ Jesus" (vv. 22-24).

The point of all of that is that you can't become saved by keeping the law. The Gentile cannot become saved by a fleshly effort to maintain the law of his conscience. The Jewish person cannot save himself by a fleshly effort to live up to the written law given to him through the Old Testament. The law has the

8

effect of showing us our sin, but we cannot keep it to the satisfaction of God in order to be granted salvation. Salvation and justification are apart from the law. They are given to us as a free gift through grace granted in Christ Jesus (v. 24).

Verse 28 continues the thought that we want to emphasize, "Therefore, we conclude that a man is justified [declared righteous] by faith apart from the deeds of the law." In other words, salvation occurs apart from some human effort to live up to the divine standard. You can't do it. All have sinned and come short. We are all incapable of reaching the standard; therefore, salvation must come another way, and it comes through the grace granted in Christ.

2. Grace establishes the law

Verse 31 says, "Do we then make void the law through faith?" In other words, if we cannot be saved by keeping the law of God in our flesh, does that mean that we are under no obligation to pay attention to the law? The answer is, "God forbid; yea, we establish the law" (v. 31*b*). That is a very broad statement, and I want to draw one thought out of it for our thinking. When a person becomes redeemed, there is never a separation between grace and law. That is a major fallacy in the thinking of many people. They want so much to purify grace that they make salvation all of grace with no responsibility or obligation. That is an effort to maintain what some have chosen to call supergrace. But grace and gracious salvation never make the law null and void—they establish the law.

That statement has all kinds of interpretive ramifications, but just one is our focus. Becoming a Christian by grace does not remove from us the obligation to obey God. Paul is saying that you cannot save yourself by your good works, but he is not saying to give up and never do good works. When you come to Christ and are justified and when you are implanted with the Holy Spirit, He then can and will produce in you those good works. It is then that you will establish and fulfill the law. That is very important for us to understand.

B. The Forbidden Separation

1. Salvation from lordship

When people want to completely separate grace from law, the logical step that follows is to separate the saviorhood of Christ from His lordship. As a result, they affirm that Jesus Christ is Savior and received purely as Savior with no other thing required for salvation. Then hopefully, at a later time, you will acknowledge Him as Lord and get on with the issue of obedience.

a) An artificial dichotomy

Now that is not germane to salvation—it is an artificial dichotomy that is not biblical. It is an effort to maintain

9

pure grace. But I think it is an ill-advised effort. There are people today who tell us that all one has to do is receive Jesus as Savior and that there doesn't need to be any manifest change in his life as a result of his salvation.

In fact, one writer says, "Believers who become agnostics are still saved; they are still born again. You can even become an atheist; but if you once accepted Christ as Savior, you cannot lose your salvation, even though you deny God" (R. B. Thieme, *Apes and Peacocks or the Pursuit of Happiness* [Houston, Texas: Berachah Church, 1973], p. 23). But 2 Timothy 2:12 says, "If we deny him, he also will deny us." So that writer is saying you can be saved and have absolutely no manifestation of it. Is that true? I don't think so.

b) An affirmation of dominion

If salvation means that the life of God is planted in the soul of man, there has to be some revelation of that life, just as there was manifestation of the life of evil before. When we teach (whether it is Matthew, or Romans, or any other book in the New Testament—even in comparison to the Old Testament), we teach that when a person comes to Christ, he receives Him as Savior and Lord, and that genuine salvation demands a commitment to the lordship of Christ. Now we don't always follow through in the way we should, but there needs to be a willingness on our part to turn from our sin and accept the responsibility to live under the lordship of Christ.

(1) John 20:28—Thomas had the right understanding when he said, "My Lord and my God." When he saw who Jesus was, he instantly affirmed that Jesus had absolute dominion and sovereignty over his life.

(2) Romans 10:9—"That if thou shalt confess with thy mouth the Lord Jesus, and shalt believe in thine heart that God hath raised Him from the dead, thou shalt be saved." That verse is based on Joel 2:32. The word "Lord" is the Hebrew word *Yahweh*—the very name for the sovereign ruler of the universe, Jehovah God Himself. Salvation is an affirmation of the sovereignty of God in my life through the mediator Jesus Christ. That is not adding works to salvation; that is a recognition of who God is.

(3) Acts 2:36—Peter, in his first sermon at the birth of the church, after the Holy Spirit had descended upon the believers, said, "Therefore, let all the house of Israel know assuredly, that God hath made that same Jesus, whom ye have crucified, both Lord and Christ." He is Lord.

(4) 1 Corinthians 12:3—"No man speaking by the Spirit of

God calleth Jesus accursed; and that no man can say that Jesus is the Lord, but by the Holy Spirit.'' That verse has reference to salvation. Nobody can be saved except through the agency of the Holy Spirit. Nobody can make the proper insight into who Christ is except by the Holy Spirit. Nobody will truly understand Jesus except by the Holy Spirit. So when the Spirit does His work in someone's life, he will say, "Jesus is the Lord."

There is no reason to dichotomize the saving work of Christ from His lordship—you do a disservice to His person, and you miss the message of true salvation.

2. Faith from obedience

In the Bible there is no way that you could ever separate faith from obedience. Romans 1:5 says, "We have received grace and apostleship, for obedience to the faith among all nations." In other words, as an apostle, Paul was proclaiming to the nations the obedience of faith. There is no such thing as a faith that has no obedience. There is no such thing as a salvation that does not acknowledge the lordship of Jesus Christ.

Yet when I have taught that, people have accused me of teaching a works salvation. In fact, when I was preaching in south Florida some years ago, I was often attacked in that regard. People would say, "You're teaching a works salvation because you're saying that you have to confess and repent of your sin, embrace Christ as Lord, and commit your life to be obedient to Him. That's a works salvation. It adulterates pure grace." I think they have a nice motive in trying to maintain the purity of grace, but in so doing I think they have emasculated the doctrine of salvation.

a) The teaching of the grace of God

Titus 2:11 says, "For the grace of God that bringeth salvation hath appeared to all men, teaching us that, denying ungodiness and worldly lusts, we should live soberly, righteously, and godly, in this present age, looking for that blessed hope, and the glorious appearing of the great God and our Savior, Jesus Christ" (vv. 11-13). In theological terms, there is no such thing as regeneration apart from sanctification. Regeneration must be the initiation of the sanctification process. When the grace of God appears to us, the first thing that it does is teach us to deny ungodliness. Verse 14 says, "Who gave himself for us that he might redeem us from all iniquity, and purify unto himself a people of his own." Purification of life, submission to the lordship of Christ, and obedience mark true salvation.

I've experienced opposition to that statement. I have received letters saying that I pervert the gospel. But I'm in good company.

(1) James S. Stewart

James S. Stewart said, "Men and movements have so often given the impression that the acceptance of the lordship of Christ is a second experience of grace, or a sort of optional addendum to the Christian life. So great has been this perversion that many congregations are astounded when they hear the true gospel of the lordship of Christ. They believe we are preaching a new gospel" (*Defective Evangelism*, p. 20).

(2) John Calvin

John Calvin said, "Therefore Christ justifies no one whom He does not at the same time sanctify . . . those whom He justifies, He sanctifies" (*Institutes* 3.16.1). What does that mean? It means that when you are redeemed, the result will be a holy life pattern. And if it isn't there, then there was no real justification.

(2) C. H. Spurgeon

Spurgeon said, "Salvation would be a sadly incomplete affair if it did not deal with this part of our ruined estate. We want to be purified as well as pardoned. Justification without sanctification would not be salvation at all" (*All of Grace* [Chicago: The Bible Institute Colportage Assoc., n.d.] p. 34).

b) The theology of the grace of God

The doctrine of salvation in Scripture is very clear. God saves us by grace through faith, not human effort. But part of God's gracious work is to bring us to repentance, confession, and submission to the lordship of Christ. Why do some people have such a hard time allowing that to be the gracious work of God? When I say that I believe the Bible teaches that you have to repent of your sin, that doesn't mean that I have decided to repent of my sin all by myself. No. That is a gracious work of God as much as any other thing. When I say you need to submit yourself to the lordship of Christ in salvation, that does not mean that I do that in my flesh; it means that God produces submission in me through His gracious act of salvation. Justification is the initiating of the sanctifying (or purifying) process, and it begins with turning from sin to God (Acts 20:21). Anything less is religious reformation. And people who religiously reform become "swept, and garnished" (Matt. 12:44*b*)—but they are still empty. Seven more spirits come back, and the end is worse than the beginning (Matt. 12:45). So when someone says that salvation is by grace through faith, I believe that.

c) The transformation by the grace of God

I also believe that in the gracious work of God, there is a

transformation of an individual's nature. That is so beautifully summed up in Ephesians 2.

(1) Dead in sin

Verse 1 begins, "And you . . . who were dead in trespasses and sins; in which in times past ye walked according to the course of this world, according to the prince of the power of the air, the spirit that now worketh in the sons of disobedience . . . in the lusts of our flesh, fulfilling the desires of the flesh and of the mind, and were by nature the children of wrath" (vv. 1-3). That is a pitiful picture. People without Christ are dead in sin and are controlled by lust, evil desire, and the reasonings of their own irrational mind. They are the pawns of Satan—the prince of the power of the air—and destined to fall under the wrath of God. They are living out a dark, dismal, sinful, vile, wretched existence.

(2) Saved by grace

Then suddenly verse 4 says, "But God, who is rich in mercy, for his great love with which he loved us." He reaches out in grace to us through Christ. Verse 8 says, "For by grace are ye saved through faith; and that not of yourselves, it is the gift of God—not of works, lest any man should boast" (vv. 8-9). But there is more.

(3) Created for good works

Verse 10 says, "For we are his workmanship, created in Christ Jesus unto good works, which God hath before ordained that we should walk in them."

There is a reversal. In the middle of Ephesians 2, salvation occurs. On the back side of salvation is a life of evil. What must there be on the front side? A life of righteousness. For someone to say, "I'm saved, but I deny God and all righteous activity," is ridiculous. Salvation has to include a transformation. "Therefore, if any man be in Christ, he is a new creation" (2 Cor. 5:17).

I don't believe that repentance, confession, and the lordship of Christ are errors added to the doctrine of salvation. I believe that those things are intrinsic elements of gracious salvation and transformation. But there are things that are added to the gospel that do corrupt it, and I want you to know what they are so you will know the difference between the real corrupters and the ones that some people think are the corrupters.

The things that corrupt the simplicity and the purity of salvation are not confession, repentance, and the lordship of Christ. Paul gives us the things that do corrupt the purity of salvation in Colossians 2. But before we can look at Colossians 2, we need to establish the context.

13

Lesson

I. THE MANIFESTATION OF GRACIOUS SALVATION

A. The Content of Salvation

1. The positional reality

   Colossians 1:20 says, "And having made peace through the blood of his cross, by him to reconcile all things unto himself—by him, I say, whether they be things in earth, or things in heaven." From verses 15-19 Paul has discussed the deity of Christ. In verse 19 he says that Christ is the fullness of God. Those verses talk about His person; verse 20 begins to talk about His work. He made peace through the cross, and that resulted in salvation in verse 21: "And you, that were once alienated and enemies in your mind by wicked works, yet now hath he reconciled in the body of his flesh through death, to present you holy and unblameable and unreproveable in his sight" (vv. 21-22). In other words, He did a sanctifying work in you.

2. The practical reality

   But that sanctifying work is valid only "if ye continue in the faith grounded and settled, and be not moved away from the hope of the gospel" (v. 23a). If somebody says, "I don't believe in God; I deny Him," but one time in his life said that he was a Christian, then is he really a Christian? Not according to verse 23, because the only thing that validates his faith is if he continues in it. If there is no manifestation of a righteous pattern, then you know that the work wasn't accomplished, because if he were truly redeemed he would have been presented holy, unblameable, and unreproveable. And that is not just a positional reality, but it should be manifested as a practical truth as well. If someone departs from the faith, you can be sure he never was truly redeemed. In John 8:31 Jesus says, "If ye continue in my word, then are ye my disciples indeed." But in response, "Many of His disciples went back, and walked no more with him" (John 6:66). They left and proved that they were not real disciples.

Sanctification and righteousness manifested, godly behavior, and holy activity are the manifestations of genuine salvation. In fact, when you read 1 John 3:10, that is all you can conclude. It says that if you don't love your brother, you're not saved. And it says that if you go on living continually in sin, you're not saved—you're the child of the devil and not the child of God. There must be a manifestation.

B. The Completeness of Salvation

Colossians 2:10 is like the hub of the wheel from which the rest of Colossians connects. Paul says, "And ye are complete in him." That is all that needs to be said. You are complete in Christ. Salva-

14

tion is complete in Him. You don't need to add anything to it. Now, why does he say that?

II. THE FALSE EFFORT OF HUMAN RELIGION

There were people attacking the Colossian church, saying that believing in Christ was not enough—He was a good start, but there had to be Christ plus something else. I think that Paul was particularly dealing with the Essene community, because the specific additions were reflective of their attitudes. But we see the same attitudes throughout the history of the church. So Paul emphasizes first that the Colossians were complete in Christ, and then he reveals the culprits that were added to salvation in order to corrupt it.

A. Philosophy

In Colossians 2:8 Paul says, "Beware lest any man spoil you through philosophy." Philosophy is human wisdom. Satan doesn't always attack the doctrine of salvation by maligning it; he usually adds to it. It is interesting that most people in the world like Jesus. He's a hero to many people. It's usually the orthodox Jewish people that get upset when you talk about Jesus. Most people are very tolerant of Him. Most people in our society say that they believe in God and in Jesus. Satan is comforted in that and will try to help them to see that Jesus isn't sufficient—that they need Jesus plus. And his first plus is philosophy.

Now, Colosse had its portion of philosophers and purveyors of human wisdom. It was a typical pagan city populated by Greeks, Romans, and Jewish people. It was about a hundred miles from Ephesus and right in the midst of Greek culture. Epaphras had no doubt made a report to Paul (prompting his letter), describing some of the dangers that were attacking and confusing the church and the people. One of the attacks that confused them was the need for a higher level of wisdom. That's why Paul says in Colossians 2:3 that in Christ are "all the treasures of wisdom and knowledge." He wanted the Colossians to see that Christ has all the wisdom and knowledge that they needed. But there is always the pressure that you need Christ plus human wisdom.

1. The strategy of philosophy

In verse 8 Paul says, "Beware [lit., "be continually being aware"] lest any man spoil you." The word "spoil" in the Greek is *sulagōgōn*. It comes from *sulē,* which means "booty" or "plunder," and *agō,* which means "to carry off." So "spoil" means "to plunder, to carry someone off, to kidnap someone, to subdue someone." Paul says, "Don't let anybody kidnap you. Don't let anybody plunder you. Don't let anybody seduce you and carry you away with their philosophy." Paul also parallels the term "philosophy" with the term "vain deceit." Philosophy equals empty deceit.

15

So we are not to think that the doctrine of salvation is Christ plus human wisdom.

2. The source of philosophy

   a) The tradition of men

   He means that philosophy flows out of human reason and thinking patterns. It is man-centered. Paul says, "But the natural man receiveth not the things of the Spirit of God; for they are foolishness unto him, neither can he know them, because they are spiritually discerned" (1 Cor. 2:14). Man says, "God is fine; the Bible is fine; and Jesus is fine as far as they go, but let me interpret them for you with my philosophy, human wisdom, and insight."

   b) The rudiments of the world

   What are the rudiments of the world? They are the ABCs—the basics, the ABCs of childish, infantile, human thinking. Man thinks he is so erudite. He has Ph.D.s and plaques on his wall to prove how intelligent he is. In his self-deceived pride, he articulates what he thinks is great, profound wisdom, but it's nothing but the ABCs of infantile, childish, human thinking.

   Christ is everything. Colossians 2:9 says, "For in him dwelleth all the fullness of the Godhead bodily." Paul is saying that Christ is enough. You don't need Christ plus human wisdom. Poverty-stricken, sin-cursed opinions of immature religious leaders can only draw truths from the heart of man, which cannot know ultimate truth as God can.

Liberal Theology Today

Liberal theology in our day says, "The Bible is true. We think Jesus is wonderful—He is the Lord and Savior." But they also tell us that parts of the Bible aren't true and believe that many of the stories really didn't occur. They attack the Scriptures and try to pull it apart with their supposed human wisdom.

Scholars who hold higher critical views of the Old Testament tell us that Moses didn't write the Pentateuch. They say that J, E, P, and D did. Who are they? Every time Jehovah is mentioned, that is supposed to represent the work of the J writer; every time Elohim is mentioned, that is the E writer; P stands for the priestly writer; and D stands for the Deuteronomist. They were said to be redactors (or editors) who corrected and edited the Pentateuch.

The same kind of thing occurs in the New Testament. One of the latest views (even coming out of evangelical schools) is that Matthew didn't write the gospel of Matthew in terms of writing an inspired book by the Holy Spirit. Matthew was just an editor who used many sources and edited the entire gospel from them.

Redaction criticism is an example of human wisdom. We are told that we can't interpret or know Christ and that we can't understand the true doctrine of salvation unless we bend to the wisdom of man. Today, human wisdom has become so sophisticated that it states Jesus isn't enough—you have to have possibility thinking or positive thinking to go with Him.

B. Ritualism

1. The true circumcision

In Colossians 2:11 Paul says, "In whom also ye are circumcised with the circumcision made without hands." Many of the Colossians were being attacked by the Essene community—a sect of the Jewish people (the other sects were the Pharisees, Sadducees, and the Zealots). The Essenes were the monastics, and they lived by the Dead Sea. They were very mystical. They said, "You Christians can't truly be in God's kingdom. You haven't had the circumcision. You can't possibly enter into a relationship with God until you've been circumcised." Some people want us to believe that salvation is Christ plus the rituals.

But Paul says, "You are complete in Christ. You don't need to have a fleshly circumcision because you have been circumcised in your heart. You have been buried with Him in baptism (v. 12). Since you have had the true washing, you don't need the ceremonial Jewish washings."

2. The triumph of the cross

In verse 14 Paul says, "The cross took care of it all. It blotted out the accusation list that was against you." In those days, when a criminal died, they would nail his crime to the cross. That is why Pilate had the soldiers nail this inscription at the top of Jesus' cross, "JESUS, OF NAZARETH, THE KING OF THE JEWS" (John 19:19b). That was His crime, and it was a mockery to the Jews. But He had no crime. Pilate said, "I wash my hands of this innocent man" (Matt. 27:24). He was an innocent man. There was no crime that they could put above Him, so Pilate mocked the Jewish people by saying that His crime was that He was claiming to be their King. When Jesus died on the cross, He took the list of your crimes, nailed them to His cross, and paid for them. When you were united with Jesus Christ in the great triumph of the cross over hell and the fallen angels (vv. 14-15), the only circumcision you needed took place. There is no need for ritual.

C. Legalism

Legalism is the religion of human achievement. In verse 16 Paul says, "Let no man, therefore, judge you in food, or in drink, or in respect of a feast day, or of the new moon, or of a sabbath day, which are a shadow of things to come; but the body [the reality] is

17

of Christ" (vv. 16-17). Legalism is salvation through external religious activities.

1. The imposition of the Judaizers

Legalism was typical of the Judaizers. They came upon the Galatians and told them that they weren't really saved because they didn't keep all of the Jewish holidays. As a result, the people returned to those things. Paul said, "How turn ye again to the weak and beggarly elements, unto which ye desire again to be in bondage?" (Gal. 4:9*b*). In Galatians 5:1 Paul says, "Stand fast, therefore, in the liberty with which Christ hath made us free, and be not entangled again with the yoke of bondage." He also says, "Ye observe days, and months, and times, and years. I am afraid of you, lest I have bestowed upon you labor in vain" (Gal. 4:10-11). The Judaizers were imposing the law on the doctrine of salvation.

2. The identification of the standards

   a) Food or drink

   In Colossians 2:16 Paul says, "Don't let people judge you in food or drink." In Romans 14:17 Pauls says, "For the kingdom of God is not food and drink, but righteousness, and peace, and joy in the Holy Spirit." Jewish people were judging in respect of those external things. They were saying, "You don't function the way we do."

   I have had people write me letters that have said, "If you're really a minister of God, how come your hair is over the top of your ears?" Some people say, "How can you possibly use humor? There is no place for that as a representative of God!" They said that to Spurgeon, too. He replied, "You ought to hear some of the things I think of and never say!" Christ plus legalism destroys salvation.

   b) Days of the week

   Feast days and new moons were all elements of Judaism. Paul even includes the Sabbath in his list. If it was still demanded for Christians, as some claim, it certainly would not be in a list of nonbinding rituals.

Paul warns against legalism. Now when you are talking about false things added to salvation, don't talk about repentance, confession, and obedience to the lordship of Christ. Instead, talk about the human philosophy that emasculates the Bible, or about ritualism, or legalism, or:

D. Mysticism

1. The recognition of mysticism

   In Colossians 2:18 Paul says, "Let no man beguile you." The word "beguile" means "to defraud, tell a lie, take away the reward." The *New American Standard Bible*'s translation of verse 18 is a little more accurate than the Authorized Version. It says, "Let no one keep defrauding you of your prize by delighting in self-abasement and the worship of the angels, taking his stand on visions he has seen, inflated without cause by his fleshly mind, and not holding fast to the head" (v. 18-19*a*). Who is the head? Christ. Here is someone who is not holding to Christ for his salvation, but is trusting in his self-immolation, self-abasement, false humility, worship of angels, and visions.

a) The center of the heresy

That was the heart of a heresy that plagued the church for centuries. That heresy later became known as Gnosticism. Gnostics believed in a series of emanations, or spirit beings (one of which was Christ), that descended from God to man and that man could ascend and meet those spirit creatures. Paul says, "Don't let anybody steal your prize. Don't let anybody defraud you of your reward. Don't let anybody rob you of the truth by making you think that true salvation and spirituality come from some kind of mystical self-immolation." Think of the Buddhist who turns himself into a torch, the priest who puts nails in his belt and wears it for years, or fills his shoes with rocks, or walks on hot irons, the Sikh who walks across nails, or the man in the Philippines who crucifies himself every year. Those are examples of people who practice self-immolation. So don't let anybody steal your prize. Don't let the legalist condemn you, don't let the ritualist condemn you, don't let human philosophy beguile you, and don't let mysticism intimidate you.

There are many people who appear so holy. The gurus look so holy and so calm. They are often found in a setting with flowers everywhere. And they sit so sedately and appear to be at peace. Their talk is pablum as they try to intimidate people with their supposed humility.

b) The claim of higher knowledge

There are within the mystics the people who claim to have a higher level of knowledge and experience. Verse 18 says that they meet with angels and worship them and follow their own visions. That can be intimidating. They say that you need to have a mystical experience—a profound exit from this world to a higher level of spiritual experience. They are the spiritual elite—the inner circle.

(1) Delighting in humility

Verse 18 says that they delight in their humility. They are so proud to be humble! There are those who think they are specially humble.

(2) Worshiping angels

There are those who worship the angels. We are not to

19

do that. When John fell down two times to worship an angel, both times the angel said, "Stand up and worship God. I am a creature like you" (Rev. 19:10; 22:9).

(3) Taking a stand on visions

In verse 18 Paul says that the mystic is "taking his stand on visions he has seen" (NASB*). I am weary of people who claim to have had many visions. One man on television said that he died and went to heaven. Whenever he wants to be reminded of what it was like, he smells the tie he wore the day he went to heaven, because the smell of heaven is still on the tie. That is very intimidating. People search for all kinds of experiences, and they base their beliefs on visions. That is sad.

2. The result of mysticism

False things added to the doctrine of salvation result in a person's being "vainly puffed up by his fleshly mind" (v. 18b). They are devoid of the Spirit and full of the flesh. And they do not hold to the head, who is Christ. They hold on to their mysticism. They don't hold to Christ—the true head who holds the whole church together (v. 19).

E. Asceticism

1. The perversion of self-denial

Verse 20 says, "Wherefore, if ye be dead with Christ from the rudiments of the world [the basic elements of human reason and religion], why, as though living in the world, are ye subject to ordinances (touch not; taste not; handle not) . . . after the commandments and doctrines of men?" (vv. 20-22). That is asceticism. Those people want to live a life of total abstinence. They deny themselves everything.

Today, self-denial is seen in the people who go into monasteries and convents. There are people who say that we should be poverty stricken and abandon everything. I met a man who gave away everything that he had in the world (he had half a million dollars). He gave me a bunch of little glow-in-the-dark praying hands that he was passing out on Hollywood Boulevard. After he had liquidated all that he had, he decided to be humble and wait in his house for the coming of the Lord (which he was convinced would happen on a certain date). Of course the Lord didn't come, and there he was on welfare for society to take care of. That is self-abnegation in the wrong sense.

2. The preoccupation of self-worship

Paul says, "Don't let people tell you to touch not, taste not, handle not. Those things are perishing with the commandments and doctrines of men" (vv. 21-22). In verse 23 he says, "They

*New American Standard Bible.

20

involve self-worship and are of no value, serving only to satisfy the flesh.'' People think that they are holy when they exhibit such behavior. They have a reputation for wisdom and holiness, but they are really unholy.

In conclusion, salvation is in Christ alone and does not call for Christ plus something else. But within genuine salvation, there will be repentance from sin and submission to the lordship of Christ. That is clear in the Bible. If you are going to accuse a person of adding to salvation, it occurs when their standard is Christ plus human reason, human wisdom, education, philosophy, and human criticism; or it is Christ plus ritual—that's sacramentalism; or it is Christ plus legalism—that is externalism; or it is Christ plus mysticism—all kinds of deeper experiences, visions, and miracles; or it is Christ plus asceticism—monasticism and self-denial. Colossians 2:10 says that salvation is Christ plus nothing—you are complete in Him. Righteousness, then, is apart from any fleshly activity, but it is not apart from the true work of God in the soul of man.

Focusing on the Facts

1. Where does the transition occur in Paul's thinking in Romans 3 (see p. 8)?

2. According to Romans 3:20, what cannot save man? What was the purpose of the law in salvation? How does a man acquire salvation (see p. 8)?

3. If man cannot be saved by keeping the law by his own effort, does that mean that Christians are under no obligation to obey the law? Why? What does grace do for the law? How is a Christian enabled to obey the law of God (see p. 9)?

4. What happens when people try to separate grace from law (see p. 9)?

5. Can a man be saved and have absolutely no manifestation of that salvation? Why? What does genuine salvation demand (see pp. 9-10)?

6. What does salvation affirm? Support your answer (see p. 10).

7. Who is the agent of salvation? How is anyone ever able to understand who Christ is (see 1 Cor. 12:3; p. 11)?

8. Can faith be separated from obedience? Explain (see p. 11).

9. When the grace of God appears to each believer, what is the first thing that it teaches? What does that mean in theological terms (see Tit. 2:11-14; p. 11)?

10. What is the doctrine of salvation according to the Scripture? What is a part of that gracious work of God (see p. 12)?

11. What initiates the sanctifying process? How does it begin (see p. 12)?

12. What happens to the nature of an individual as a result of the gracious work of God? Describe the steps of that transformation as indicated in Ephesians 2:1-10 (see pp. 12-13).

13. When is the sanctifying work of Jesus Christ valid? Explain (see Col. 1:23; p. 14).

14. Which verse in Colossians is the key to the letter? Why did Paul emphasize that the Colossians were complete in Christ (see pp. 14-15)?

15. What are the five additions that corrupt salvation (see pp. 15-21)?

16. How does Satan often attack the doctrine of salvation (see p. 15)?

17. Why did Paul have to tell the Colossians to beware of philosophy (see p. 15)?

18. What were the two sources of the philosophy that was attacking the Colossians? Explain them (see p. 16).

19. Who are the J, E, P, and D writers? What is one opinion of how Matthew wrote his gospel (see p. 16)?

20. What were the Essenes teaching regarding salvation? What did Paul teach in response to their teaching (see Col. 2:11; p. 17)?

21. What inscription did Pilate have nailed above the cross of Christ? Why did he have that done (see p. 17)?

22. What did Jesus do with the list of crimes against all Christians? Why did He do that (see Col. 2:14; p. 17)?

23. What is legalism (see p. 17)?

24. What group of people in Paul's time were legalists? What did they believe was necessary for salvation (see p. 18)?

25. What do the mystics believe is necessary for salvation (see p. 19)?

26. What heresy plagued the church for centuries? What did it eventually become known as? What did it teach (see pp. 19-20)?

27. What three things were characteristic of those who claimed to have a higher level of knowledge and experience (see pp. 19-20)?

28. What happens to those who want to add mysticism to salvation (see Col. 2:18b; p. 20)?

29. What do ascetics believe is necessary for salvation (see p. 20)?

Pondering the Principles

1. In their effort to separate grace from law, many people separate faith from obedience. Look up the following verses: John 3:36; Romans 1:5; 15:18; 16:19, 26; 2 Thessalonians 1:8; Hebrews 3:18-19; 4:2, 6; 11:8. According to those verses, what is the relationship between faith and obedience? What are the different ways in which they are the same? Look up the following verses: Luke 24:47; Acts 2:38; 5:31; 11:18; 20:21; Romans 2:4; 2 Peter 3:9. According to those verses, what is the relationship between faith and repentance? Look up the following verses: Isaiah 1:15-17; Ezekiel 33:11; Luke 16:27-31; Hebrews 6:1; Revelation 2:20-21; 3:15-19; 9:21. According to those verses, how is repentance related to the issue of sin? Based on this brief study, what can you conclude about genuine salvation?

2. What does the New Testament teach in regard to what it means to be saved? Look up the following verses: 1 Corinthians 1:30; Ephesians 2:8-10; 2 Thessalonians 2:13; 1 Timothy 4:7-10; Titus 2:11-14; James 2:14-26. According to those verses, what is the relationship between justification and sanctification? Look up the following verses: John 14:15; 2 Corinthians 6:16—7:1; Philippians 2:12-13; 1 Timothy 6:11; Titus 2:13-14; Hebrews 5:9; 12:14; 1 John 2:4; 3:1-10. According to those verses, are obedience and holiness options in the Christian life? Why? Look up the following verses: Matthew 5:17-19; 7:23; John 14:15; 1 Corinthians 9:21; Galatians 5:6; 6:2; Titus 2:14; James 1:22—2:13; 1 John 2:4; 3:4. According to those verses, what is the standard rule of conduct for Christian living? What are Christians to keep, or fulfill? Based on this brief study, what does the New Testament teach about what it means to be saved?

3. Have you ever had anyone try to tell you that your salvation is incomplete? What have they told you is necessary for your salvation? Does their addition come under the heading of philosophy, ritualism, legalism, mysticism, or asceticism? Were you intimidated to the point that you tried to add something to your salvation in order to make it valid? Why? As a result of this study, how will you plan to respond to anyone who tries to tell you that you need to add something to your salvation? What key verse in Colossians can you use to support the fact that your salvation is complete? Thank God for His Word that teaches you about the reality of your salvation.

2
How to Be Right with God—Part 1

Outline

Introduction
A. The Darkness of Man
   1. The question
     a) Of Job
     b) Of man
   2. The answer
     a) Of religion
     b) Of the Bible
       (1) In the New Testament
         (*a*) Romans 3:9
         (*b*) Romans 1:18
         (*c*) Romans 2:2-3
         (*d*) Romans 2:11-12
         (*e*) Romans 3:10-20
       (2) In the Old Testament
B. The Light of God
   1. The dispelling of darkness
   2. The revelation of righteousness
     a) The source of that righteousness
     b) The singularity of righteousness
       (1) Author
       (2) Nature
         (*a*) Fulfilling the precept
         (*b*) Fulfilling the penalty
       (3) Duration
     c) The significance of this righteousness

Lesson
I. Apart from Legalism
  A. The Principle
  B. The Passages
    1. Romans 3:28
    2. Romans 4:6
    3. Galatians 2:16, 21
    4. Galatians 3:10-11
    5. Ephesians 2:8-10

6. 2 Timothy 1:8*b*-10
7. Titus 3:4-5
8. Philippians 3:8-9
II. Built on Revelation
A. The Importance of Revelation
B. The Illustrations of Righteousness
1. Abraham
2. David
III. Acquired by Faith
A. The Instrument of Righteousness
1. Romans 4:5
2. Romans 5:1
3. Ephesians 2:8
4. Romans 4:20-22
B. The Identification of Faith
1. False faith
a) John 8:30-32
b) James 2:17
2. True faith
a) The elements of true faith
(1) The will
(2) The emotion
(3) The intellect
b) The embodiment of true faith

Introduction

Romans 3:21-25*a* is one of the most profound portions in all of Holy Scripture, written by Paul under the inspiration of the Holy Spirit: "But now the righteousness of God apart from the law is manifested, being witnessed by the law and the prophets, even the righteousness of God which is by faith of Jesus Christ unto all and upon all them that believe; for there is no difference. For all have sinned, and come short of the glory of God, being justified freely by his grace through the redemption that is in Christ Jesus, whom God hath set forth to be a propitiation through faith in his blood." So much is said in those few verses, that all the sermons of all the ages cannot exhaust the ramifications of its truth.

A. The Darkness of Man

The major message that comes out of that portion of Scripture is how to be right with God.

1. The Question

a) Of Job

Job asked the most important question that any person could ever ask. In Job 9:2 he says, "How should man be just [right] before God?" And having asked that question, he penned these words: "Though one wished to dispute with him, he could not answer him one time out of a thousand.

His wisdom is profound, his power is vast. Who has resisted him and come out unscathed? He moves mountains without their knowing it and overturns them in his anger. He shakes the earth from its place and makes its pillars tremble. He speaks to the sun and it does not shine; he seals off the light of the stars. He alone stretches out the heavens and treads on the waves of the sea. He is the Maker of the Bear and Orion, the Pleiades and the constellations of the south. He performs wonders that cannot be fathomed, miracles that cannot be counted. When he passes me, I cannot see him; when he goes by, I cannot perceive him. If he snatches away, who can stop him? Who can say to him, 'What are you doing?' God does not restrain his anger; even the cohorts of Rahab cowered at his feet. How then can I dispute with him? How can I find words to argue with him? Though I were innocent, I could not answer him; I could only plead with my Judge for mercy. Even if I summoned him and he responded, I do not believe he would give me a hearing. He would crush me with a storm and multiply my wounds for no reason. He would not let me regain my breath but would overwhelm me with misery. If it is a matter of strength, he is mighty! And if it is a matter of justice, who will summon him? Even if I were innocent, my mouth would condemn me; if I were blameless, it would pronounce me guilty" (Job 9:3-20, NIV*).

Job is saying, "Since God is the kind of God He is, how can I ever approach Him? How can I ever be right with Him? How can I ever get an audience with Him? How can I ever have a relationship with a God who is so mighty, so holy, and so powerful?" That is the question. Can a man be right with a God like that? Can a man have a right relationship with the holy, infinite, mighty God? That is the question answered by our text, and the answer is yes.

b) Of man

Throughout human history men have asked themselves the same question. Religion exists because man seeks to be right with God. How else can a man escape a sense of lostness, a sense of guilt, a sense of cosmic loneliness, a sense of emptiness, and a sense of meaninglessness? How else can he eliminate the fear of death and the dread of punishment from a holy God?

2. The answer

a) Of religion

Every religion in the world offers an answer to that question. Every religion in the world suggests to man how he can

*New International Version.

be right with God. And those religions tell man that he can be right with God if he does certain things based on his own effort. That is the religion of human achievement—the religion of works, the religion of self, the religion of human activity.

b) Of the Bible

The Bible clearly demonstrates that a man can be right with God, but not on the basis of anything that he does. In that respect, Christianity stands distinct from every other religion in the world. In fact, there are only two religions in the world—the religion of human achievement, which encompasses every human religion, and the religion of divine accomplishment, which alone is Christianity.

The Bible says that a man can be right with God, but he can't do that from his end of things. If men are to be right with God, that has to happen from God's end of things. There must be a way to be right with God, and Paul gives the answer in Romans 3:21-25.

(1) In the New Testament

In the first part of his epistle Paul has shown that nobody can be right with God on the basis of his own effort.

(*a*) Romans 3:9—"What then? Are we better than they? [Are Jews better than Greeks?] No, in no way; for we have before proved both Jews and Greeks, that they are all under sin."

(*b*) Romans 1:18—"For the wrath of God is revealed from heaven against all ungodliness and unrighteousness." Paul shows that all men are under sin. Therefore, God will judge them all.

(*c*) Romans 2:2-3—When God does judge, He will judge according to the facts. "But we are sure that the judgment of God is according to truth against them who commit such things. And thinkest thou this, O man, that judgest them who do such things, and doest the same, that thou shalt escape the judgment of God?" In other words, all men are sinners, and God is going to judge them on the basis of the facts. Even the man who condemns someone else condemns himself because he does the same things. Whether you are irreligious or religious, you will be judged.

(*d*) Romans 2:11-12—"For there is no respect of persons with God [He doesn't prefer one over the other]. For as many as have sinned without law shall also perish without law; and as many as have sinned in the law shall be judged by the law." Both the Jewish person and Gentile (those who know and those who don't know the law) are sinful. All of them will be judged by the facts, whether they had the law or not.

(e) Romans 3:10-20—"As it is written, There is none righteous, no, not one: There is none that understandeth, there is none that seeketh after God. They are all gone out of the way, they are together become unprofitable; there is none that doeth good, no, not one. Their throat is an open sepulcher; with their tongues they have used deceit; the poison of asps is under their lips; whose mouth is full of cursing and bitterness. Their feet are swift to shed blood; destruction and misery are in their ways; and the way of peace have they not known. There is no fear of God before their eyes" (vv. 10-18). That is a characterization of sinful man.

The climax comes in verse 19: "Every mouth may be stopped, and all the world may become guilty before God." There is no defense—nothing to say. You say, "What about the people who do good things?" Verse 20 says, "Therefore, by the deeds of the law there shall no flesh be justified in his sight."

A man cannot be right with God from his own end. All men are sinners and under condemnation whether they are religious or irreligious. They will be judged according to the facts of their unrighteousness. For three chapters Paul has revealed the condemnation of man. When man is brought to the judgment bar of God and given all of his defense, every mouth is stopped—there is nothing more to say.

That is a particularly devastating truth to religious people who like to think that they can get right with God on their own terms by some kind of spiritual activity. The Jewish people were like that. They believed that they could be right with God by meticulous attention to the law. But they had to face the fact that they couldn't keep the law. People will often ask, "What is the law of God for if you can't keep it?" Its purpose is to show that you can't keep it. You wouldn't know you were a sinner unless you knew you couldn't keep the standard. So, you have to know the standard. Paul says, "When the law came, I knew I was sinful. When I saw the law, I saw my sin as against the law" (Rom. 7:7). God has given the law (the revealed law in the Word of God as well as the law of conscience) not so men can live up to it and be righteous, but so men can know they can't live up to it.

The way to God is not by human effort.

(2) In the Old Testament

The same was true in the Old Testament. Many people think that Old Testament men and women became right with God because of their sacrifices and rituals. But that is not true. Those things were just the activities of their faith—the result of the fact that they were already right with God. Otherwise, those things would have been pure hypocrisy and unacceptable to God. Micah says, "With what shall I come before the Lord, and bow myself before the High God? Shall I come before him with burnt offerings, with calves of a year old? Will the Lord be pleased with thousands of rams, or with ten thousand rivers of oil? Shall I give my first-born for my transgression, the fruit of my body for the sin of my soul?" (Mic. 6:6-7). In other words, "What am I going to do to be right with God? Bring Him what He says is the prescription for sacrifice? Bring Him ten thousand sacrifices? Offer my son on the altar? What am I going to do to be right with God?" The implied answer is: Nothing. You can't do anything.

All sinners are under judgment. All sinners are equally unable and incapable of making things right with God to avoid that judgment. Every mouth is stopped. There are none righteous. That simply means that nobody is right with God. The plight of man is dark, dismal, and despairing. He is bound for hell, and there is no remedy in his world. That is why Christianity hates religions that espouse human achievement and say that men can reach God with religious activity. That damning lie provides false security for people.

As we come to Romans 3:21, man is in the dark. The lights are out, and there is no escape. Man is backed into a corner in a state of frenzy because he can't solve the problems of his life, much less the problems of his death and eternal destiny.

B. The Light of God

1. The dispelling of darkness

No sooner is man locked into a corner, where the law of God shows how rotten he is, than the light breaks in Romans 3:21. It flickered in Romans 1:16 when Paul said, "For I am not ashamed of the gospel of Christ; for it is the power of God unto salvation." He gave us a glimpse that there was a salvation. And in verse 17 he says, "The just shall live by faith."

The key phrase at the beginning of Romans 3:21 is welcome: "But now." The word "but" is an adversative conjunction with the following meaning in verse 21: "As opposed to the darkness comes this." The word "now" takes us into the welcome present tense. Paul says, "Now the light has dawned. Now the darkness is dispelled." It is time for the dawn of hope, time for the light to break, time to find a solution and a way of escape.

2. The revelation of righteousness

The phrase "but now" means "at this present time." Paul says that at a crucial moment in redemptive history—which Paul calls "the fullness of the time" in Galatians 4:4—God revealed a kind of righteousness. Romans 3:21 says, "But now the righteousness of God apart from the law is manifested." That is what man needs. He can't generate it on his own.

a) The source of that righteousness

People often ask, "What does righteousness mean?" It simply means "to be right with God." According to verse 21, there is a kind of righteousness. But notice that it is not the righteousness of man; it is the righteousness of God. The righteousness of man can't make man right with God. Isaiah said: "All our righteousnesses are as filthy rags" (Is. 64:6*a*). The original Hebrew means "menstrual rags." That is the best that man can do. Man can't be right with God if he approaches righteousness from the human side of things; it has to be approached from God's side of things. The light comes from above, not from below. God comes to the rescue and delivers man from his impossible situation.

The Bible talks about the light of the glorious gospel that shines in the darkness (2 Cor. 4:4). When Jesus was born, He was said to be "A light to lighten the Gentiles" (Luke 2:32*a*). John 1:9 says He "was the true Light, which lighteth every man that cometh into the world." In John 8:12 Jesus says, "I am the light of the world; he that followeth me shall not walk in darkness, but shall have the light of life." The light came, and God came to the rescue in the midst of man's darkness.

b) The singularity of that righteousness

The righteousness of God is different from any other kind of righteousness. The word *righteousness* means "to be right, to be good as opposed to evil, to be holy as opposed to unholy, to be pure as opposed to dirty." It means "to be right before God."

(1) Author

Isaiah 45:8 says, "Drop down, ye heavens, from above, and let the skies pour down righteousness; let the earth open, and let them bring forth salvation, and let righteousness spring up together; I, the Lord, have created it." What did He create? Righteousness. Why is this righteousness different? God made it.

(2) Nature

It is a different righteousness by nature because it is comprehensive. It is the kind of righteousness that fulfilled both the precept and the penalty of the law.

(*a*) Fulfilling the precept

Jesus came as the utter fulfillment of God's righteousness. He was right with God. He was absolutely perfect. He always followed the Father's will, spoke the Father's Word, never violated the Father, never moved against the Father's will, never sinned a sin, thought an evil thought, or said an evil word of any kind. He was absolutely without sin. Therefore, He had a righteousness that perfectly fulfilled the law. Why? It followed all of the law's precepts. He kept every law of God in perfection. That in itself makes that righteousness more than anything ever generated by men. In Matthew 5:20 Jesus says, "Except your righteousness shall exceed the righteousness of the scribes and Pharisees, ye shall in no case enter into the kingdom of heaven." There is a righteousness of men, but it doesn't get them anywhere. The righteousness of God fulfills the whole law without a flaw.

(*b*) Fulfilling the penalty

When Jesus went to the cross, He again fulfilled righteousness. Since God is right and holy, He has to punish sin. Jesus totally and completely bore the sins of every human being that has ever and will ever live. No man could have done that. In addition, Christ rose from the dead and conquered death, hell, Satan, and sin.

The righteousness of God is different because of its author and its nature. It is the kind of righteousness that can perfectly keep the law. Third, it is distinct from any other righteousness because of its:

(3) Duration

God's righteousness is everlasting (Ps. 119:142; Dan. 9:7). Hebrews 9:12 talks about an eternal redemption that is provided for us. Hebrews 10:14 says, "For by one offering he hath perfected forever them that are sanctified."

God is saying, "Here is manifested a righteousness unlike man's." The author is God—He created it. Jesus Christ demonstrated that it is a righteousness that can perfectly fulfill God's law because He kept the law and satisfied its penalty. It is a righteousness that lasts forever. God manifests a righteousness that He created—and anything that God creates is as perfect as the One who created it. His righteousness provides the ability for total obedience, and it lasts forever. Now that's the kind of righteousness anyone would like to have! And what amazes me is the love God has to grant that righteousness, because He didn't have to do it.

    c) The significance of this righteousness

The key term in Romans 3:21-30 is "righteousness" in one form or another. The root word translated as "righteousness," "just," "justifier," or "justified" is used nine times in that brief passage. And it is used over sixty times in Romans. Paul's epistle to the Romans is all about how to be made right with God.

When Paul says, "The righteousness of God . . . is manifested," he is saying that the deepest, most profound question in the human heart has an answer. Can a man be made right with God? Paul says, "Yes." How can a man be made right with God? Paul says, "The righteousness of God is revealed from heaven." Since all men are evil, God can take any man and make him right with Himself. Paul loves to talk about how God justifies the ungodly (Rom. 4:5) and how God, who is rich in mercy, makes men right with Himself (Eph. 2:4-5).

Now, let's look at the key points that interpret the righteousness of God.

Lesson

I. APART FROM LEGALISM (v. 21*a*)

"But now the righteousness of God apart from the law is manifested."

Whenever you see the Greek word *nomos* (or "law"), you need to be very careful about how you interpret it, because Paul uses it in different ways. Sometimes he uses it to refer to legalism, sometimes he uses it to refer to the ceremonial law of God, sometimes he uses it to refer to the moral law of God, sometimes he uses it to refer to the Old Testament scripture, and sometimes he uses it to refer to a principle (or general law). In fact, he uses it in two different ways in Romans 3:21. First he says, "This righteousness is apart from the law," and then he says, "But it is witnessed by the law." Let's look at the first one.

A. The Principle

When Paul says that righteousness is apart from the law, I believe he uses the word in the sense of legalism. God's righteousness is apart from any human effort. The order of the words of verse 21 in the Greek are: "But now apart from the law, the righteousness of God is manifested." The phrase "apart from the law" is in the emphatic position. What does it mean? It means that God's righteousness is apart from man's effort to keep a system of rules. We don't gain God's righteousness by the things that we are able to do in our own strength. There are many people in this world who don't understand that. Some people light candles, crawl on their knees, and try to live up to certain rules and standards. In the process of following those rules they think they are becoming righteousness before God, but that isn't the case.

The law of God only works wrath (Rom. 4:15). It gives God the right to condemn people because nobody can keep it. It justifies God's wrath. In other words, God has a right to be angry because you can't keep the law. If you spend your life trying to make yourself right with God, all you will do is justify God's wrath.

B. The Passages

1. Romans 3:28—"Therefore, we conclude that a man is justified by faith apart from the deeds of the law." Men do not become right with God by something they do.

2. Romans 4:6—"Even as David also describeth the blessedness of the man unto whom God imputeth righteousness apart from works."

3. Galatians 2:16, 21—If Romans is the mind of Paul on the righteousness of God, Galatians is the heart of Paul. This is a more impassioned plea, "Knowing that a man is not justified by the works of the law." The works of the law won't justify a man. Verse 21 says, "I do not make void the grace of God; for if righteousness come by the law, then Christ is dead in vain." If you could make yourself right with God without Christ dying on the cross, then Christ wasted His time.

4. Galatians 3:10-11—"For as many as are of the works of the law are under the curse." All of the people who try to get to God by their works and their own self-righteousness keep themselves under the curse. Why? Verse 10 continues, "Cursed is everyone that continueth not in all things which are written in the book of the law, to do them." If you try to live by the law, you will be cursed because you will come short of the whole law. So verse 11 says, "But that no man is justified by the law."

5. Ephesians 2:8-10—"For by grace are ye saved through faith; and that not of yourselves." Salvation is not based on anything you do. Verse 8 continues, "It is the gift of God—not of works, lest any man should boast. For we are his workmanship" (vv. 8*b*-10*a*).

6. 2 Timothy 1:8*b*-10—"God, who hath saved us, and called us with an holy calling, not according to our works, but according to his own purpose and grace, which was given us in Christ Jesus before the world began, but is now made manifest by the appearing of our Savior, Jesus Christ." When Christ came, God's righteousness was manifest. That is what the phrase "but now" means in Romans 3:21: "But now, at this marvelous time in redemptive history, when Christ has come, God's righteousness is made abundantly clear."

7. Titus 3:4-5—"But after the kindness and love of God, our Savior, toward man appeared, not by works of righteousness which we have done, but according to his mercy he saved us."

8. Philippians 3:8-9—Paul says, "That I may win Christ, and be found in him, not having mine own righteousness, which is of the law, but that which is through the faith of Christ, the righteousness which is of God by faith."

There is a righteousness that can make us right with God, but it isn't the righteousness of men; it is the righteousness of God. It doesn't rise from below; it comes down from above. It is authored by God, its very nature is perfection, and its duration is eternal. It is not like man's righteousness. Man's righteousness comes up from man, it is not perfect, it cannot keep the whole law, it doesn't last very long, and it falls infinitely short of God's standards. We are to be right with God on God's terms. His righteousness is unlike any other. The greatest error of religion in the world is that it allows people to try to make themselves right with God on their own, and there is no place for that.

Having affirmed that the righteousness of God is apart from legalism, let's look at the second point.

II. BUILT ON REVELATION (v. 21b)

"Being witnessed by the law and the prophets."

A. The Importance of Revelation

A Jewish person reading Romans 3:21 might say, "Paul is introducing something new. How can he say that righteousness is apart from the law? We are the people who hold to the law and love the law [they practically worshiped it]. We are the ones who strive with all of our might to keep the law, and now he says that righteousness is apart from the law. Is that something new?" Paul says, "No. It is witnessed to by the law and the prophets." The phrase "the law and the prophets" is an expression used by the Jewish people to refer to the Old Testament. Paul is saying, "That is what was witnessed to in the Old Testament. It isn't anything revolutionary."

In Amos God says, "I hate your feasts and I despise your sacrifices. Stop worshiping Me with your songs" (Amos 5:21-23). The writer of Hebrews tells us that no one was ever justified by the blood of bulls and goats (Heb. 10:4). According to Paul, the law was given for only one reason—to show us our sin (Rom. 3:20). The law didn't make people righteous in the Old Testament; it showed them how sinful they were and threw them on the mercy of God. A Jewish person was to look at the law of God, realize he couldn't keep it, cry out for mercy and grace, and believe that God would provide.

People in the Old Testament were redeemed in the same way people were in the New Testament—they believed God, knew they were sinful and needed a Savior, and acknowledged God as their Savior. Although they did not fully understand Christ since He hadn't come, they still knew that they needed a Savior. The sacrifices in the Old Testament depicted a Savior who had to die for them. So Paul's teachings were not something new; they were that which the Old Testament promised.

B. The Illustrations of Righteousness

   1. Abraham

      Romans 4:2 says, "For if Abraham were justified by works, he hath something of which to glory, but not before God. For what saith the scripture? Abraham believed God, and it was counted unto him for righteousness" (vv. 2-3). Abraham was justified by faith. He believed God. The Old Testament witnessed to the fact that in order to be made right with God, righteousness had to come from God's end of things.

   2. David

      In Romans 4:7-8 Paul quotes David as saying, "Blessed are they whose iniquities are forgiven, and whose sins are covered. Blessed is the man to whom the Lord will not impute sin." David saw God's mercy, love, and grace.

The ceremonies and the sacrifices of the Old Testament couldn't give life, forgive sin, or make people right with God. People in the Old Testament were made right with God when they believed Him and acted in faith on His Word. You say, "How much of His Word?" As much as had been revealed. When they believed God and acted in faith on His Word, they were saved by God's grace, mercy, and forgiveness. Then, in obedience, they carried out the ceremonies and sacrifices, which pictured their forgiveness. So the Old Testament saw the need for a sacrifice and a righteousness beyond that of man's ability. The gospel of Jesus Christ, contrary to what a Jewish person might think, is not a subversion of the Old Testament. The Old Testament was simply the shadow, and the New Testament is the substance.

The righteousness of God is apart from legalism, built on revelation, and third:

III. ACQUIRED BY FAITH (v. 22a)

"Even the righteousness of God which is by faith of Jesus Christ."

A. The Instrument of Righteousness

   The righteousness of God comes by faith—just like it did for Abraham and David, and as it will for anyone else. It is not the righteousness of man that comes through works; it is the righteousness of God, and it comes through faith.

   1. Romans 4:5—"But to him that worketh not, but believeth on

him that justifieth the ungodly, his faith is counted for righteousness." There is nothing for us to do but believe.

2. Romans 5:1—"Therefore, being justified by faith."

3. Ephesians 2:8—"For by grace are ye saved through faith." Faith is only an instrument. It is the hand that reaches out and takes the righteousness of God.

4. Romans 4:20-22—"He [Abraham] staggered not at the promise of God through unbelief, but was strong in faith, giving glory to God, and being fully persuaded that, what he had promised, he was able also to perform. And therefore it was imputed to him for righteousness." How did Abraham become right with God? He believed that what God said He would do, He would do.

How is a man made righteous? Ephesians 2:8-9 says, "It is the gift of God—not of works." You say, "What does he need to do?" He needs to believe; he needs to have faith. Faith in what? Faith in God. Faith in what about God? Faith in all that God said about Himself. He says more now than He did in Abraham's time. But we still have to believe all that God has said about Himself in order to be true believers. And when you believe that by faith, you are made righteous.

B. The Identification of Faith

   1. False faith

   There is such a thing as false faith. There are people who try to make faith simple and easy. But I want you to be aware that there is a false faith and a true faith.

   a) John 8:30-32—"As he spoke these words, many believed on him. Then said Jesus to those Jews who believed on him, If ye continue in my word, then are ye my disciples indeed; and ye shall know the truth, and the truth shall make you free." One thing that we learn about false faith is that it tends to be momentary, whereas true faith tends toward continuance in obedience to the Word of God.

   b) James 2:17—"Even so faith, if it hath not works, is dead." That's false faith.

   Faith that has no fruit is like rocky soil where there is no root, or thorny ground, where the seed is choked out by the world's system (Matt. 13:5, 7). There is that kind of faith. It may even look good at the beginning. There is the immediate joy as seen in the parable in Matthew 13:20. There may be the apparent germination of faith in the seed that falls in the thorny soil, but it is false faith because it doesn't bear fruit or continue in the Word (Matt. 13:22).

   2. True faith

   We are saved by faith alone, but it is by a true faith. A. W.

Tozer said this, "But something has happened to the doctrine of justification. . . . The faith of Paul and Luther was a revolutionizing thing. It upset the whole life of the individual and made him into another person altogether. It laid hold on the life and brought it under obedience to Christ. It took up its cross and followed along after Jesus with no intention of going back. It said good-bye to its old friends as certainly as Elijah when he stepped into the fiery chariot and went away in the whirlwind. It had a finality about it. It snapped shut on a man's heart like a trap; it captured the man and made him from that moment forward a happy love-servant of his Lord" (*The Root of the Righteous* [Harrisburg, Pa.: Christians Publications, 1955], pp. 45, 46).

Many people have redefined faith to mean "a passive agreement with facts about Jesus." But saving faith is not that at all—it is a placing of oneself totally in submission to the Lord Jesus Christ.

a) The elements of true faith

Romans 6:17 says, "But God be thanked, that whereas ye were the servants of sin." In other words, you used to be a servant of sin, implying that now you are a servant of the Lord Jesus. How did that happen? There are three elements, "Ye have obeyed from the heart that form of doctrine which was delivered you" (v. 17*b*). The word that is connected with salvation is "obedience."

(1) The will

True faith is an exercise of the will. Paul says, "Ye have obeyed." There is an obedience to the faith (Rom. 1:5). The will responds in obedience to the lordship of Christ.

(2) The emotion

Paul says, "Ye have obeyed from the heart." I see that as referring to not only the mind but the emotions and senses awakened to sin and stirred by the Spirit of God. The response rises from deep within a man.

(3) The intellect

Paul says, "Ye have obeyed from the heart that form of doctrine which was delivered you." Those are the facts.

Moving backward through the list, you first heard the facts, then they stirred your mind and heart; and then you responded with obedience in submission to Christ. That is the makings of true faith. It is a deep commitment. You heard the true doctrine of the gospel—that form of doctrine properly declaring Jesus Christ. You internalized it in your mind, heart, and senses—your emotions were awakened. They then triggered your will, and you acted in obedience. Each one builds on the other. So, the righteousness of God

37

is made available by true faith.

b) The embodiment of true faith

Romans 3:22 says that true faith is faith in Jesus Christ, not just faith in God. This is no vague attitude. True faith is faith directed at the Lord Jesus Christ. He is the embodiment of righteousness. He is the One whose death on the cross revealed God's righteousness to us. On the one hand, He showed us God's righteousness by demonstrating a perfect life. On the other hand, He showed us God's righteousness by dying on the cross. God is righteous, and He has to punish sin. When Christ died, we saw how righteous and loving God truly is.

What have we learned about the righteousness of God? It is apart from anything we do—it is not by our works or legalism. It is that which the Old Testament taught. And it is ours by faith—not false faith, but true faith in the Lord Jesus Christ.

Focusing on the Facts

1. What is the most important question that anyone could ask (see Job 9:2; p. 25)?

2. What answer do the religions of the world offer man in his quest to be right with God (see pp. 26-27)?

3. Name the only two religions in the world. What do they teach (see p. 27)?

4. How does Paul prove that a man cannot be made right with God on the basis of his own effort? Support your answer with Scripture (see pp. 27-28).

5. What was the purpose of the law of God (see Rom. 3:20; p. 28)?

6. What is the great transition that we find in Romans 3:21 (see p. 29)?

7. What does *righteousness* mean? What is the source of the righteousness that makes man right with God (see p. 30)?

8. Why is the righteousness of God different from any other kind of righteousness (see pp. 30-31)?

9. What two aspects of the law did the righteousness of God fulfill? Explain how Christ fulfilled each one (see p. 31).

10. What are the different ways in which Paul uses the Greek word *nomos*? How does he use it in Romans 3:21 (see p. 32)?

11. What does Paul mean when he says, "The righteousness of God apart from the law" (see Rom. 3:21; p. 32)?

12. What does Paul mean when he says that the law of God works wrath (see Rom. 4:15; p. 33)?

13. What does the phrase "the law and the prophets" refer to (see Rom. 3:21; p. 34)?

14. How were people in the Old Testament redeemed? What was the purpose of the sacrifices that they performed (see pp. 34-35)?

15. How does a man acquire the righteousness of God (see Rom. 3:22; pp. 35-36)?

16. What does man need to believe about God (see p. 36)?

17. What is false faith? What is true faith? Support your answers (see pp. 36-37).

18. What are the elements of true faith (see Rom. 6:17; p. 37)?

19. Toward whom is our faith to be directed? Why (see p. 38)?

Pondering the Principles

1. How do you perceive God? In your own words, in a paragraph or two, write down your answer. Then read Job 9:3-20. How is your perception of God similar to Job's? How is it different? What is your standing before God? Are you right with Him, or is there sin in your life that is preventing you from communicating with Him? If there is sin, confess and repent of it. Begin to perceive God as He truly is, not just how you think He is.

2. What was your life like before you came to Christ? What had the darkness of the world done to you? What were the circumstances surrounding your conversion? Now that the light of God has come into your life, what is different? As you dwell on those circumstances, thank God for choosing to make you right with Himself. And as a result of His righteousness in your life, make the commitment to be obedient to Him.

3. Read Romans 6:14-23. According to verse 18, what happened to you as a result of being made right with God? Are you a happy love-servant of Jesus Christ? If you are not responding in obedience to God's righteousness, what are you obeying? What fruit was yielded in your former manner of life? What fruit is yielded as a result of being a servant of righteousness? Which do you prefer? As a true Christian, what are you a servant of? Thank God for having freed you from sin.

3
How to Be Right with God—Part 2

Outline

Introduction
A. Man's Basic Question
B. Man's Eternal Quest
  1. Solomon's prayer
  2. Jeremiah's petition
    a) The request of the people
    b) The response of the people

Review
  I. Apart from Legalism
 II. Built on Revelation
III. Acquired by Faith
   A. The Instrument of Righteousness
   B. The Identification of Faith
    1. False faith
    2. True faith
     a) The elements of true faith
     b) The embodiment of true faith

Lesson
     c) The establishment of true faith
     d) The enablement of true faith
      (1) Ephesians 2:8
      (2) Romans 10:17
      (3) Isaiah 61:10
IV. Provided for All
   A. The Comprehensiveness of the Provision
    1. Romans 4:11
    2. Acts 13:39
    3. Galatians 2:16
    4. John 6:37
   B. The Categorization of the Recipients
    1. They are all the same
    2. They are all sinners
     a) The illustrations
     b) The introspection

        c) The interpretation
V. Given Freely Through Grace
  A. Righteousness Is Imputed
  B. Righteousness Is Unmerited
VI. Accomplished Through Redemption
  A. The Ransom
  B. The Redeemer
    1. 1 Timothy 2:6
    2. 1 Peter 1:18-19
VII. Paid for with Blood
  A. Satisfied by Christ
  B. Saved by Faith
    1. Colossians 2:12
    2. Philippians 1:29

Introduction

What a sad commentary it is when those of us who have known the Lord Jesus Christ for a long time so easily drift away from the initial joy we had when we first discovered how to be right with God. For some people, the truth becomes the end of a lifelong search—the most marvelous, incomprehensible, fantastic, and thrilling thing they have ever known. That truth is contained in Romans 3:21-25*a,* "But now the righteousness of God apart from the law is manifested, being witnessed by the law and the prophets, even the righteousness of God which is by faith of Jesus Christ unto all and upon all them that believe; for there is no difference. For all have sinned, and come short of the glory of God, being justified freely by his grace through the redemption that is in Christ Jesus, whom God hath set forth to be a propitiation through faith in his blood." Those verses tell us how to be right with God.

A. Man's Basic Question

On one occasion when I was traveling by plane, the man sitting next to me noticed that I was reading the Bible. He said, "Sir, excuse me, but you wouldn't know how a person could have a right relationship with God, would you?" I said, "I think I can help you with that." That is the question that has been on the heart of man throughout history.

1. Job

Job asked that question. He gives words to the longing of many hearts in Job 9:2 when he says, "How should man be just before God?"

2. The Philippian jailer

This man asked the apostle Paul, "What must I do to be saved?" (Acts 16:30*b*).

3. The Jewish people

Hearing Peter preach of sin and the Savior at Pentecost, the Jewish listeners said, "What shall we do?" (Acts 2:37*b*).

41

4. Paul

   While he was lying on the ground with his face in the dirt, Paul said: "Lord, what wilt thou have me to do?" (Acts 9:6a). That is essentially the same question: What do I do to get right with God?

5. Bildad, the Shuhite

   This man echoed Job's question, "How then can man be justified with God? Or how can he be clean?" (Job 25:4).

6. The hearers of John the Baptist

   When John the Baptist preached the message of repentance, the people cried, "What shall we do, then?" (Luke 3:10b).

7. The crowd at Galilee

   The crowd our Lord fed at Galilee sought only material fulfillment and ignored eternal issues. He condemned them for their sin, and in John 6:28 they responded by saying, "What shall we do, that we might work the works of God?"

8. The demon-possessed girl

   In Acts 16:16, Paul and Silas are followed by a demon-possessed girl at Philippi. As she followed them, she said, "These men are the servants of the Most High God, who show unto us the way of salvation" (Acts 16:17). Even in her demon-possessed condition, she followed those who spoke of the way to be right with God.

9. Thomas

   Thomas asks the key question in John 14:5, "Lord, we know not where thou goest; and how can we know the way?"

10. Micah

   Micah the prophet asked, "With what shall I come before the Lord, and bow myself before the High God? Shall I come before him with burnt offerings, with calves of a year old? Will the Lord be pleased with thousands of rams, or with ten thousands of rivers of oil? Shall I give my first-born for my transgression, the fruit of my body for the sin of my soul?" (Mic. 6:6-7). He was saying, "What does God want to make me right with Him? Does He want me to go to the point of slaying my own son or daughter?"

11. The rich young ruler

   In Matthew 19:16 this man says, "What good thing shall I do, that I may have eternal life?"

12. A lawyer

   A lawyer came to Jesus burdened with the issue of how to be right with God. He said, "Master, what shall I do to inherit eternal life?" (Luke 10:25b).

13. The psalmist

Looking at the depth of his sin, the psalmist cried out, "If thou, Lord, shouldest mark iniquities, O Lord, who shall stand?" (Ps. 130:3). Later he said, "In thy sight shall no man living be justified" (Ps. 143:2b).

Man throughout history has sought to be right with God and has wondered how that might happen. That is why there are religions scattered across the earth. That is inevitably why man is a religious creature. Even in the midst of his blindness, man is faced with an awareness of his sinfulness, the anticipation of judgment, and the reality that he is disconnected from the God of the universe. He seeks to be made right with God. But the religions of the world offer him a plethora of wrong answers.

B. Man's Eternal Quest

How is a man made right with God? Romans 3:20 says that it is not by the deeds of the law. In other words, a man doesn't become righteous by any good or religious thing that he does. Isaiah the prophet said, "All our righteousnesses are as filthy rags" (Is. 64:6). If a man is going to be right with God, the solution will not come from the man—it will come from God. How can a person be right with God when He is holy and we are sinful? How can we overcome that disparity? How can we who are sinful be made right with a God who is infinitely holy? That is man's age-old longing.

1. Solomon's prayer

In 1 Kings 8:46 Solomon prayed for his people, "If they sin against thee (for there is no man who sinneth not), and thou be angry with them, and deliver them to the enemy, so that they carry them away captives unto the land of the enemy, far or near; yet if they shall take it to their hearts in the land where they were carried captives, and repent, and make supplication unto thee in the land of them who carried them captives, saying, We have sinned, and have done perversely, we have committed wickedness; and so return unto thee with all their heart, and with all their soul, in the land of their enemies, who led them away captive, and pray unto thee toward their land, which thou gavest unto their fathers, the city which thou hast chosen, and the house which I have built for thy name, then hear thou their prayer and their supplication in heaven, thy dwelling place, and maintain their cause, and forgive thy people who have sinned against thee, and all their transgressions in which they have transgressed against thee, and give them compassion before them who carried them captive, that they may have compassion on them; for they are thy people, and thine inheritance, whom thou broughtest forth out of Egypt, from the midst of the furnace of iron; that thine eyes may be open unto the supplication of thy servant, and unto the supplication of thy people, Israel, to hearken unto them in all that they call for unto thee. For thou didst separate them from among all the people of the earth, to be thine inheritance" (vv. 46-53a). Solomon says, "God, when the people come to You and seek to be made right, make them right. When they are in the midst of their captivity, and they look at their situation and reach out to You, reach out to them. Make them right." Solomon affirmed that righteousness can only come from God's side.

2. Jeremiah's petition

a) The request of the people

Jeremiah sought God on behalf of others in Jeremiah 42: "All the people from the least even unto the greatest, came near, and said unto Jeremiah, the prophet, Let, we beseech thee, our supplication be accepted before thee, and pray for us unto the Lord, thy God, even for all this remnant (for we are left but a few of many, as thine eyes do behold us), that the Lord, thy God, may show us the way in which we may walk, and the thing that we may do. Then Jeremiah, the prophet, said unto them, I have heard you; behold, I will pray unto the Lord, your God, according to your words; and it shall come to pass that, whatsoever thing the Lord shall answer you, I will declare it unto you; I will keep nothing back from you. Then they said to Jeremiah, The Lord be a true and faithful witness between us, if we do not even according to all things for which the Lord, thy God, shall send thee to us. Whether it be good, or whether it be evil, we will obey the voice of the Lord, our God, to whom we send thee, that it may be well with us, when we obey the voice of the Lord, our God" (vv. 1-6).

The people said, "Jeremiah, say to God, 'How do we get right with you?' And whatever God says, tell us and we'll do it. We want to be right with God." So Jeremiah went before God. Verse 7 says, "And it came to pass after ten days, that the word of the Lord came unto Jeremiah." He got his answer from God.

b) The response of the people

Jeremiah responded to the people, "For ye dissembled in your hearts, when ye sent me unto the Lord, your God, saying, Pray for us unto the Lord, our God; and according unto all that the Lord, our God, shall say, so declare unto us, and we will do it. And now I have this day declared it to you, but ye have not obeyed the voice of the Lord, your God, nor any thing for which he hath sent me unto you. Now, therefore, know certainly that ye shall die" (vv. 20-22a).

What happened? The people said, "We want to know the

way to God." Jeremiah came back ten days later and said, "Here's what God says." But the people said, "We don't want to hear it." And that is still going on. People around the world are saying, "How do you get right with God?" But when someone tells them the answer, they walk away. It isn't enough to know how to be right with God; we need to obey Him. Men seek the answer, but they don't always want the answer they get. Most of those who heard John the Baptist weren't interested in responding when they got their answer. When the crowd at Galilee heard Jesus say that they should eat His flesh and drink His blood, they went away (John 6:56, 66). The rich young ruler, the lawyer, and Jeremiah's people didn't respond either. So we learn something very basic about man—he wants to know how to be right with God, but he doesn't always respond when he finds out the truth. Still, we must continually proclaim the truth.

Review

Romans 3:21 begins, "But now." Up to that point Romans has been full of sin, ugliness, hopelessness, darkness, despair, hell, damnation, and judgment. Man stands at the bar of God's judgment with no defense. Romans 3:19 says that his mouth is stopped. Verse 20 says that by his own works he cannot be made right with God. Verse 21 then says, "But now the righteousness of God apart from the law is manifested." When man has come to the end of his resource—to the limit of his capability—and he realizes that he can't be right with God, then God moves in with righteousness that comes from above. Only God can make a man right with Himself. Man can't do that on his own. That is a monumental reality because all of the religions that have ever existed or ever will exist, apart from the true Christian faith, have said that men can be right with God by their own effort. There are only two kinds of religions: the religion that says man can be righteous on his own, and the one that says he can't. The latter is the biblical one. In love, God provides a righteousness that man can never generate.

Illustrating the Fury of God

In the *Iliad* of Homer, there is a story of the great warrior Hector. He was eventually slaughtered by Achilles, according to Greek mythology. But before he went to battle, he said farewell to his wife and child—it would be the last time that he would ever see them. He wanted to embrace his little child, but as he reached out, his fierce armor and helmet so terrified the boy that he cried and buried his head in his nurse's shoulder. So, Hector took off his armor and then reached out for his child. Instantly he jumped into his father's arms and embraced him. He found the father he loved behind the armor.

In a sense, God takes the armor off in Romans 3:21. He is no

45

longer the warrior of the first three chapters, He is the loving Father. He has been the judge and executioner. His fury has been poured out in the promises of those first three chapters. But now, behind all of that armor, we find a God of love who offers His righteousness to men who could never gain it on their own.

What makes us right with God? What kind of righteousness is the righteousness of God? How can we describe it?

I. APART FROM LEGALISM (v. 21a; see pp. 32-34)

"But now the righteousness of God apart from the law is manifested."

II. BUILT ON REVELATION (v. 21b; see pp. 34-35)

"Being witnessed by the law and the prophets."

The purpose of the Old Testament was to show men that they couldn't be righteous on their own. Romans 3:20 says, "For by the law is the knowledge of sin." The law was given to condemn people. Jesus reiterated the purpose of the Old Testament when He preached the Sermon on the Mount. He told people what God's standard was as opposed to what they did. Why did He tell them that? So they would keep God's standard? No. He told them so they would know that they couldn't keep it. Jesus said, "I'm here because you can't reach God by your righteousness. But God has brought His righteousness to you and offers it as a gift."

There are at least three hundred thirty prophecies in the Old Testament concerning Jesus Christ. His coming as the embodiment of God's righteousness was the fulfillment of the Old Testament.

III. ACQUIRED BY FAITH (v. 22a; see pp. 35-38)

"Even the righteousness of God which is by faith of Jesus Christ."

A. The Instrument of Righteousness (see pp. 35-36)

The righteousness of God doesn't come by good works; it comes by faith. The two are distinct. Salvation by good works involves things that you do—an effort that you embark on. Salvation by faith is something that God does, that you believe, accept, and trust in. There is nothing to add to it. For example, Jesus said on the cross, "It is finished" (John 19:30b). He had accomplished the work of salvation. The Bible says that if you believe Christ finished that work, if you believe in its significance, if you believe in who Christ is, and if you believe in His death and resurrection, then that's all that is necessary to be saved. He did everything pertaining to salvation—you only need to believe that. Romans 10:9-10 says, "That if thou shalt confess with thy mouth the Lord Jesus, and shalt believe in thine heart that God hath raised him from the dead, thou shalt be saved. For with the heart man believeth unto righteousness."

B. The Identification of Faith (see pp. 36-38)

1. False faith (see p. 36)

2. True faith (see pp. 36-38)

    a) The elements of true faith (see pp. 37-38)

    b) The embodiment of true faith (see p. 38)

Lesson

    c) The establishment of true faith

    From the Old Testament to the New Testament we hear this refrain, "The just shall live by faith." That is why Hebrews 11 lists the heroes of faith. Then Hebrews 12:1 says, "Wherefore, seeing we also are compassed about with so great a cloud of witnesses, let us"—the implication is, "also live by faith." If there are that many godly people who attest to the validity of a life of faith, then that is the kind of life we ought to live. The writer of Hebrews closes by saying that we ought to be "Looking unto Jesus, the author and finisher of our faith" (Heb. 12:2). Even your faith isn't yours—Jesus Christ authors and finishes it.

    d) The enablement of true faith

    (1) Ephesians 2:8—"For by grace are ye saved through faith; and that not of yourselves, it is the gift of God."

    (2) Romans 10:17—"So, then, faith cometh by hearing, and hearing by the word of God." Faith is a gift of God. We depend totally on God granting saving faith because we cannot muster such faith on our own. It comes from God.

    (3) Isaiah 61:10—"I will greatly rejoice in the Lord, my soul shall be joyful in my God; for he hath clothed me with the garments of salvation, he hath covered me with the robe of righteousness."

The righteousness of God is apart from legalism, built on revelation, acquired by faith, and fourth:

IV. PROVIDED FOR ALL (v. 22*b*-23)

A. The Comprehensiveness of the Provision (v. 22*b*)

"Unto all and upon all them that believe."

The provision of salvation is made for anyone who believes.

1. Romans 4:11—"And he [Abraham] received the sign of circumcision, a seal of the righteousness of the faith which he had yet being uncircumcised, that he might be the father of all them that believe." Anybody can be saved who believes.

2. Acts 13:39—"All that believe are justified." You say, "You mean it doesn't matter how bad or irreligious people are?" No, that is not the issue. The issue is, do they believe?

3. Galatians 2:16—"Knowing that a man is not justified by the works of the law, but by the faith of Jesus Christ, even we have believed in Jesus Christ, that we might be justified by the faith of Christ, and not by the works of the law; for by the works of the law shall no flesh be justified." God-haters, criminals, murderers, child molesters, rapists, brutal and bitter people, religious hypocrites, false teachers, and false prophets are all made right with God if they believe.

4. John 6:37—Jesus said, "Him that cometh to me I will in no wise cast out."

B. The Categorization of the Recipients (vv. 22c-23)

1. They are all the same (v. 22c)

"For there is no difference."

You say, "I'm a very moral person. I belong to philanthropic organizations. I give my money to poor people. I work hard. I'm a good provider. I love my wife and my kids. Basically, I'm a good person." No, you are just the same as a child molester, a rapist, a murderer, or an irreligious, God-hating, Christ-cursing, hell-bound sinner. That is very hard for people to understand, but that is what Paul says. People think they are good because they think good is relative. But good is not relative; it's absolute. Evil is relative. Technically, some people are worse than others, but they are all infinitely far from God.

You say, "Can God save anybody?" Yes. There is no difference between us; we are all wretched, vile, godless sinners. There may be a relative difference in our surface appearance, but the fact remains that we are all in the same category. So if He can save any of us, He can save all of us. Somebody can't say, "You can't save me; I'm too far gone," because God sees no difference among men.

2. They are all sinners (v. 23)

"For all have sinned, and come short of the glory of God."

Every human being on the face of the earth comes short of the glory of God. We are in the same category as everybody else.

a) The illustrations

Suppose you lined up all the people of Los Angeles on the beach at San Pedro and said, "We are going to see who can jump to Catalina Island." Everybody could start as far back as he wanted before he jumped. Some people would stumble before they got to the water. Some people would jump about two feet. Some professional athletes, who know how to long jump, might jump twenty-four to twenty-five feet. But nobody would land at Catalina. And that is what Paul is saying. It doesn't matter what the relative variables are—you are too far from God's glory. Romans 3:23 doesn't prove how far we are from God; it proves how savable we are.

As another comparison, measure the height of everybody in the city of Los Angeles. There would be midgets, dwarfs, small children, and heights ranging to as much as a seven-foot-eight inch basketball player. What would be the standard of comparison? We will say that the standard is the nearest star. Seven feet eight inches is a long way from the nearest star. And even the nearest star cannot approach the infinite holiness of God.

Evil is evil. Everybody is in the same boat—we are infinitely separated from a holy God. So God provides salvation for all because everybody is in the same category. Everybody needs salvation, and God is able to save everybody who believes.

b) The introspection

Some of the people we think are the best of men are in truth the worst of sinners. For example, at one time Paul described himself as, "Circumcised the eighth day, of the stock of Israel, of the tribe of Benjamin, an Hebrew of the Hebrews; as touching the law, a Pharisee [keeping all the minutia of the law]; concerning zeal, persecuting the church; touching the righteousness which is in the law, blameless" (Phil. 3:5-6). That sounds like a good guy. But he also said this about himself in 1 Timothy 1:15: "I am the chief of sinners."

There is no way to change our situation, and no one is any better than the other. All have sinned and fallen short. If someone says that he doesn't sin, he is contradicting the Word of God.

c) The interpretation

Paul says that all have come short of the glory of God. Now, God's glory is God's perfection, and men come short of that divine standard. To "come short" means "to be destitute of," or "to lack." It is the term used of the prodigal son (Luke 15:14). It refers to a condition with no resources. Man fails to live up to God's glorious, holy standard. But God can redeem him because everybody is in the same predicament. And if God can redeem anybody, He will redeem those who come in faith.

The righteousness of God is apart from legalism, built on revelation, acquired by faith, provided for all, and:

V. GIVEN FREELY THROUGH GRACE (v. 24a)

"Being justified freely by his grace."

I believe verse 24 connects with verse 22, "Even the righteousness of God which is by faith of Jesus Christ unto all and upon all them that believe." Verse 22b-23 is a parenthesis describing how everybody can be saved because they are all the same. Then verse 24 picks up the main point by saying that those who believe are made right with God freely by His grace.

A. Righteousness Is Imputed

Some people say that the word *justified* means "to declare someone righteous." They say, "Justified means 'Just-as-if-I'd-never-sinned.' " But God isn't saying, "I'm going to pretend that it was just as if they never sinned." To justify doesn't mean to declare you are righteous when you're not; it means to make you righteous. That is an important distinction.

Paul's usage of the word *justify* was drawn from the Old Testament concept. The equivalent in the Hebrew is the verb *tsadeq*, which primarily means "to cause someone to be righteous." God doesn't say, "I'm going to pretend you are righteous"—He makes us righteous. It is the opposite of condemnation. It is a transformation. If we believe that God is saying we are righteous when we are not, then conversion isn't a transformation. But justification makes us righteous. And I believe we are made right with God—that we receive an actual acquittal, an actual imputation of the righteous nature granted to us.

B. Righteousness Is Unmerited

God grants that righteous nature freely by His grace. The word "freely" means "as a gift." The idea is that His righteousness is given without payment, without human merit. (For example, Isaiah 55:1 says, "Come, buy wine and milk without money.") The word "freely" is translated "needlessly" in Galatians (2:21, NASB). It means "for nothing, without a cause, without a price." We were justified without any price to pay on our part. You don't have to earn your way into heaven. To say you do is a lie right out of the pit of hell because it discredits God's grace. And grace mingled with law isn't grace. We are saved freely by grace. Grace is undeserved love granted to the guilty. Paul used that term approximately one hundred times in his epistles.

You say, "If God graciously gives us His salvation freely, and all we have to do is believe, then it didn't cost anything." I didn't say that. It didn't cost you anything, but it cost God a great deal. God's loving, gracious act is granted to us freely, but it was extremely costly to Him.

VI. ACCOMPLISHED THROUGH REDEMPTION (v. 24b)

"Through the redemption that is in Christ Jesus."

What does that mean? That means that somebody had to pay a price.

A. The Ransom

Whenever you see the word *redeemable,* it means that something can be used as money to buy something else. To redeem something is to ransom it by paying a price. There was a price to pay for justification. You or I don't pay it, but somebody paid it.

B. The Redeemer

Romans 3:24 says that Jesus Christ paid the price. Redemption is illustrated in buying a slave out of the slave market in order to set him free. It is also illustrated by the kinsman redeemer in the wonderful story of Ruth and Boaz (Ruth 4:6-13). Christ Jesus paid the price. The Greek text could allow us to read the verse like this: "Through the redemption that is *by* Christ Jesus."

Man is a slave to sin; he cannot be righteous on his own. But God provides righteousness by faith. And the only way God can do that is for Christ to pay the price to free that man. Man is a prisoner sentenced to die. Somebody had to pay his penalty. The redeeming price was paid by the blessed Lord Jesus Christ. He paid the price to set us free.

1. 1 Timothy 2:6—"Who [Christ Jesus] gave himself a ransom." The price was Himself. He had to die in our place.

2. 1 Peter 1:18-19—"Forasmuch as ye know that ye were not redeemed with corruptible things, like silver and gold, from your vain manner of life . . . but with the precious blood of Christ, as of a lamb without blemish and without spot."

What did God say the price had to be? "For the wages of sin is death" (Rom. 6:23*a*). The price was death, and Christ died that death by shedding His blood.

The righteousness of God is available apart from legalism, built on revelation, acquired by faith, provided for all, given freely through grace, accomplished by redemption, and:

VII. PAID FOR WITH BLOOD (v. 25*a*)

"Whom God hath set forth to be a propitiation [the covering over of our sins] through faith in his blood."

God required sacrifice and death. Jesus became that sacrifice. God could not simply forgive and not deal with justice. Love could forgive but justice had to be met. Justice required a penalty, and the penalty had to be paid.

A. Satisfied by Christ

Jesus became the satisfaction. He became the covering. The Greek word for "propitiation" is *hilastērion,* which means "a place where sins are blotted out." In Hebrews 9:5, the word is used to refer to the Mercy Seat. When the priest went into the Holy of Holies on the Day of Atonement, he sprinkled the blood on the Mercy Seat, which pictured the blotting out of sins (Heb.

9:6-8). Christ became the place where sins are blotted out (Heb. 9:11-12). He became the *kapporeth* (Hebrew for Mercy Seat). Jesus Christ, by His blood, provided satisfaction. We are redeemed by the precious blood of Jesus Christ, a lamb without spot or blemish.

To Christians, the cross is everything. God's righteousness could not have come to us apart from the cross. Jesus died in our place. We were all hell bound. We could not become right with God on our own, so God came to earth with a plan to make us right. Through that plan He gave us His righteousness. You say, "How could He do that?" He had to deal with our sin first. The penalty for sin had to be paid, and it was paid in the death of Jesus Christ.

B. Saved by Faith

Romans 3:25 adds this final word: Christ's propitiation is appropriated "through faith." That takes us back to the most important of all truths we saw in verse 22: salvation comes by faith, not by anything we do.

1. Colossians 2:12—"Buried with him in baptism, in which also ye are risen with him through the faith of the operation of God."

2. Philippians 1:29—"For unto you it is given in the behalf of Christ, not only to believe on him but also to suffer for his sake." If you believe, it has been given to you to believe. Belief is from God, but it requires a true, genuine faith.

This exchange of our unrighteousness for His righteousness is marvelously summed up in 2 Corinthians 5:21: "For he [God] hath made him [Christ], who knew no sin, to be sin for us, that we might be made the righteousness of God in him." That's the plan. Having said that, I don't fully understand it. Salvation is a supernatural, divine miracle. And I confess to you that I believe in it, and that's what God asks.

Horatius Bonar, a nineteenth century hymn writer, preacher, and poet, wrote:

> Not what my hands have done
> Can save my guilty soul;
> Not what my toiling flesh has borne
> Can make my spirit whole.
> Not what I feel or do
> Can give me peace with God;
> Not all my prayers and sighs and tears
> Can bear my awful load.
>
> Thy grace alone, O God,
> To me can pardon speak;
> Thy power alone, O Son of God,
> Can this sore bondage break.
> No other work save thine,
> No other blood will do;

No strength save that which is divine
Can bear me safely through.

We are not left with the condemnation of Romans 1:18—3:20. We are brought to Romans 3:21, and the righteousness of God is given to us by faith. That's what it means to be saved. Salvation is not what we have done for ourselves; it is what He has done for us.

Focusing on the Facts

1. What is man's basic question? Who are some of the people that have asked that question (see pp. 41-43)?

2. Why is man a religious creature (see p. 43)?

3. What did Solomon ask for when he prayed on behalf of the people in 1 Kings 8:46-53 (see pp. 43-44)?

4. How should people respond when they are told how they can be right with God? What is the actual response of the majority of people? Give some examples (see pp. 44-45).

5. What do the religions of the world teach about how to be right with God? What does Christianity teach (see p. 45)?

6. What was the purpose of the Old Testament? Why was the law given (see Rom. 3:20; p. 46)?

7. What is it that people need to believe in order to be saved (see p. 46)?

8. What does Jesus do to our faith (see Heb. 12:2; p. 47)?

9. Who can be saved? What is the condition for salvation? Support your answer with Scripture (see pp. 47-48).

10. Can God save anybody who believes? Explain (see Rom. 3:22; pp. 47-48).

11. Illustrate how men come short of the glory of God (see pp. 48-49).

12. What does Romans 3:23 prove (see p. 49)?

13. What is God's glory? What does Paul mean when he says that men have "come short of the glory of God (see Rom. 3:23; p. 49)?

14. How is the righteousness of God given (see Rom. 3:24; pp. 49-50)?

15. What do many people think that the word *justified* means? Where did the concept of the word come from and what does it mean (see p. 50)?

16. What is meant by the fact that God's righteousness is given "freely" (see p. 50)?

17. What is grace (see p. 50)?

18. What did the righteousness that was freely given to us cost God? Who paid the price for the righteousness that we have received (see Rom. 3:24b; pp. 50-51)?

19. How was our righteousness paid for (see Rom. 3:25; p. 51)?

20. What does the word "propitiation" mean? How did Jesus become a propitiation? What Old Testament picture did Jesus fulfill (see pp. 51-52)?

Pondering the Principles

1. Read Hebrews 11-12:14. What did the cloud of witnesses in Hebrews 11 testify to? Be specific. Based on Hebrews 12:1, what is the race that we are to run with patience? What was the race that Jesus ran? Why is Jesus the "author and finisher of our faith" (v. 2)? Why does God chasten believers? Why should we welcome that chastening? Based on those verses, how are we to live? What changes do you need to make in your life in order to live like that?

2. When you are presenting the gospel, how do you respond to someone who says that they are good enough on their own to make it to heaven? How would you explain that he needs to be saved just as much as the worst criminal? Write out the important points you would need to tell him, based on Romans 3:22-23. As an exercise, look up other verses that might help to communicate his need for salvation. If you are acquainted with a person who believes that he doesn't need salvation, pray that God would begin to soften his heart to receive your witness.

3. Look up the following verses: Matthew 26:28; John 6:53-56; Acts 20:28; Romans 5:9; Ephesians 1:7; 2:13; Colossians 1:20; Hebrews 9:13-14; 1 John 1:7; Revelation 1:5. What do each of those verses teach about the blood of Jesus Christ? What effect does His blood have for you? According to Matthew 26:28, Christ's blood had to be shed. Meditate on Christ's sacrifice on the cross. Considering what Christ had to pay for you to be redeemed, how much do you think you are worth to Him? Memorize 1 Peter 1:18-19, "Forasmuch as ye know that ye were not redeemed with corruptible things, like silver and gold, from your vain manner of life received by tradition from your fathers, but with the precious blood of Christ, as of a lamb without blemish and without spot." Thank the Lord for His sacrifice on your behalf.

4
How Christ Died for God—Part 1

Outline

Introduction
A. The Satisfaction of Self
  1. Manifested in the world
  2. Manifested in Christianity
B. The Glory of God
  1. The primary objective
    a) Of Christians
      (1) Illuminating the objective
        (*a*) Colossians 1:16
        (*b*) Psalm 115:1
        (*c*) Isaiah 45:5, 21-23
        (*d*) 1 Corinthians 10:31
      (2) Identifying the objective
      (3) Illustrating the objective
    b) Of salvation
      (1) The effect of the cross
        (*a*) On the angels
        (*b*) On Satan and his demons
        (*c*) On man
        (*d*) On God
          i) Philippians 2:5-11
          ii) Romans 1:5
      (2) The explanation of heaven
    c) Of Jesus Christ
  2. The perfect satisfaction
    a) Summary of salvation
      (1) The source of salvation
      (2) The agent of salvation
      (3) The revelation of salvation
      (4) The satisfaction of salvation
      (5) The sacrifice of salvation
      (6) The appropriation of salvation
    b) Satisfaction through sacrifice

Lesson
I. Declares God's Righteousness

A. The Revealed Truth
  1. The problem raised
    a) Associated with paganism
    b) Attributed to God
  2. The purpose related
    a) Presupposing God's injustice
      (1) God's patient tolerance of sin
        (*a*) Defined
        (*b*) Described
      (2) God's apparent violation of justice
        (*a*) How can God be holy and pass by sin?
          i) Habakkuk 1:13
          ii) Malachi 2:17
          iii) Psalm 78:38
        (*b*) How can God forgive without forfeiting His justice?
    b) Preserving God's justice
      (1) The substitution
      (2) The satisfaction
B. The Repeated Truth
  1. The righteous Redeemer
  2. The right response

Introduction

We are all very much aware that Jesus died for men. We are less aware that Jesus also died for the sake of God.

A. The Satisfaction of Self

  1. Manifested in the world

  We live in a man-centered era—everything focuses on us. People live for self-fulfillment, self-gratification, and little else. People in our society are absorbed with their own feelings, emotions, possessions, and successes—they seldom look outside their ego. You could sum up our society by saying that it suffers from the severe and fatal disease of selfism.

  2. Manifested in Christianity

  Sadly, selfism has even found its way into Christianity. Christians, and many who call themselves Christians, manifest a pervading selfism. For example, many people come to Christ only because they think He will solve their problems, give them peace, joy, happiness, keep them out of hell, and make life worth living. When many people come to Christ, they find themselves preoccupied with their personal satisfaction. Further, they are often instructed that if they will be obedient, they will be blessed; if they go to church, they will be blessed; if they learn certain spiritual truths, they will be blessed; and if they give, they will be blessed. The idea of self-fulfillment runs rampant even through our perceptions of the Christian faith. We know little about glorifying and worshiping God, but a lot

56

about seeking satisfaction—even in a spiritual dimension.

B. The Glory of God

  1. The primary objective

    a) Of Christians

The Bible teaches, contrary to that perspective, that the primary objective of life is the glory of God in everything a man or woman does as a believer in Jesus Christ. Through the years, that has been the major theme of my teaching and preaching because it is the major theme of Scripture. Ultimately, everything is for God's glory.

(1) Illuminating the objective

    (*a*) Colossians 1:16—"All things were created by him, and for him." Everything is for God's glory. Somehow, in great measure, we have evaded that basic truth in our society.

    (*b*) Psalm 115:1—"Not unto us, O Lord, not unto us, but unto thy name give glory, for thy mercy, and for thy truth's sake." In great measure, that sums up the believer's perspective of God—the glory belongs to Him.

If God alone is God, and there is no other, then He has the right to be glorified as God. If He is the holy God, the Creator of the universe, then He has a right to our worship, our adoration, and our ascribing to Him the glory that is properly due His name. The Bible makes it abundantly clear that since He is the only God, we are required to glorify Him.

    (*c*) Isaiah 45:5, 21-23—"I am the Lord, and there is none else, there is no God beside me; I girded thee, though thou hast not known me" (v. 5). God is saying, "Even though you don't know who I am, I still am who I am—the only God." In verse 21 He says, "There is no God else beside me, a just God and a Savior; there is none beside me. Look unto me, and be saved, all the ends of the earth; for I am God and there is none else" (vv. 21-22). God's point is: "Look to Me and be saved, not because of your need, but because of who I am. I am worthy of your worship." Verse 23 begins, "I have sworn by myself." If you are to swear by something, you swear by something greater than yourself. Nothing is greater than God, so He swears by Himself. Verse 23 continues, "The word is gone out of my mouth in righteousness, and shall not return, that unto me every knee shall bow, every tongue shall swear." When we swear, we swear by God, who is greater than all. When He swears or affirms His truth, He does not do it by someone higher than Himself because there is no one higher. There is no other God. If the Lord is God, as He claims to be, then He is to be worshiped and glorified. We are not to seek for ourselves that which only belongs to the Lord. We are to seek that God be glorified.

(d) 1 Corinthians 10:31—"Whether, therefore, ye eat, or drink, or whatever ye do, do all to the glory of God." There is nothing as mundane, as routine, as neutral, or as inconsequential in a spiritual dimension as eating and drinking. Yet, when you are involved in the mundane, menial, daily, inconsequential acts of life, they too are to be done for the glory of the Lord. God's people, instead of being consumed with their own feelings, spiritual blessedness, and rewards, are to be lost in the wonder of giving praise, adoration, and glory to God.

(2) Identifying the objective

As you study the Word of God, time after time people are called to glorify God. That truth is beautifully summed up in 1 Chronicles 16, where David continuously gives glory to God. We are to be consumed with how God feels and not how we feel, with what honors God and not with what makes us happy. You say, "What about our happiness?" Don't worry about that. Seek first the kingdom and the exaltation of God, and your happiness will be taken care of (Matt. 6:33). If you seek happiness, you will fail to glorify God and end up with a cheap substitute for real happiness.

The attitude of spiritual selfism that pervades the church is the key reason why many people do not aggressively evangelize the lost. For the most part, we are not moving out into the world for the sake of Jesus Christ because we are more concerned with our comfort than the glory of God. We seek personal blessing and peace. We seek to be relieved from tensions, anxieties, and problems. We spend hours being counseled and discipled to overcome our anxieties. In many ways, we are even consumed with our own comfort in a spiritual context. I believe that is an ultimately debilitating perspective. It prevents us from being confrontive with the gospel because we are afraid of what people might say that would cause us discomfort. We are content to stay at home rather than go where God is calling us because we don't like the thought of changing our material circumstances. Instead of pursuing the glory of God in our attempt to win souls, we are content with our own comfort.

(3) Illustrating the objective

Hudson Taylor, while in Brighton, England, in June of 1865, became tremendously burdened for the land of China. John Stott says, "He found the self-satisfied, hymn-singing congregation intolerable. He looked round him. Pew upon pew of prosperous bearded merchants, shopkeepers, visitors; demure wives in bonnets and crinolines, scrubbed children trained to hide their impatience; the atmosphere of smug piety sickened him. He seized his hat and left. 'Unable to bear the sight of a congregation of a thousand or more Christian people rejoicing in their own security, while millions were perishing for lack of knowledge, I wandered out on the sands alone, in great spiritual agony.' And there on the beach he prayed for "twenty-four willing skillful laborers" (*One People* [Downer's Grove, Ill.: InterVarsity, 1968]). Out of that prayer came the China Inland Mission. Today there are between twenty-five and thirty million Christians in mainland China in spite of the social revolution. God used that man because he wasn't centered on himself.

b) Of salvation

Of all the spiritual realities that are designed to glorify God, I believe that the greatest thing that glorifies God is salvation. It is like a many-faceted diamond. The Bible approaches it in a myriad of ways, all of which glorify God. God speaks of Himself as a saving God. He gains glory by saving sinful men. Salvation is the first and foremost way of glorifying God. How we miss the point of salvation when we only make it a way to make man better rather than a way to glorify God! Salvation must glorify God. The fact that is does something for us is secondary.

(1) The effect of the cross

(*a*) On the angels

The cross affected the angels, but it didn't redeem them. The fallen angels have no redemption; the holy and elect angels need no redemption. The plan of salvation demonstrated the wisdom of God to the angels.

(*b*) On Satan and his demons

The saving act of Jesus Christ on the cross delivered a crushing blow to the kingdom of darkness. That kingdom threw all its fury at our Lord but couldn't kill Him, so it was defeated. Even the devils will bow eternally in the lake of fire.

(*c*) On man

The cross of Jesus Christ had a dramatic affect on

man: it provided redemption.

(c) On God

Primarily, the purpose of the cross was to glorify God. In that sense, Jesus died for God's sake.

i) Philippians 2:5-11—Let this mind be in you, which was also in Christ Jesus, who, being in the form of God, thought it not robbery to be equal with God, but made himself of no reputation, and took upon him the form of a servant, and was made in the likeness of men; and, being found in fashion as a man, he humbled himself and became obedient unto death, even the death of the cross'' (vv. 5-8). When Jesus came into the world, became obedient unto death, and died on the cross, He saved us. Verses 9-11 say, "Wherefore, God also hath highly exalted him, and given him a name which is above every name, that at the name of Jesus every knee should bow, of things in heaven, and things in earth, and things under the earth, and that every tongue should confess that Jesus Christ is Lord, to the glory of God, the Father.'' Salvation is primarily for the glory of God.

ii) Romans 1:5—It is through Christ that "we have received grace and apostleship, for obedience to the faith among all nations, for his name.'' It is for His name, not for ours.

Salvation is for God's glory. The primary reason you ought to be saved is not so you will know the love and blessing of God and be prevented from going to hell forever; the main reason you should be saved is that God is worthy of your adoration.

(2) The explanation of heaven

When you think about heaven, if you're like most Christians, you think about streets of gold, gates of pearl, and angels sitting on clouds and playing harps. You think of a place that has no problems, no pain, no tears, no sorrow, no death, no dying, no disease. You think about a pure river and the tree of life nearby. We tend to think about heaven from our perspective. But that isn't the way to think about it. Heaven is where you go to glorify God unhindered forever. On his death bed, David Brainerd said this to his biographer, Jonathan Edwards, "My heaven is to please God and glorify Him, and give all to Him, and to be wholly devoted to His glory. . . . I do not go to heaven to be advanced, but to give honor to God. It is no matter where I shall be stationed in heaven, whether I have a high or low seat there, but to live and please and glorify God" (*The Life of David Brainerd* [Grand Rapids: Baker, 1980], pp. 330-31). Brainerd knew that salvation was for God and not for him.

You were made to glorify God—that's your purpose. Salvation, and all of its attendant blessings, is not mainly for you, but for Him. And if you glorify God, there will be bliss beyond description in return. The purpose of salvation is God's glory.

c) Of Jesus Christ

The chief purpose in Christ's death was to glorify God. In John 17:4 He says, "I have glorified thee on the earth." When He went to the cross, Jesus was glorifying God.

That is what Paul wants us to understand in Romans 3:25-31. Salvation glorifies God.

2. The perfect satisfaction

a) Summary of salvation

Paul has already declared the sinfulness of man in Romans 1:18—3:20. That picture was dark. But beginning in Romans 3:21, he speaks of the salvation of God—that God redeems sinful man. Then, beginning in verse 25, he sums up what he said in verses 21-24 about salvation, "Christ Jesus, whom God hath set forth to be a propitiation through faith in his blood" (vv. 24b-25a).

(1) The source of salvation

Verse 25 begins, "Whom God hath set forth." That means the source of salvation is God. Obviously, sinful man can't generate his own salvation, so God has to be the source.

(2) The agent of salvation

The antecedent of verse 25 is at the end of verse 24, so Christ Jesus is the One whom God has set forth. Jesus is the agent of salvation.

(3) The revelation of salvation

Then verse 25 says that God set Him forth. That refers to revelation. God sent Christ into the world—He revealed him in the incarnation. He is the Savior.

(4) The satisfaction of salvation

Verse 25 says that God sent Christ to earth "to be a propitiation." The Greek word for propitiation is *hilastērion,* which basically means "a satisfaction." Jesus was a satisfaction. Whom did He satisfy? God. Jesus met God's righteous requirements when He died.

61

(5) The sacrifice of salvation

The satisfaction is through His blood. It was a sacrificial, substitutionary death.

(6) The appropriation of salvation

Finally, salvation is appropriated through faith.

We find a summary of salvation in just one part of a verse. In Romans 3:24b-25a, we see God, the source of salvation, and Christ, the agent of salvation, who dies a sacrificial, substitionary death as the satisfaction of God's law and requirement. We also see the incarnation and revelation in the phrase "set forth," and the appropriation of the work of Jesus Christ through faith. That is a tremendous statement! Through the death of Jesus Christ on the cross, God is satisfied. If you believe in Him, your sins are forgiven.

b) Satisfaction through sacrifice

The sacrifice of Jesus Christ was different from sacrifices in the Old Testament. In all the millions of animals that were slain in the Old Testament, God was never satisfied. Ultimately, He was satisfied only with the sacrifice of Jesus Christ. You say, "What did all those sacrifices do?" They symbolized the one sacrifice that would satisfy God. They were not that different from our communion service. Are you saved because you drink the cup and eat the bread? No, they are symbols of what did satisfy God—the body and blood of Jesus Christ. On this side of the cross, we have our symbols. They don't satisfy God; only Christ's sacrifice does. Those on the Old Testament side of the cross had their symbols, but they didn't satisfy God either—only Christ did. Primarily, Christ died to satisfy God, not men. And faith imparts to the individual that which satisfied God.

The death of Christ was primarily for God's sake—to glorify Him. How does it do that? Let me give you four ways that the death of Christ glorifies God: one, by declaring His righteousness; two, by exalting His grace; three, by revealing His consistency; and four, by confirming His Word.

Lesson

I. DECLARES GOD'S RIGHTEOUSNESS (vv. 25-26)

A. The Revealed Truth (v. 25)

1. The problem raised (v. 25a)

"Whom God hath set forth [put on public display] to be a propitiation [satisfaction] through faith in his blood, to declare his righteousness."

Why did God set forth Christ into the world to humble Himself and die on a cross? For you, secondarily, but first for Himself in order to declare His righteousness. That element of the cross is missing in the thinking of many people.

What does the phrase "declare his righteousness" mean? A synonym for *righteousness* is *just*. It is used in verse 26 and means "doing that which is right." God wanted to show the world that He did what was right. You say, "Were people questioning that?" Sure.

a) Associated with paganism

Pagan people have always had deities. They had many during the time of Paul and the time of our Lord. There is one important thing to learn about pagan deities—they are always both good and bad. For example, in Greek and Roman literature, pagan gods could be found acting in a benevolent manner at one time and acting in a devastating, destructive manner at another. On the one hand, they are doing what is good, and on the other hand, they are involved in immoral affairs with other gods. They are capricious, whimsical, and inconsistent. They demand righteous behavior from their subjects, but deny that very behavior by their actions.

Whenever men invent gods, those deities turn out to be like themselves because men don't invent perfect gods. So it was very typical for pagans to accuse their own gods of being capricious, whimsical, and inconsistent.

b) Attributed to God

You say, "Would people accuse Jehovah God of that?" Sure. God could be accused of that. They would say this: "If your God is so righteous, so just, and so holy that He can't look on sin, tolerate evil, or give in to disobedience, then how come many people get away with sin? How can He overlook that? Christians tell us that when we believe in Him, He forgives our sin. How can He be a just and holy God and do that?" For example, if a criminal was brought into court before a judge and the criminal said, "I'm guilty," but the judge said, "I'm attracted to you. Go free," would we say that man is a just judge who upholds the law? No, we would say that judge is worse than the criminal—he has no sense of justice and injustice. He would cease to be a true judge. The accusers of God were saying the same thing: "You say your God is holy, righteous, just, and good. Then how can He be forgiving people all the time and say, 'I'm attracted to you, so become My children and I will forget your sin'?"

2. The purpose related (v. 25*b*)

"For the remission of sins that are past, through the

forbearance of God."

a) Presupposing God's injustice

    (1) God's patient tolerance of sin

        (*a*) Defined

The word "forbearance" means "patient toler-ance." It is used in Romans 2:4 to describe the "for-earance and long-suffering" of God. The phrase "sins that are past" describes the sins before Christ. Throughout that era of history, God was patient. The word "remission" does not mean "forgive-ness"; it basically means "to pass over." In a sense He closed His eyes to those sins but didn't forgive them.

During that tremendous time in history, God, by patient tolerance, passed over the sins that were committed and said to the people, "I'm not going to hold you responsible for those sins." But the natural response to that is: "Don't tell me that You are a just, holy, and righteous God; You're just like everybody else's god: capricious and inconsistent."

Through all of man's sinful history since the Fall, God has overlooked sin—not in every single case, but in many cases. On the occasions when people believed in Him, He actually did overlook their sin. And, in looking forward to the cross, He went as far as forgiving it.

        (*b*) Described

In the context of Acts 17, Paul is on Mars' Hill talk-ing about God's part in history. In verses 30-31, he describes man's paganism in the past: "And the times of this ignorance God overlooked, but now commandeth all men everywhere to repent, because he hath appointed a day, in which he will judge the world in righteousness by that man [Christ] whom he hath ordained; concerning which he hath given assurance unto all men, in that he hath raised him from the dead." After the cross, God said that all must repent, but in the past He overlooked sin— and not only among His own people—for He even overlooked some of the sins of the Gentile nations (Acts 14:14-18).

    (2) God's apparent violation of justice

        (*a*) How can God be holy and pass by sin?

How can He be just and overlook evil? How can He be righteous and pass by sin? Several scriptures will help our understanding. For example:

i) Habakkuk 1:13—"Thou art of purer eyes than to behold evil, and canst not look on iniquity." Habakkuk is saying, "God, You are too holy to ignore sin and iniquity." Yet for thousands of years, God passed over sin.

ii) Malachi 2:17—The Jewish people of Malachi's day accused God just as Romans 3 indicates He would be accused. They said, "Every one that doeth evil is good in the sight of the Lord, and he delighteth in them; or, Where is the God of justice?" That was the same accusation: Where is the God of justice? He must delight in evil since everyone that does evil is so prosperous.

iii) Psalm 78:38—"But he, being full of compassion, forgave their iniquity, and destroyed them not; yea, many a time turned he his anger away, and did not stir up all his wrath." Since God turned away His anger, and did not stir up His wrath, you have a right to ask the question, "How can God be holy and pass by sin?"

(b) How can God forgive without forfeiting His justice?

At this point somebody will say, "But God is loving, merciful, and gracious. He wants to forgive, He wants to make people right, and He wants to invite them to Himself." Yes, we believe that, but how can He do that to the point of overruling His justice? That question is summed up in verse 26, "How can God be just and at the same time be the justifier of those who believe in Jesus?" In other words, how can He be gracious, merciful, and forgiving yet still maintain His holy justice?

A look at God in the Old Testament makes Him appear as if His love is overbalanced—as if He loved so much that He had to forfeit His justice. If that's true, then forgiveness is a moral evil, because God violated His holy nature. If God had to overrule His justice to forgive people, then God did evil because He violated the virtue of justice. As a result, a thick veil hung over the Old Testament and covered the justice of God. When Micah says, "Who is a God like unto thee, who pardoneth iniquity, and passeth by the transgression" (Mic. 7:18a), is he impugning the justice of God? For four thousand years a scandal existed in the universe because God appeared to be unrighteous.

65

b) Preserving God's justice

Then came the death of Christ. What does the death of Christ say? It says that God is righteous.

(1) The substitution

Sin had to have a punishment, so God's justice and God's mercy kissed each other at the cross. The penalty was paid, but we were spared from paying it ourselves by the substitutionary death of Jesus Christ. As a result, God's mercy can be extended to us with no loss of His justice. That's why I say that the death of Jesus Christ was primarily for the sake of God. It preserved God from the accusation that He is unjust and upheld the glory of God. We have just plumbed the depths of the meaning of Calvary's cross.

(2) The satisfaction

God was satisfied because He wants to be worshiped and glorified. He has a right to that and becomes very jealous if anybody gets in the way. When God was impugned by people saying, "You're not a righteous God because you passed by sin," He did not receive glory from that. So God had Christ die primarily that the world might see that His holiness and righteousness and justice were never set aside, even if it meant He had to come down to earth in a human body and pay the penalty Himself. He could not pass by His justice. So He is just, and at the same time He is the justifier of those who believe in Jesus (Rom. 3:26).

The real issue behind the gospel is not how to get sinful men to holy God but how to get holy God to sinful men without violating His justice. That's the issue. God has the problems, not us. We don't have any virtue to hang on to, but He does. How can an infinitely, absolutely holy God approach sinful men without violating something of His holy perfection?

B. The Repeated Truth (v. 26)

"To declare, I say, at this time his righteousness, that he might be just, and the justifier of him who believeth in Jesus."

Isn't that profound? From now on it is clear that the cross frees God from any thought of injustice.

Why You Should Confess Your Sin

Most people think that the reason you confess your sin is to get blessed, but that's secondary. The primary reason you confess your sin is so when you get chastened for your sin, God is not thought of as an evil Father. For example, if you were to visit me, you might see me spank one of my children. You might conclude, "What kind of a father is he? He was really hitting that poor little kid." But if my child went up to you and said, "I deserved that. I confessed the evil that I had done. I deserved what I received. My father was only bringing loving judgment on me," then you would see what God is looking for in your confession of sin. The primary reason He wants you to confess your sin is not so you can get blessed, but so that He can be glorified if He chooses to chasten you and not be thought of as an evil Father. That's why Joshua 7:19 says, "Give, I pray thee, glory to the Lord God of Israel, and make confession." Why? Achan was about to be stoned to death along with his entire family because of his sin, but before they were stoned to death, God wanted to be sure that everybody knew that Achan was getting what he deserved. The confession came out of his own lips.

1. The righteous Redeemer

No matter how you look at salvation, God wants glory. He is the justifier. That means He makes sinful men right with Himself. But He is also just. Somebody had to die, and Jesus did. Now do you see the meaning of the death of Jesus? It satisfied God, and freed Him to forgive the one who believes in Jesus. Mercy and truth kissed each other at the cross.

Elizabeth Clephane wrote:

> And though the road be rough and steep,
> I go to the desert to find my sheep.
> But none of the ransomed ever knew
> How deep were the waters crossed,
> Nor how dark was the night that the Lord passed
>   through
> Ere He found His sheep that was lost.

None of us will ever understand that intricate miracle of miracles that holy God Himself became the very sacrifice to His own justice.

2. The right response

The only right response to the gospel is to believe that man can be right with God, knowing that God has abundant love, grace, and mercy, and knowing that He can still be the just and holy God that He is. That is what made Isaac Watts, the writer of "When I Survey the Wondrous Cross," say this:

> When I survey the wondrous cross,
> On which the Prince of glory died,
> My richest gain I count but lost—
> And pour contempt on all my pride.

67

Were the whole realm of nature mine,
That were a present far too small;
Love so amazing, so divine—
Demands my soul, my life, my all!

God first had to satisfy Himself before He could be free to
satisfy all the needs of your heart. He loved us so much that
He went to the length of satisfying His own nature in order to
forever satisfy His redeemed people.

Focusing on the Facts

1. For whom did Jesus die (see p. 56)?

2. What disease does our society suffer from? How does that disease affect Christianity (see p. 56)?

3. What is the primary objective of life for every Christian? What are some scriptures that illuminate that objective? Explain them (see pp. 57-58).

4. Are there various mundane situations in life when we need not be concerned about glorifying God? Explain (see 1 Cor. 10:31; p. 58).

5. What is the Christian to be consumed with? How should the Christian seek for his own happiness (see Matt. 6:33; p. 58)?

6. Why do many Christians not take an aggressive approach in their evangelization of the lost (see p. 58)?

7. What is the greatest thing that glorifies God (see p. 59)?

8. How does the cross affect the angels? Satan and his demons? Man? God (see pp. 59-60)?

9. What perspective should Christians have of heaven (see p. 60)?

10. What was the chief purpose of Christ's death? What verse could you use to support your answer (see p. 61)?

11. Who is the source of salvation? the agent? What is the revelation of salvation? the satisfaction? the sacrifice? the appropriation (see Rom. 3:25; pp. 61-62)?

12. What was the purpose of the Old Testament sacrifices? What is the purpose of the communion service (see p. 62)?

13. What are four ways that Christ's death on the cross glorified God (see p. 62)?

14. Why did God want to "declare his righteousness" (see p. 63)?

15. Why were people questioning the fact of God's righteousness? What did they accuse Him of (see p. 63)?

16. In the time prior to Christ, how did God treat sin in many cases (see p. 64)?

17. How did God treat sin after Christ's death on the cross? What does He command each man to do? Why (see Acts 17:30; p. 64)?

18. What act preserved God's justice? How could He be gracious, merciful, and forgive sin yet still maintain His righteousness (see p. 66)?

19. What is the real issue behind the gospel of Jesus Christ (see p. 66)?

20. Why should you confess your sin (see pp. 66-67)?

21. What is the right response to the gospel (see p. 67)?

Pondering the Principles

1. What is the primary objective of your life—the glory of God or the satisfaction of yourself? Be honest in your appraisal. In what ways do you manifest that the objective of your life is the glory of God? In what ways do you manifest that your main concern is to satisfy yourself? Based on your answers, what would the majority of people you know conclude about your main objective in life? Do you think you are glorifying God to the greatest extent that you can? What changes do you need to make in order to glorify Him more?

2. How confrontive are you when you share the gospel with an unbeliever? What fears are present within you at the thought of sharing Christ with an unbeliever? Be honest with yourself. How many of those fears are related to your self-comfort? What attitude do you think Jesus would want you to have? Read Matthew 28:19-20. Is there an option to spreading the gospel? Read Romans 1:16. Why wasn't Paul ashamed of the gospel? Based on those verses, how can your fear be controlled when you witness to someone? How important is your self-comfort in comparison with Jesus' commission for you to share the gospel of the kingdom?

3. What does *righteousness* mean? How often do you do what is right? How often do you not do what is right? Recently, what opportunities have you had to do the right thing, but didn't? What happens when you do what is right? What happens when you don't do what is right? Read Philippians 3:4-14. What was Paul's perspective of the righteousness he had generated on his own? According to verse 9, what kind of righteousness did he need? According to verses 12-14, what was Paul's perspective of doing right? Is that your perspective? What is the best way you can declare God's righteousness?

4. Read the two verses of the hymn *When I Survey the Wondrous Cross* (see pp. 67-68). As you survey the cross of Christ, what meaning does it have for your life? What is your attitude toward the things of the world that you could count as gain? Read Philippians 3:7. What was Paul's attitude? How do you treat your pride? Do you have contempt for it, or do you build it up? Consider all that is in the world that could be gained. In your eyes, is it small in comparison to the gift of God's love, or is God's love small in comparison to what you could gain? God's love demands all of your life. Are you giving it to Him? If not, will you today? Make the commitment to do so by praying to God right now.

5
How Christ Died for God—Part 2

Outline

Introduction
A. The Importance of the Cross
B. The Impact of the Cross
  1. On believers
     a) 1 Thessalonians 1:10
     b) Romans 5:8-10
     c) 2 Corinthians 5:18
     d) Titus 2:13-14
  2. On Satan and his dominion
     a) Hebrews 2:14
     b) Colossians 1:13
  3. On Jesus
     a) He would be glorified
     b) His word would be verified
     c) His enemy would be defeated
     d) His love would be demonstrated
  4. On God

Review
I. Declares God's Righteousness
  A. The Revealed Truth
     1. The problem raised
     2. The purpose related
        a) Presupposing God's injustice
        b) Preserving God's justice
           (1) The substitution
           (2) The satisfaction
  B. The Repeated Truth

Lesson
II. Exalts God's Grace
  A. The Exclusion
     1. The provision
        a) 1 Corinthians 1:26-31
        b) Romans 4:2
        c) Ephesians 2:8-9

2. The principles
   a) Works
   b) Faith
      (1) Luke 18:10-14
      (2) Romans 4:5
      (3) Romans 5:1
      (4) Romans 8:3
      (5) Galatians 2:16
      (6) Galatians 3:8, 11
      (7) Romans 10:9
   B. The Conclusion

I. Invalid Indicators of Saving Faith
   A. Visible Morality
      1. Of the Pharisees
      2. Of the young man
   B. Intellectual Knowledge
      1. Romans 1:21
      2. Romans 2:17-20
   C. Religious Involvement
   D. Active Ministry
   E. Conviction of sin
      1. Acts 24:25
      2. John 16:8
      3. John 8:37, 40
      4. Revelation 16:9, 11, 21
   F. Assurance
   G. The Time of Decision
II. Valid Indicators of Saving Faith
   A. Love for God
      1. The definitions
         a) The unsaved
         b) The saved
      2. The delineation
         a) Matthew 10:37
         b) Psalm 73:25
         c) Psalm 42:1-3
      3. The direction
   B. Repentance from Sin
      1. The tears of repentance
         a) Proverbs 28:13
         b) Psalm 51:1-4
      2. The triumph of repentance
      3. The test of repentance
   C. Genuine Humility
      1. Illuminated in the Beatitudes
      2. Illustrated by the prodigal son
   D. Devotion to God's Glory
      1. The desire

      2. The direction
  E. Continual Prayer
      1. The heart that cries to God
      2. The hypocrisy that won't cry to God
  F. Selfless Love
      1. John 2:9-10
      2. 1 John 3:14
      3. 1 John 4:7-8
  G. Separation from the World
      1. 1 John 5:4-5
      2. 1 John 2:15
      3. James 4:4
      4. 1 Corinthians 2:12
  H. Spiritual Growth
      1. The parables
        a) The soils
        b) The growing seed
      2. The passages
        a) 1 Peter 1:23
        b) Ephesians 4:13
        c) 1 John 2:12-13
        d) Philippians 1:6
  I. Obedient Living
      1. 1 John 2:3-5
      2. Ephesians 2:10

Introduction

Perhaps as much as any passage in the Scripture, Romans 3:25-31 has been dissected, expanded, and applied by theologians through the years since it was written. It is the very heart and soul of the Christian faith because it describes the doctrine of justification by faith—that man is made right with God through faith. Throughout the history of the church, that doctrine has been lost and found many times. It has been misrepresented and misunderstood; it has been understated and overstated. The doctrine has been confused and has been taught properly.

Whenever the church fully understands the doctrine of justification by faith, it understands the reality of the gospel. When it does not, it misses the gospel message. And if we are wrong about the gospel, souls are unknowingly damned. Justification by faith is an essential doctrine. Yet, in spite of all of that, there is a profound simplicity in Romans 3:21-31. Paul says, "But now the righteousness of God apart from the law is manifested, being witnessed by the law and the prophets, even the righteousness of God which is by faith of Jesus Christ unto all and upon all them that believe; for there is no difference. For all have sinned, and come short of the glory of God, being justified freely by his grace through the redemption that is in Christ Jesus, whom God hath set forth to be a propitiation through faith in his blood, to declare his righteousness for the remission of sins that are past, through the forbearance of God; to declare, I say, at this time his righteousness, that he might be just, and the justifier of him who believeth in Jesus. Where is boasting then? It is excluded. By what law? Of works? Nay, but by the law of faith. Therefore, we conclude that a man is justified by faith apart from the deeds of the law. Is he the God of the Jews only? Is he not also of the Gentiles? Yes, of the Gentiles also, seeing it is one God, who shall justify the circumcision by faith, and uncircumcision through faith. Do we then make void the law through faith? God forbid; yea, we establish the law.''

Initially, the text can leave us baffled by its intricacy. That is why it has demanded such close scrutiny and attention through the years. It is not complicated. It is simple, but it is also profound. Once the doctrine is understood, it becomes all the more profound because its ramifications are so sweeping.

At the beginning of Romans, an indictment was set forth against sinners. Romans 1:18-3:20 presents a terrifying picture of sin and its inevitable judgment. The sinner is indicted, but beginning in Romans 3:21, he is offered redemption. A statement of redemption is made in verses 21-31, and an illustration of it follows in Romans 4, with a further expansion of it in Romans 5. Presently, we are studying the section that deals with our being justified by faith, that is, being made right with God through faith.

A. The Importance of the Cross

As we have learned so far in our study, the key to our justification is found in Romans 3:24-25. We are justified—made right with God—by "grace through the redemption that is in Christ Jesus, whom God hath set forth [manifested] to be a propitiation [satisfaction] through faith in his blood" (vv. 24-25a). The word "blood" is the key. God manifests Christ as a satisfaction through His blood. And that takes us to the cross, which becomes the focal point in the matter of justification. The key event is the death of Jesus Christ. That provided man's only hope for deliverance from the penalty, the power, and ultimately, the presence of sin.

The cross of Christ is central to us as Christians. It is the theme of our hymns. It is the theme of our testimonies. It is the theme of our worship. The cross is the central focus of the Lord's table, and it is the central picture in the baptismal service, for an individual is depicted as dying in order to rise again. The death of Jesus Christ is at the very heart of our faith.

B. The Impact of the Cross

The death of Christ has a sweeping impact.

1. On believers

The death of Jesus Christ saves those who believe from sin and, consequently, from death and eternal hell. The death of Christ is the source of salvation.

a) 1 Thessalonians 1:10—"Jesus . . . delivered us from the wrath to come."

73

b) Romans 5:8-10—"But God commendeth his love toward us in that, while we were yet sinners, Christ died for us. Much more then, being now justified by his blood, we shall be saved from wrath through him. . . . we were reconciled to God by the death of his son." We are saved by the death of Jesus Christ. That truth is repeated over and over in the pages of the New Testament.

c) 2 Corinthians 5:18—"And all things are of God, who hath reconciled us to himself by Jesus Christ." It is through Christ and His death on the cross that we are saved. There is no other source.

d) Titus 2:13-14—"Our Savior, Jesus Christ . . . gave himself for us that he might redeem us."

2. On Satan and his dominion

The "serpent's head" was bruised at the cross (Gen. 3:15).

a) Hebrews 2:14—"Forasmuch, then, as the children are partakers of flesh and blood, he also himself likewise took part of the same, that through death he might destroy him that had the power of death, that is, the devil." When Jesus died on the cross, He destroyed Satan. Why? Because Satan's great weapon is death, and when Jesus died, He rose again and thus conquered Satan's only weapon.

b) Colossians 1:13—"[God] hath delivered us from the power of darkness, and hath translated us into the kingdom of his dear Son." Based on the victory won at the cross, Christ will one day cast Satan into the lake of fire, where he will burn forever.

3. On Jesus

We rarely consider this question: What did Jesus' death mean to Him?

a) He would be glorified

John 14:28 says, "Ye have heard how I said unto you, I go away, and come again unto you. If ye loved me, ye would rejoice, because I said, I go unto the Father; for my Father is greater than I." That is the first thing that Jesus said His death meant to Him. When He died, He knew He would be able to go to the Father. That is a satisfying thing for Him, as is indicated when He said, "My Father is greater than I" (v. 28*b*). What did He mean by that? He meant this: "In My present incarnation, I am in submission to My Father. He has a place of authority over Me. But I long to return to the place where I am not under Him, but face-to-face with Him. If you really thought about My death in unselfish terms, you would think about what My death means to Me." Instead of telling Jesus not to go to the cross, the disciples should have encouraged Him in this sense:

Having accomplished His work, Christ would be restored to His face-to-face relationship with the Father, His servitude and humiliation coming to an end.

b) His word would be verified

In John 14:29-30 He says, "And now I have told you before it come to pass, that, when it is come to pass, ye might believe. Hereafter I will not talk much with you; for the prince of this world cometh, and hath nothing in me." He is saying, "You should be glad about the cross, because when I am there, My word will be verified. Everything I told you is going to come to pass. You will see the fulfillment of all the promises. There's not going to be much talk anymore; there's going to be some action."

c) His enemy would be defeated

He says, "The prince of this world cometh, and hath nothing in me" (v. 30*b*). He would come, but his attack would be unsuccessful because Jesus had no vulnerability. Satan couldn't strike anywhere because Christ was the perfect Son of God.

d) His love would be demonstrated

John 14:31 says, "But that the world may know that I love the Father, and, as the Father gave me commandment, even so I do. Arise, let us go from here." He is saying, "There's a fourth reason you ought to rejoice in the meaning of My death for Me—it demonstrates to the world that I love the Father." Why? He willingly accepted the Father's will and died, not only to redeem us, but to give us a pattern for our own obedience.

So Jesus says, "Instead of thinking about yourself, why don't you think about what my death means to Me? It allows Me to be glorified, it verifies My promises, it defeats My enemy, and it demonstrates My love. The cross, as the focal point of all of history, has a profound impact on men—it saves them. It has profound impact on demons—it damns them. And it has profound impact on Jesus Christ—His work is finished, and He returns to the glory of the Father. But most importantly, in Romans 3:25-31, we need to understand that the death of Christ has great impact:

4. On God

Everything ultimately resolves itself in God's majestic glory, and the death of Christ is no different. While it has a saving impact on men, a damning impact on demons and the ungodly, and a fulfilling impact on Christ, it has a glorifying impact on God Himself.

There are four ways the cross glorifies God. It is very important for us not

75

to see everything from our perspective. We need to see from the divine perspective of God's glory.

Review

I. DECLARES GOD'S RIGHTEOUSNESS (vv. 25-26; see pp. 62-68)

  A. The Revealed Truth (v. 25; see pp. 62-66)

    1. The problem raised (v. 25a; see pp. 62-63)

    "Whom God hath set forth to be a propitiation through faith in his blood, to declare his righteousness."

    2. The purpose related (v. 25b; see pp. 63-66)

    "For the remission of sins that are past, through the forbearance of God."

      a) Presupposing God's injustice (see pp. 64-65)

God received criticism that He was not righteous because He was tolerant of sin in the past. He appeared to be so merciful, gracious, kind, generous, and loving that He just passed by sin. As a result, critics say that He is capricious, whimsical, inequitable, unjust, unrighteous, and inconsistent, like the deities of the pagan world, because He passed by sin. If He were truly holy, righteous, and just, He couldn't do that—He would have to exact the penalty that the crime deserved. If He were a just, holy, righteous God, He could not overlook sin. So critics posed this question: "How could a righteous God forgive sinners, pass by their sin, and eliminate the penalty?" And the answer is: He couldn't.

God Himself claims to be holy and to be unable to pass by sin. In the Old Testament God says that He will not pass by their iniquity. Habakkuk 1:13 says, "Thou art of purer eyes than to behold evil, and canst not look on iniquity." Exodus 34:7 says that He "will by no means clear the guilty."

Sin has to be punished. It is impossible for sin to be excused. It cannot fade away or be put aside. Sin hangs on, wreaking its deadly havoc in judgment. No amount of optimism, no amount of love, no amount of grace, and no amount of mercy can put aside sin. The Bible makes it very clear that "the wages of sin is death" (Rom. 6:23). Sin demands death, and a holy God could never eliminate that penalty.

      b) Preserving God's justice (see p. 66)

        (1) The substitution

At the cross, God vindicated His righteousness by putting His Son to death as a substitute. In a divine miracle, He gathered up all the sin of the ages and put it on Christ. Jesus Christ became sacrifice, paying the price for all that sin, and God was proven to be a just God. He does not pass by sin without its penalty being met.

You say, "If God is a just and holy God, why didn't He slaughter everybody and send them all to hell?" But He is also a merciful God, and had to find the absolute balance between His love and His justice. That balance was found in the full execution of the penalty for sin on a substitute. Those who believe in that substitute can go free. Every sin I ever committed or will commit has been paid for by Christ. Because I believe in Him, His sacrifice is applied on my behalf. God wrote across the list of my transgressions, "Paid for in full!" And with that, God remains a just and righteous God.

Romans 1:18 says, "For the wrath of God is revealed from heaven against all ungodliness and unrighteousness." All of God's wrath against ungodliness and unrighteousness was revealed at the cross. You ask, "What does a Christian receive when he is punished and chastened by the Lord?" He receives remedial instruction so he won't sin again. The Christian's sins have been paid for in full if he knows and believes in the Lord Jesus Christ. At the cross God declared His righteous nature.

A Great Truth of the Old Testament

One of the great truths of the Old Testament is God's righteousness.

1. Deuteronomy 32:4—"He is the Rock, his work is perfect; for all his ways are justice; a God of truth and without iniquity, just and right is he." He will always do what is just and right. That is why sin had to be paid for.

2. Psalm 89:14—"Righteousness and justice are the habitation of thy throne." They are intrinsic to God.

3. Exodus 23:7—"I will not justify the wicked." And not without an adequate penalty, which was death.

Second Corinthians 5:21 says, "For he hath made him, who knew no sin, to be sin for us, that we might be made the righteousness of God in him." That's the heart and soul of the Christian message.

The Son of Man Must Suffer

That phrase is used several times in the New Testament (Mark 8:31; 9:12; Luke 9:22; 17:25; Acts 9:16; Heb. 9:26). The Son of Man must suffer. Why? In order to preserve the integrity of God's character as a righteous God. You say, "What about the Old Testament sacrifices? Didn't they preserve God's integrity?" Not at all. They were only symbols. Hebrews 10:4 says, "For it is not possible that the blood of bulls and of goats should take away sins." A bull can't die for you, a goat can't die

77

for you, even a man can't die for you—only the God-Man could go into the grave, conquer death, and come out the other side.

(2) The satisfaction

In Romans 3:25 a key word is *"propitiation."* It is the Greek word *hilastērion,* which basically means "to be satisfied." When Jesus died on the cross, God was satisfied. How do we know that? When Jesus finished His work on the cross, the Father exalted Him to His right hand. Hebrews 1:3 says, "When he had by himself purged our sins, sat down on the right hand of the Majesty on high" (cf. Phil. 2:9-11; Heb. 10:12). He did what no man could do.

Psalm 49:7-8 says, "None of them can by any means redeem his brother, nor give to God a ransom for him (for the redemption of their soul is precious)." The psalmist is saying that no man could redeem another because the price is too high. Only Christ—God incarnate, the sinless, spotless lamb of God—could. He was a holy, special, harmless, and undefiled sacrifice. He took our place.

B. The Repeated Truth (v. 26; see pp. 66-68)

"To declare, I say, at this time his righteousness, that he might be just, and the justifier of him who believeth in Jesus."

Lesson

II. EXALTS GOD'S GRACE (vv. 27-28)

A. The Exclusion (v. 27)

1. The provision (v. 27*a*)

"Where is boasting then? It is excluded."

Why is boasting excluded? What did you do to gain righteousness? Nothing. God, to vindicate His own righteousness, revealed His Son, and put Him on a cross to bear our sins. He offers us the free gift of salvation, and says, "Believe." Where is there room for boasting? There is no place for self-congratulation or for self-satisfaction.

a) 1 Corinthians 1:26-31—"For ye see your calling, brethren, how that not many wise men after the flesh, not many mighty, not many noble, are called; but God hath chosen the foolish things . . . the weak things . . . and base things . . . and things which are despised" (vv. 26-28). Why? "That no flesh should glory in his presence. But of him are ye in Christ Jesus . . . that, according as it is written, he that glorieth, let him glory in the Lord" (vv. 29-31). If you

78

are going to boast, then boast in the Lord. You didn't deserve or earn anything.

b) Romans 4:2—"For if Abraham were justified by works, he hath something of which to glory." Was he justified by works? Not at all. Nobody in this world has ever been saved by anything they did, including religious activity.

c) Ephesians 2:8-9—"For by grace are ye saved through faith; and that not of yourselves, it is the gift of God—not of works, lest any man should boast." If salvation came by works, we would all be telling each other how we accomplished it. Then the glory is ours, not God's. But God designed a plan of salvation that would reveal His righteous character and exalt His great grace. You say, "Well, I believed." Sure, but even the ability to do that was from Him. Verse 8 says, "For by grace are ye saved through faith; and that not of yourselves, it is the gift of God."

2. The principles (v. 27b-c)

a) Works (v. 27b)

"By what law [principle]? Of works? Nay."

If we were saved by works, would that exclude boasting? No. If we were saved by works, that would invite boasting.

b) Faith (b. 27c)

"But by the law [principle] of faith."

If salvation is an act of simply believing—if redemption comes to you by believing in what God has done and not holding to what you have done, then what have you got to boast about? Nothing.

(1) Luke 18:10-14—"Two men went up into the temple to pray. . . . The Pharisee stood and prayed thus with himself, God, I thank thee that I am not as other men are, extortioners, unjust, adulterers, or even as this tax collector. I fast twice in the week; I give tithes of all that I possess" (vv. 10-12). He was patting himself on the back and telling God how marvelous he was. Verse 13 says, "And the tax collector, standing afar off, would not lift up so much as his eyes unto heaven, but smote upon his breast, saying, God be merciful to me a sinner." In verse 14 Jesus says, "I tell you, this man went down to his house justified rather than the other." You could title that passage, "The good man that went to hell, and the bad man that went to heaven." That is exactly what salvation is all about. The issue of salvation is believing in it, not trying to earn it. What staggers me is how the Roman Catholic system has missed the teaching of justification by faith through the centuries and bound its people in a horrible and eternally

consequential system of works.

(2) Romans 4:5—"But to him that worketh not, but believeth on him that justifieth the ungodly, his faith is counted for righteousness." It is not the seemingly godly one that works for salvation, but the ungodly one that believes that receives God's righteousness.

(3) Romans 5:1—"Therefore, being justified by faith, we have peace with God through our Lord Jesus Christ."

(4) Romans 8:3—"For what the law could not do, in that it was weak through the flesh, God sending his own Son, in the likeness of sinful flesh and for sin, condemned sin in the flesh." Paul means that the law couldn't fulfill righteousness in us. We couldn't live up to the standards. We couldn't do enough good works to be saved.

(5) Galatians 2:16—"Knowing that a man is not justified by the works of the law, but by the faith of Jesus Christ, even we have believed in Jesus Christ, that we might be justified by the faith of Christ, and not by the works of the law." The biggest lie of false religion across the earth is that men are justified by their works. The cults all teach justification by works. And that takes the glory from God and gives it to man.

(6) Galatians 3:8, 11—"And the scripture, foreseeing that God would justify the Gentiles through faith, preached before the gospel unto Abraham. . . . no man is justified by the law in the sight of God, it is evident; for, The just shall live by faith."

(7) Romans 10:9—"If thou shalt confess with thy mouth the Lord Jesus, and shalt believe in thine heart that God hath raised him from the dead, thou shalt be saved."

The apostle Paul cuts away the ground from underneath the one who says, "I always do the best I can. I certainly live a decent life. If there's a good God up there, He couldn't possibly send me to hell." That stance is eliminated when Paul tells him that he is made right with God only through faith.

B. The Conclusion (v. 28)

"Therefore, we conclude that a man is justified by faith apart from the deeds of the law."

You can't earn your way into the kingdom. A works salvation system blasts the glory of God. Man becomes a usurper who boasts that he has earned his way to God. But that violates the intent of salvation. Romans 3 teaches that salvation is for God's sake. Jesus died for the sake of God so that God's righteousness might be revealed and that His grace might be exalted. Edward Mote said the following in the hymn "The Solid Rock":

> My hope is built on nothing less
> Than Jesus' blood and righteousness.
> I dare not trust the sweetest frame,
> But wholly lean on Jesus' name.

In 1 Corinthians 15:10 Paul says, "But by the grace of God I am what I am." That certainly makes me thankful that I have been redeemed—not on the basis of anything that I have done or deserve, but purely by the grace of God. It is a staggering thought that fills my heart with thanksgiving.

What is saving faith? We are saved by faith according to Romans 3:22, 25, and 28. We are saved by believing in Jesus according to Romans 3:26. It is important to understand what that faith is. What is saving faith? Many people say that they believe in Jesus. There is a continual discussion about faith: "What kind of faith is saving faith? How much of it do you need to have?" In the parable of the soils from Matthew 13:1-8, there were many people who initially latched on, but they eventually died out (vv. 4-7). They didn't have saving faith because there was no fruit. So let's look at faith to see if we can discern saving faith from non-saving faith. I know there are many people who identify with Christianity, but how do we know if they are really saved? Here is the test.

I. INVALID INDICATORS OF SAVING FAITH

Invalid indicators neither prove nor disprove saving faith. If you look at somebody's life and see those things, you can't know for sure if they are saved.

A. Visible Morality

If a person is outwardly moral, that does not necessarily mean he has saving faith. But many people would say they believe in Jesus because they are outwardly moral. As you look at their lives, there is a visible morality. Do you know what that proves? Nothing.

1. Of the Pharisees

The Pharisees were moral on the outside. Jesus said, "For ye are like whited sepulchers, which indeed appear beautiful outward, but are within full of dead men's bones, and of all uncleanness" (Matt. 23:27b).

2. Of the young man

In Matthew 19:16 a young man came to Jesus and said, "Good Master, what good thing shall I do, that I may have eternal life?" What kind of system was he in? Works salvation. He was saying, "What other good thing do I need to do since I've done so many good things?" In verse 17 the Lord says, "Why callest thou me good? There is none good but one, that is, God." Jesus established that He is God. In verses 18b-20a He says, "Thou shalt do no murder, Thou shalt not commit adultery. Thou shalt not steal, Thou shalt not bear false witness, Honor thy father and thy mother; and, Thou shalt love thy neighbor as thyself. The young man saith unto him, All these things have I kept from my youth up." His visible morality didn't mean anything. The young man asked, "What lack I yet? Jesus said unto him, If thou wilt be perfect, go and sell what thou hast, and give to the poor" (vv. 20b-21a). You say, "Are you saved by doing that?" No, but you will get a big barrier out of the way, and that was what was standing between that man and the Lord. Verse 22 says, "But when the young man heard that saying, he went away sorrowful; for he had great possessions." He didn't want to part with his money. His visible morality meant absolutely nothing.

Morality is a mark of a Christian if it comes from a proper internal motive, and not from an external one. A second mark that doesn't prove or disprove saving faith is:

B. Intellectual Knowledge

This could also be called "biblical knowledge." Sometimes you might meet someone who knows the Bible well enough to quote many verses, and even interpret some of them. They might have an amazing ability to understand the truth.

1. Romans 1:21—"When they [men] knew God, they glorified him not as God." It is possible to know all about God, yet have no personal relationship with Him. So, when somebody knows the Bible, it doesn't necessarily mean that they are saved.

2. Romans 2:17-20—"But if thou . . . makest thy boast of God, and knowest his will, and approvest the things that are more excellent, being instructed out of the law, and art confident that thou thyself art a guide of the blind, a light of them who are in darkness, an instructor of the foolish, a teacher of babes, who hast the form of knowledge." In verse 24 Paul says, "For the name of God is blasphemed among the Gentiles through you." They only had a form of knowledge. In fact, when the Jewish people were given the full knowledge of the Messiah, many rejected Him (John 15:24).

C. Religious Involvement

In the Old Testament, God continually condemned Israel for being religiously involved but totally lacking in a vital relationship with Him. That was also the error of the Pharisees. There are all kinds of people who are involved in religious activity.

A good illustration is from the parable found in Matthew 25:1-12: "Ten virgins . . . took their lamps, and went forth to meet the bridegroom. And five of them were wise, and five were foolish.

They that were foolish took their lamps, and took no oil with them; but the wise took oil in their vessels with their lamps. While the bridegroom tarried, they all slumbered and slept. And at midnight there was a cry made, Behold, the bridegroom cometh, go ye out to meet him. Then all those virgins arose and trimmed their lamps. And the foolish said unto the wise, Give us of your oil; for our lamps are gone out. But the wise answered, saying, Not so, lest there be not for us and you" (vv. 1b-9a). They missed the whole marriage. The implication is given in verse 13, "You had better be ready when the Son of Man comes."

What is interesting about that parable are the similarities between the two sets of women. They are all virgins. What do virgins represent? Purity, chastity, virtue—they are religious people. They are properly involved, doing what religious virgins should do—trimming their lamps, and attending to the religious environment. The only thing one set doesn't have is what they need (the oil). But that is the only difference. You wouldn't have been able to pick out the fools from the wise in that group of ten until the fools said, "We don't have any oil." Religious involvement doesn't prove anything. You can be involved in a church all of your life and still be lost.

D. Active Ministry

One of the most active prophets in the Old Testament was Balaam, but he didn't serve God; he served the highest bidder (2 Pet. 2:15). And then there was Judas, a public preacher of the gospel of the kingdom, and there was never more a son of hell than that man.

Matthew 7 says, "Many will say to me in that day, Lord, Lord, have we not prophesied in thy name? And in thy name have cast out demons? And in thy name done many wonderful works? And then will I profess unto them, I never knew you; depart from me" (vv. 22-23a). Visible morality, intellectual knowledge, religious involvement, and active ministry don't prove anything. And fifth, neither does:

E. Conviction of Sin

Mental hospitals all over this nation are filled with people who are convicted of their sin but haven't been delivered from it. They have been beaten into insanity by guilt.

1. Acts 24:25—Felix trembled under the preaching of Paul, but he delayed responding to his conviction.

2. John 16:8—The Holy Spirit convicts the world of sin, righteousness, and judgment, but not all people will respond.

3. John 8:37, 40—When Jesus convicted the Pharisees of sin, they didn't confess it; they became infuriated and sought to kill Him.

4. **Revelation 16:9, 11, 21**—When the Lord begins to pour out judgment on sin, people will become aware that God is judging them for their sin; but instead of repenting, they will blaspheme the God of heaven.

There are some people who respond to the conviction of sin. They feel bad about their sin, so they confess it and amend their ways. People do reform. There are alcoholics, drug addicts, and criminals who have been rehabilitated. They decide to reform, but God isn't necessarily involved in that reform. A person could sense his sinfulness and guilt, and still not necessarily exercise saving faith. He could say, "I believe in Jesus. I'm convicted about my sin," but that doesn't automatically mean that he has truly come to Jesus Christ.

F. Assurance

You say, "Do you mean that a person could be sure he was saved and still be lost?" That's right. This world is full of people like that. If they didn't believe they were saved, do you think they would stay in the false religion they are involved in? They think they are OK. There are all kinds of people saying, "I'm a good person; God wouldn't do anything to me." The world is full of legalists who believe that. Gardner Spring wrote, "If to be strongly persuaded that we are Christians would make us Christians, there would be no such thing as being deceived by false hopes and delusive presumption." Men couldn't be deceived if they didn't have the opportunity to think they were saved when they weren't. So many people say, "I'm good; I'll be fine—I'm not worried." But they are lost.

G. The Time of Decision

A person will come to be baptized and very often say, "I received the Lord ten years ago, but nothing ever happened in my life for the next ten years." But an individual doesn't get transformed by the Son of God and translated out of the kingdom of darkness into the kingdom of His dear Son and have nothing happen. Jesus said, "Ye shall know them by their fruits" (Matt. 7:16*a*). They will have to manifest some fruit—"some an hundredfold, some sixtyfold, some thirtyfold" (Matt. 13:8*b*). Just because there was a moment when you walked down an aisle, went into a prayer room, signed a card, or raised your hand, it doesn't mean that your decision for Christ was necessarily valid.

That was a list of invalid indicators of faith. Look at your life. Ask yourself this question: "Is my faith real, saving faith?" If you look at yourself and say, "I'm a moral person; I know the Bible; I'm involved at church; I have a ministry; I feel bad about my sin; I feel like I'm OK with God; I can remember the moment I was saved"—don't think those things indicate anything one way or another about the validity of your faith. All kinds of people think those things are true about themselves, and they are deceived—self-deceived. When they arrive at the situation in Matthew 7:23, they receive the shock of all shocks when the Lord says, "I don't know you." A man may be completely committed to moral development, well instructed in the doctrines of the Bible, manifest a form of religion, proceed in a ministry with marvelous giftedness, have been subject to conviction in his heart, believe himself to be converted and regenerated, and still be lost.

II. VALID INDICATORS OF SAVING FAITH

A. Love for God

1. The definitions

a) The unsaved

The basic definition of an unsaved person is bound in Romans 8:7: "The carnal [fleshly] mind is enmity against God." That means, "the carnal mind hates God." That is a classic definition of an unregenerate person. They resist God; they hate Him.

b) The saved

The saved person loves God. The first commandment is, "And thou shalt love the Lord thy God with all thy heart, and with all thy soul, and with all thy mind, and with all thy strength" (Mark 12:30a). When a person is truly exercising saving faith, I believe there is a great love for God in his heart. His delight is in the law of God, and he meditates on it day and night (Josh. 1:8). Psalm 42:1 says, "As the hart panteth after the water brooks, so panteth my soul after thee, O God." His delight is in the excellency of God. The first and highest affection rising out of his renewed soul is that God should be honored and glorified. God is his chief happiness.

2. The delineation

Most people in this world are consumed with their own happiness. There are many people who say they are Christians, but they are consumed with their own happiness. They don't pass the first test.

a) Matthew 10:37—"He that loveth father or mother more than me, is not worthy of me." If God is not your highest affection, check yourself. Is He your greatest love? Is He your supreme delight? Do you long from the deepest part of your heart to love God, to bask in the warmth of the relationship with Him, and to draw nigh unto Him? That is a mark of saving faith and a regenerated heart.

b) Psalm 73:25—Asaph says, "Whom have I in heaven but thee? And there in none upon earth that I desire beside thee."

c) Psalm 42:1-3—"As the hart panteth after the water

brooks, so panteth my soul after thee, O God. My soul thirsteth for God, for the living God; when shall I come and appear before God? My tears have been my food."

The heart that craves God, that adores Him, is what marks true saving faith. If you have truly been redeemed, you will love God. He will be your greatest desire. Your deepest longing will be to be in His presence and to fulfill His glory.

3. The direction

There will be times when we fail to do that. Nonetheless, that will still be the direction of our lives if not the perfection. When I fail to love God as I ought, to seek Him as my highest good, to pour out my affection, to be jealous for His holy name, and to live for His glory—that in itself breaks my heart.

B. Repentance from Sin

I believe that is the corollary of the first principle. If you love God, you hate sin. The two are obviously connected. That which gives us a love for God gives us a hatred of sin.

1. The tears of repentance

a) Proverbs 28:13—"He that covereth his sins shall not prosper, but whoso confesseth and forsaketh them shall have mercy." Mercy is given to those who confess and forsake their sins.

b) Psalm 51:1-4—David had the same attitude after he had committed a terrible sin. He said, "Have mercy upon me, O God, according to thy loving-kindness; according unto the multitude of thy tender mercies blot out my transgressions. Wash me thoroughly from mine iniquity, and cleanse me from my sin. For I acknowledge my transgressions, and my sin is ever before me. Against thee, thee only, have I sinned, and done this evil in thy sight." In other words, he realized, in his great love for God, how terrible his sin was against Him.

A true Christian—a person with saving faith—hates sin. Even though he commits a sin, he hates it. In Romans 7:15 Paul says, "I do what I don't want to do, and I don't do what I want to do." Even though our humanness draws us into sin, we hate it. You may not hate sin when you first get involved in it, but you sure hate it when you realize what you have done. So a believer is marked by a love for God and a hatred of sin.

2. The triumph of repentance

In 2 Corinthians 7:9 Paul says, "Now I rejoice, not that ye were made sorry but that ye sorrowed to repentance; for ye were made sorry after a godly manner." Many people are sorry about their sin. It makes them feel bad, it reaps bad fruits, and it brings bad consequences. Many people who don't know God are sorry about their sin, but they don't sorrow unto repentance—they are not so sorry that they stop doing it and turn from it. Verse 10 says, "For godly sorrow worketh repentance to salvation." Salvation comes to those who sorrow unto repentance. In other words, I'm not just to be sorry about my sin; I'm to be so sorry about it that I want to turn from it and be delivered from it. That is the kind of sorrow that is attached to salvation. A proper love for God results in a hatred of sin and a grief over it. True penitents are born of God.

3. The test of repentance

In 1 John, John gives us a test. He says, "If we are believers, we will confess our sins. A non-believer denies his sin." First John 1:8-10 says, "If we say that we have no sin, we deceive ourselves, and the truth is not in us. If we confess our sins, he is faithful and just to forgive us" (vv. 8-9a). In others words, forgiveness belongs to sin-confessors, not to sin-deniers. Verse 10 says, "If we say that we have not sinned, we make him a liar, and his word is not in us." A truly forgiven and saved person is one who turns from sin.

Ask yourself these questions: "Do I hate sin? Is sin a bitter and evil thing? Am I convicted deep within my heart when I see it in my life? Do I hate it not only because it is ruinous to my soul, but because it is offensive to my God? Which gives you more anxiety—your sins or your misfortunes in life?" That is a good test. The one born of God is overwrought with his sin.

One writer said, "When God touches, He breaks the heart. Where He pours out the spirit of grace, there are not a few transient sighs that agitate the breast—there are heart-rending pangs of sorrow." The true believer is marked by a hatred of sin and repentance from it.

C. Genuine Humility

This test is linked with the previous one. Where there is a sense of the love of God, there will be a sense of the hate of sin. And when sin is hated, there will be humility, because as you look at your life and see your sin, you are humbled.

1. Illuminated in the Beatitudes

In the Beatitudes, we see that one who wants to enter into the kingdom mourns, comes begging in spirit, hungers and thirsts, and seeks mercy (Matt. 5:3-4, 6-7).

2. Illustrated by the prodigal son

The story of the prodigal son is an illustration of salvation (Luke 15:11-32). The son runs away to riotous living, and spends all he has. But he comes back, and his father receives him. That is a picture of salvation. What the son said is so much a part of true saving faith: "Father, I . . . am no more worthy to be called thy son" (Luke 15:21*b*). That is humility and a mark of saving faith.

An individual with humility doesn't offer himself to God as if he were something very valuable. He doesn't say, "Here I am, God. Aren't You blessed to get me?" The Lord seeks a broken spirit and a contrite heart (Ps. 51:17). The Bible says, "God resisteth the proud, but giveth grace unto the humble" (James 4:6*b*). There is humility in saving faith. Matthew 16:24 says, "If any man will come after me, let him deny himself."

Look at your life. Do you see a love for God? Even though you fail, do you sense that great love and delight in Him? Do you see a hatred for sin and the desire to turn from it? Do you find in your heart no good thing? And are you humbled because of your sin in the presence of the God you love?

D. Devotion to God's Glory

1. The desire

I believe that true saving faith is marked by the desire to glorify God above everything else. There is a certain sense in which you need to set aside your own glory, designs, will, comfort, and enterprise in order to seek that which brings honor to God. The person who is truly experiencing salvation is one who is consummately committed to God's glory. Paul's testimony is: "According to my earnest expectation and my hope, that in nothing I shall be ashamed, but that with all boldness, as always, so now also Christ shall be magnified in my body, whether it be by life or by death" (Phil. 1:20). I believe that one who is truly exercising saving faith will have his life marked by a desire for the glory of God.

2. The direction

Now I know that desire is not going to be true all of the time in our lives. As I said before, if it is not the *perfection* of our lives, at least it is the *direction* of our lives. We, like Paul, can say, "I have not already attained it, but I'm running on the track, seeking God's glory" (Phil. 3:12). A person who seeks only his own glory, his own will, his own aggrandizement, and his own reputation could not be exercising saving faith because his own self had not yet died. One who has been saved and transformed will have the glory of God as the direction of his life.

Those tests are all general patterns, much like the tests John gives in 1 John. There are exceptions to those patterns, and that is why we need a high priest who intercedes for us.

E. Continual Prayer

1. The heart that cries to God

Galatians 4:6 says, "And because ye are sons, God hath sent

88

forth the Spirit of his Son into your hearts, crying, Abba, Father." What is it that marks a Christian? A heart that cries to God, a heart that seeks communion. I admit to you that I don't pray as much as I should, but perhaps none of us has the sense of having arrived in our prayer life. But I can also say that my heart longs to commune with God. When any problem comes into my life, my first response is to take it to God. When I face any task that I know is significant, my first response is to depend on Him. I believe that a true Christian, one marked by saving faith, will express his heart in communion with God.

2. The hypocrisy that won't cry to God

In Job 27:10, Job demands that a hypocrite be evaluated. He says, "Will he delight himself in the Almighty? Will he always call upon God?" That was Job's test for saving faith. If you want to determine the identity of a hypocrite, find out if he calls on God all the time. If he doesn't, then he is a hypocrite. Jonathan Edwards, the great preacher, gave a sermon titled, "Hypocrites Deficient in the Duty of Secret Prayer." True believers commune with God.

Test yourself. Do you love God? Do you hate sin? Do you find your heart broken in humility? Are you devoted to God's glory? And do you find yourself continually drawn into communion with Him? Those are the tests.

F. Selfless Love

I also believe that true saving faith is marked by the love believers have for each other.

1. 1 John 2:9-10—"He that saith he is in the light, and hateth his brother, is in darkness even until now. He that loveth his brother abideth in the light." In other words, the light is the light of redemption. The truly redeemed love their brothers. Do you love the fellowship of believers? Are you enriched, thrilled, and enthralled by the fellowship of those of like precious faith? Do you rejoice with them and care for them as well?

2. 1 John 3:14—"We know that we have passed from death unto life, because we love the brethren." If I have my choice between being with the people of the world and being with the people of the Lord, it's not much of a choice. I have no desire to fellowship with the people of the world. I love to be with God's people; I love the fellowship of the saints!

3. 1 John 4:7-8—"Beloved, let us love one another; for love is of God, and everyone that loveth is born of God, and knoweth God. He that loveth not knoweth not God; for God is love." If you have true saving faith and have been genuinely redeemed, you are going to love the brethren.

G. Separation from the World

When we were saved, we were delivered out of the world in a very real sense.

1. 1 John 5:4-5—"Whatever is born of God overcometh the world; and this is the victory that overcometh the world, even our faith. Who is he that overcometh the world, but he that believeth that Jesus is the Son of God?" True faith, believing in Jesus as the Son of God, results in overcoming the world.

2. 1 John 2:15—"If any man love the world, the love of the Father is not in him." What do you love? Do you love the world, or do you separate yourself from the world?

3. James 4:4—"The friendship of the world is emnity with God? Whosoever, therefore, will be a friend of the world is the enemy of God." The true test is separation from the world. There are times when we drift, but the main pursuit of our life is away from the world.

4. 1 Corinthians 2:12—"Now we have received, not the spirit of the world, but the Spirit who is of God." Our hearts are drawn to Him.

H. Spiritual Growth

I believe that saving faith will demonstrate itself in growth.

1. The parables

a) The soils

If we have learned anything from the parable of the soils, we have learned that you can distinguish true faith by its fruit—its product (Matt. 13:8). True faith grows and develops. Life reproduces life, and spiritual life reproduces spiritual life.

b) The growing seed

In Mark 4:26-29 the Lord says, "So is the kingdom of God, as if a man should cast seed into the ground; and should sleep, and rise night and day, and the seed should spring and grow up, he knoweth not how. For the earth bringeth forth fruit of itself: first the blade, then the ear, after that the full grain in the ear. But when the fruit is brought forth, immediately he putteth in the sickle, because the harvest is come." You plant seed and it grows.

2. The passages

a) 1 Peter 1:23—Peter says that there is an incorruptible seed planted in the heart of the believer.

b) Ephesians 4:13—Paul constantly taught that the life of God produces fruit, results, and growth. He said that we all are growing "unto the measure of the stature of the fullness of Christ."

  c) 1 John 2:12-13—You start out as little babes, become spiritual young men, and then mature to become spiritual fathers.

  d) Philippians 1:6—"He who hath begun a good work in you will perform it until the day of Jesus Christ."

You need to grow. Growth is the sign of true spiritual life.

I. Obedient Living

  1. 1 John 2:3-5—"And by this we do know that we know him, if we keep his commandments. He that saith, I know him, and keepeth not his commandments, is a liar, and the truth is not in him. But whosoever keepeth his word, in him verily is the love of God perfected; by this know we that we are in him." You know you are saved when you live a life of obedience.

  2. Ephesians 2:10—"For we are his workmanship, created in Christ Jesus unto good works, which God hath before ordained that we should walk in them."

The overwhelming habit of our life is not disobedience; it is obedience. There will be disobedience in our lives, but as we grow, it will decrease. I believe with all my heart that if a person has exercised true saving faith, he has a great desire to live a life of obedience. Show me someone who doesn't, and I have every right to ask the question, "Do you have saving faith?" no matter what he claims.

The next time you want to know if someone is a Christian, or even if you want to examine your own heart, here is what you are looking for: Do I love God above all else? Do I hate sin and desire to turn from it? Am I genuinely aware of my nothingness and feebleness? In true humility do I come to the God of mercy, unworthy to be called His son? Am I devoted above all things to the expression of God's glory? Am I continually drawn into sweet communion with Him? Am I selfless and given to loving others? Do I find myself longing to be utterly separated from the world? Can I look at my life and see spiritual growth? Is the deep hunger of my heart to obey, even during those times of disobedience? Those are the marks of a Christian—one with true saving faith.

When you have asked those questions, and the answers are positive, you can go back to the first list. Those things may be true about a Christian. When you display the true marks of saving faith, I believe you will have a visible, genuine morality. I believe you will have a proper knowledge of the Word of God. You will be involved in the activities of the church—you will have a ministry. You will sense guilt over sin. You will have assurance. The time of your decision will have meaning to you. But those things can't stand alone. We must continually examine ourselves to see whether we are in the faith. That is the issue. Are you in the faith?

Focusing on the Facts

1. What doctrine is the very heart and soul of the Christian faith? Why (see p. 72)?

2. In what ways is the death of Jesus Christ central to Christians (see p. 73)?

3. What kind of impact did the death of Christ have on believers? On Satan and his dominion? Support your answer with Scripture (see pp. 73-74).

4. What four things did Jesus' death mean to Him? Explain the importance of each one (see pp. 74-75).

5. Why was God criticized in the past? How was He vindicated (see pp. 76-77)?

6. Since God is just and holy, why didn't He slaughter everyone and send them all to hell (see p. 77)?

7. What happened to every sin that every Christian has committed or will commit (see p. 77)?

8. What does the Old Testament teach about God's righteousness? Support your answer with Scripture (see p. 77).

9. Why did the Son of Man have to suffer (see p. 77)?

10. How do we know that God was satisfied by Jesus' death on the cross (see p. 78)?

11. According to Romans 3:27, boasting is excluded. Why? Support your answer (see pp. 78-79).

12. Fill in the blanks: Boasting is not excluded by the law of _____ _____, but by the law of _____ (see Rom. 3:27; p. 79).

13. Why does a works salvation system blast the glory of God (see p. 80)?

14. Give examples of things that neither prove nor disprove saving faith (see pp. 81-85).

15. When is visible morality a true mark of a Christian? When is it not (see p. 82)?

16. Discuss some verses that explain how some people can know a great deal about the Bible yet not be saved (see p. 82).

17. How does the parable of the ten virgins from Matthew 25:1-12 illustrate the error of religious involvement (see pp. 82-83)?

18. Fill in the blanks: Many people are convicted of their sin, but haven't been _____ _____ _____ (see p. 83).

19. How can a person be sure he is saved but still be lost (see p. 84)?

20. What is needed in the life of a person who claims he is saved because of his time of decision for Christ (see p. 84)?

21. Give a definition of an unsaved person. Give a definition of a saved person. What does a truly saved person delight in (see p. 85)?

22. Discuss some Scriptures that demonstrate the heart that craves God (see pp. 85-86).

23. What kind of sorrow over sin results in salvation? How must the individual with that sorrow react to sin (see 2 Cor. 7:9-10; pp. 86-87)?

24. In 1 John 1:8-10, what is the test John gives to determine a believer from a non-believer (see p. 87)?

25. Why is genuine humility the result of hating sin (see p. 87)?

26. How does the prodigal son illustrate the humility necessary in true saving faith (see Luke 15:21; pp. 87-88)?

27. What marks true saving faith above all else? Give a scriptural example of someone who attempted to do just that (see p. 88).

28. What should be your first response when any problem comes into your life or when you are faced with a significant task (see p. 89)?

29. What was Job's test for evaluating a hypocrite (see Job 27:10; p. 89)?

30. Why is selfless love a true mark of saving faith? Support your answer with Scripture (see p. 89).

31. What verses support the fact that those who are truly saved have separated themselves from the world? Discuss them (see p. 90).

32. As a Christian grows in the faith, what will happen to the disobedience in his life (see p. 91)?

Pondering the Principles

1. Jesus Christ died primarily for God, but He also died for you. What was the impact of Christ's death for you? Look up the following verses: Romans 5:8-11; 6:3-5; 8:32; 2 Corinthians 5:15-21; 8:9; Galatians 2:20; 4:4-5; Colossians 1:20-22; 2:14-15; Titus 2:14; Hebrews 10:19-20; 12:2; 1 Peter 1:18-21; 2:21; 3:18; 1 John 1:7; 3:16. According to those verses, list the benefits you have received through Christ's death on the cross. Which of those benefits have the most meaning for you? Thank God for all that He has given you.

2. Review the section that deals with the impact that Jesus' death had on Himself (see pp. 74-75). Read John 14:28-31. Why didn't the disciples rejoice with Jesus? What is your reaction when God does certain things in your life that you don't necessarily approve of? Are you selfishly concerned about your own problems and needs, or are you more concerned with glorifying God? What is the primary focus of your life—how things affect you or how things affect the cause of Christ? What must you do in order to take your focus off of yourself and onto God? Pray that God will cure you of your selfishness so you can be totally obedient to Him.

3. Have you ever boasted about the fact that you are a Christian? Why? Read 1 Corinthians 1:26-31 and Ephesians 2:8-9. Why shouldn't you boast about your salvation? Examine your lifestyle. Are there times in your life when you boast about your Christianity in very subtle ways

and are not even aware that you are doing so? In those cases, could your behavior cause a non-believer to feel inferior to you because you are a Christian? Read Luke 18:10-14. Could you be accused of behaving more like the Pharisee than the publican? What does God want from you? How will you respond in the future to what God wants from you?

4. Do you have the desire to be visibly moral? Why? Do you want to appear moral for the benefit of others, or do you want God to change your life on the inside so that your outward morality will be a reflection of your internal commitment to God? What should your internal commitment consist of?

5. Ask yourself these questions. Is my faith true saving faith? Do I base my faith on the fact that I am a moral person? Do I base my salvation on the fact that I know the Bible? Is it based on my religious involvement? Am I basing my salvation on the fact that I feel the conviction of sin? Do I think I'm saved because I'm sure that I am? Am I basing my salvation on the day I made a decision for Christ? If your responses to those questions indicate that those things are the results of your true faith, praise God! But if you see them as the basis of your salvation, ask God to show you the reality of the salvation He has for you in Jesus Christ. Invite Jesus to be the Lord and Savior of your life. Let Him change you on the inside. Read and memorize Romans 10:9, "If thou shalt confess with thy mouth the Lord Jesus, and shalt believe in thine heart that God hath raised him from the dead, thou shalt be saved."

6. Is God your highest affection? Is He your greatest love? Is He your supreme delight? Is the deepest longing of your heart to love God, to bask in the warmth of a close relationship with Him, and draw near to Him? Look up the following verses: Psalm 37:3-5; 42:1-3; 63:1-7; 73:25; 84:2. Are those verses reflective of your desire? If not, why? Read Philippians 3:3-14. Are you still holding on to what you were before you came to Christ? You need to have the perspective of Paul. What did he desire most in his life? If you are having trouble in giving God your full commitment, you may be stuck at verse 13. Do you have trouble forgetting the things that you have left behind? If you do, compare those things to what Christ has given you (see Pondering the Principles, question 1, p. 93). Then move on in your faith like Paul did.

7. Examine your heart. Do you love God above all else? Do you hate sin and desire to turn from it? Are you genuinely aware that you are nothing compared to God? Do you approach the God of mercy in humility, realizing that you are not worthy to be called His son? Are you devoted to the expression of God's glory? Are you continually drawn into sweet communion with Him? Are you selfless and given to loving others? Do you find yourself longing to be separated from the world? Can you look at your life and see spiritual growth? Is the deep

hunger of your life to obey God? Certainly you will not fulfill those marks perfectly, but are they the direction of your life? If they are not, begin to move in that direction as you make them more a part of your life every day.

6
How Christ Died for God—Part 3

Outline

Introduction
A. The Record of Justification
   1. Imputation
   2. Impartation
      a) A genuine transformation
      b) A genuine righteousness
         (1) The analogy
            (*a*) The reign
            (*b*) The reality
         (2) The analysis
B. The Reality of Justification
   1. Regeneration
   2. Indentification
   3. Redemption
   4. Adoption
C. The Result of Justification
   1. 2 Corinthians 5:17
   2. 2 Peter 1:4
   3. Galatians 2:20
D. The Ramifications of Justification
   1. A new creature
   2. A new righteousness

Review
 I. Declares God's Righteousness
II. Exalts God's Grace

Lesson
III. Reveals God's Consistency
   A. One God of All
      1. The fundamental truth of Judaism
         a) Deuteronomy 6:4
         b) Isaiah 45:5-6
         c) Isaiah 45:22
      2. The foundational truth of Christianity
         a) The premise

        b) The principle
           (1) Illustrations from the Old Testament
             (*a*) Jonah
             (*b*) Ruth
             (*c*) Naaman, the Syrian
           (2) Illustrations from the New Testament
             (*a*) Mark 16:15
             (*b*) Acts 4:12
             (*c*) John 14:6
   B. One Salvation for All
      1. One level of humanity
      2. One way of salvation
         a) In the Old Testament
           (1) Before the national theocracy
             (*a*) Noah
             (*b*) Moses
             (*c*) Abraham
           (2) During the national theocracy
         b) In the New Testament
IV. Confirms God's Law
   A. Questioning the Law
      1. Psalm 119:126
      2. Jeremiah 8:8
   B. Establishing the Law
      1. By the penalty
      2. By the purpose
         a) Stirring up sin
         b) Signifying a Savior
      3. By the potential

Introduction

In Romans 3, Paul describes the human condition from the divine viewpoint. Men have chosen to glorify themselves rather than God. Consequently, all men—both religious and irreligious, moral and immoral—are under the wrath of God. They are under the condemnation of God's judgment. But God also made it possible for men to avoid that judgment and made men right with Him. He poured out His wrath on Christ, who became the substitute for men. Christ suffered our pain and died our death. His death satisfied God's just requirement and allowed God's love, mercy, and grace to be given to man because the penalty was paid. Paul told us that we are not made right with God according to works or law. Salvation, the gift of God, is received by faith. It is provided for all who will respond in faith; it is given freely and paid for by the sacrifice of Christ. That is how God makes man right with Himself. The purpose of justification by faith is to make men right with God and acceptable to Him. It enables us to have fellowship with God now and forever.

   A. The Record of Justification

      Justification by faith encompasses two things:

1. Imputation

   It is a declaration, a statement, and an affirmation. God says, "Based upon the merit, death, and righteousness of Jesus Christ, and your faith in Him, I declare you to be right with Me. I declare you to be just and righteous." Romans 4:11 says that righteousness is imputed to those who believe. Based on the work of Christ, God declares us righteous.

   Now, in a very real sense we are not righteous; we are unrighteous. By believing we don't make ourselves righteous. Rather, God declares that we are righteous. He imputes His righteousness to us because Jesus Christ has paid the penalty for our sin.

2. Impartation

   Many people believe justified means "just-as-if-I'd-never-sinned." In other words, God says, "I count you righteous even though you're really not." It is true that God makes that declaration, but there is also a reality of righteousness. We are not only declared righteous; we are made righteous. There is not only imputation—the declaration of righteousness—but there is impartation—the granting of real righteousness. God is not guilty of some legal fiction. He is not play acting, that is, saying something is true that isn't.

   a) A genuine transformation

   If God says you are righteous, then you are righteous. That is obvious, because God doesn't make up things. There is a genuine transformation. Second Corinthians 5:21 says, "For he [God] hath made him [Christ], who knew no sin, to be sin for us, that we might be made the righteousness of God in him." The verb "be made" means "to become" righteous in Him.

   b) A genuine righteousness

   An Old Testament word for righteous is the Hebrew word *tsadeq*. It means "to cause to be righteous." It is not a statement of something that isn't true; it is a statement of something that is true. We are made righteous. In salvation, God actually causes us to become righteous.

   (1) The analogy

   (*a*) The reign

   Romans 5:17 says, "For if by one man's offense death reigned by one, much more they who receive abundance of grace and of the gift of righteousness shall reign in life by one, Jesus Christ." That is a very good analogy. One man's offense brought death on everybody. Who was that one man? Adam. When he sinned, everybody was bound up in sin. We are not just declared sinners; we really are sinners. So just as death reigned in the rest of us by one man's offense, we have received the gift of righteousness by Jesus Christ. In the parallelism of that text, we are made real sinners in Adam and made righteous in Christ.

(*b*) The reality

The same thought but with different terms is found in Romans 5:19, "For as by one man's disobedience many were made sinners [not just counted as sinners, but made sinners], so by the obedience of one shall many be made righteous." The word "made" is *kathistēmi,* and it basically means "to make." Justification is not simply a declaration. God is not saying, "You are just as rotten and wretched as you've ever been, but I'm going to pretend you are righteous." No, there is a reality of righteousness. Matthew 24:45 says, "Who, then, is a faithful and wise servant, whom his lord hath made ruler." The word is used that way again and again in Scripture, and it simply means "to make."

(2) The analysis

I'm convinced that the reason God can declare us righteous is that we are truly made righteous. Otherwise, God is saying something that isn't true about us. I know that there have been many people who have tried to teach that we are only declared to be righteous and not actually made righteous. They then have this excuse: "Since we are not made righteous, there doesn't have to be the result of righteousness in our lives." But that is not the case.

B. The Reality of Justification

Galatians 3:24 says, "Wherefore, the law was our schoolmaster to bring us unto Christ, that we might be justified by faith." Justification by faith is the terminology of the Reformers. It is the great heart of Christian doctrine. We are made righteous by faith. What does that involve? Is it only a declaration, or is it a reality?

1. Regeneration

Galatians 3:26 says, "For ye are all the sons of God by faith in Christ Jesus." If you are justified "by faith" and made a son of God "by faith," being justified and being made a son of God are the same thing. So justification involves regeneration. We were enemies; now we are sons. We have been born again, born of the Spirit, born of incorruptible seed (John 3:3, 6; 1 Pet. 1:23). John 1:12 says that we have become the sons of God (cf. 1 John 3:1). We have been born into the family of

99

God. There is a new birth and a new life. There is an actual transformation. Justification by faith must encompass the concept of regeneration to prove the reality of God's righteousness.

2. Identification

Galatians 3:27 says, "For as many of you as have been baptized into Christ have put on Christ." That is called "identification" by the theologians. First Corinthians 6:17 says, "But he that is joined unto the Lord is one spirit." We are truly transformed. We become one with Christ and are clothed in Him.

It is virtually impossible to determine where your will stops and where Christ's begins. I can't tell. When I live in obedience to Him and walk in the Spirit, I don't know where my will ends and His begins because we are one by His indwelling presence. In verse 27, Paul may be referring to the *toga virilis,* a garment that was given to a Roman boy when he reached the age of manhood. When the boy put on the toga, he received all of the rights and privileges of adulthood and was no longer treated as a child. Paul is saying, "When you came to Jesus Christ, you received the covering of Christ's righteousness, and you were united with Him in His death and resurrection. You are in an eternal, indivisible union with the living Christ." That is what identification is. We have no fear of judgment because we are clothed in Christ.

Further, justification by faith not only encompasses regeneration and identification; it also embraces the concept of:

3. Redemption

Galatians 3:28-29 says, "There is neither Jew nor Greek, there is neither bond nor free, there is neither male nor female; for ye are all one in Christ Jesus. And if ye be Christ's, then are ye Abraham's seed, and heirs according to the promise." You are also the partakers of the covenant—recipients of covenant blessing. You are regenerated into the family of God, identified with Jesus Christ in an eternal and indivisible union, and then identified with the blessings, promises, and redemption that springs from the loins of Abraham. And that is not a racial designation; it is a designation of faith. Abraham is the father of all who trust in God. He is the father of the faithful because he believed God.

4. Adoption

Verse 29 says that we become "heirs according to the promise." We receive all the promises of God; we are blessed with all spiritual blessings in the heavenlies (Eph. 1:3). Galatians 4:5-6 says that the Lord redeemed "them that were under the law, that we might receive the adoption of sons. And because ye are sons, God hath sent forth the Spirit of his Son into your hearts, crying, Abba, Father." In other words, there is marvelous intimacy with God. "Abba, Father" means "daddy." Galatians 4:7 says, "Wherefore, thou art no more a servant, but a son; and if a son, then an heir of God through Christ."

Don't think that justification by faith is simply a statement God makes apart from reality; there is a reality in justification. You are regenerated into the family of God—you are born again. The new birth involves the implanting of a new nature. You are identified with Christ; you are cloaked in Christ. You become a part of the redeemed seed of faith. You become heir to all the promises of God. And you become the temple of the resident Holy Spirit of God.

C. The Result of Justification

When justification by faith occurs, a person is transformed. He is given a new "I"—a new ego, a new life.

1. 2 Corinthians 5:17—"Therefore, if any man be in Christ, he is a new creation; old things are passed away; behold, all things are become new."

2. 2 Peter 1:4—"Ye might be partakers of the divine nature." Your death will be less of a change for you than your conversion because you have already been fitted for eternity. You have been transformed, you are sons of God, members of the covenant family with all of the blessings, heirs of all that God promised, and possessors of the indwelling Holy Spirit, who is the guarantee (engagement ring) of our glorious future. We are literally made righteous. We are transformed!

3. Galatians 2:20—"I am crucified with Christ: nevertheless I live; yet not I, but Christ liveth in me; and the life which I now live in the flesh I live by the faith of the Son of God, who loved me and gave himself for me."

You are a new creation. You are the possessor of a divine nature. The Spirit of God lives in you, and you are cloaked with Christ. That is transformation—you have been made righteous.

D. The Ramifications of Justification

What are the implications of being made righteous? When I say you are made righteous, what do I mean?

1. A new creature

First, I don't mean that you're perfect and sinless. If you were, the New Testament would be a waste of time, because there is no sense in commanding you to do something if you are obedient in everything. When I say you are made righteous, I don't mean that you are sinless or perfect; I mean that God has recreated you into an eternally righteous, transformed person fit for eternity. But during your time on earth, that new creation is encompassed within the flesh—our humanness. And that humanness restricts the full manifestation and development of that potentially righteous creature. That new creation is encased in your humanness. That is why Paul says, "It is no more I that do it, but sin that dwelleth in me" (Rom. 7:17). When he says "I," he means his new creation; when he says "but sin that dwelleth in me," he refers to the sin that is in him. We are not perfect because that new creation is encased in our humanness. When we die, we fly from our humanness and flesh to see the fullness of our new creation. That is why John says, "When he shall appear, we shall be like him; for we shall see him as he is" (1 John 3:2b).

2. A new righteousness

The righteousness that you and I have as Christians is not our own since God gave it to us. We couldn't earn it now any more than we could before we were redeemed. He granted His righteousness to us. Without God's gift of righteousness, we would be just like unregenerate people. But until that humanness is burst asunder, we won't know the fullness of that righteousness. However, the more you walk in the Spirit and obey the Lord, the more that new "I" overpowers the flesh. In Romans 7 Paul repeatedly fights against the flesh, but in Romans 8:2 he acknowledges the Holy Spirit and says, "You take over." That's when he begins to see the new "I" have victory over his sinfulness.

Philippians 3:7-9 says, "But what things were gain to me, those I counted loss for Christ. Yea doubtless, and I count all things but loss for the excellency of the knowledge of Christ Jesus, my Lord; for whom I have suffered the loss of all things, and do count them but refuse, that I may win Christ and be found in him, not having mine own righteousness . . . but that which is through the faith of Christ, the righteousness which is of God by faith." Ours is a real righteousness given by God, and it becomes ours by faith. We become right with God. That is not only a declaration; it is a reality. When we become Christians, we can do that which glorified God for the first time in our lives because we have a new nature.

There is a need for both the declaration and the reality of righteousness. The only kind of religion that means anything is the one that transforms as well as forgives. A. W. Tozer said, "I have not said that religion without power makes no changes in a man's life; only that it makes no fundamental difference. Water may change from liquid to vapor, from vapor to snow and back to liquid again and still be fundamentally the same. So powerless religion may put a man through many surface changes and leave him exactly where he was before." You can't change a man by saying different things about him. Our faith in the Lord Jesus Christ does not leave us with an incurable disease, it makes us acceptable to God. We have a great Savior who has given us a great salvation.

We have seen what salvation does for us in Romans 3:21-25a. Now Romans 3:25b-31 shows us what it does for God. Salvation is important for us, but it is even more important for God. Four great truths about Christ's death are stated in that passage.

Review

I. DECLARES GOD'S RIGHTEOUSNESS (vv. 25-26; pp. 76-78)

II. EXALTS GOD'S GRACE (vv. 27-28; pp. 78-81)

Lesson

III. REVEALS GOD'S CONSISTENCY (vv. 29-30)

A. One God of All (vv. 29-30a)

"Is he the God of the Jews only? Is he not also of the Gentiles? Yes, of the Gentiles also, seeing it is one God."

Paul preached justification by faith. The Jewish leaders believed you were justified by works (or law). This verse attacks that belief in a very interesting way.

1. The fundamental truth of Judaism

Do you know what the fundamental truth of all Judaism is? Do you know what every Jewish person knows first as the definition of his religion? He knows that there is only one God.

a) Deuteronomy 6:4—"Hear, O Israel: The Lord our God is one Lord." That is the essence of all Jewish faith—the first article of the manifesto of Judaism. That truth is repeated throughout the Old Testament. God is one God—there are no other gods. The Lord will tolerate no other worship. All of the idols are wood and stone, and they cannot answer (Hab. 2:19-20). There are no other gods, only the one true God.

b) Isaiah 45:5-6—"I am the Lord, and there is none else, there is no God beside me . . . that they may know from the rising of the sun, and from the west, that there is none beside me. I am the Lord, and there is none else."

c) Isaiah 45:22—"Look unto me, and be saved, all the ends of the earth; for I am God, and there is none else." If people are to look to Him to be saved, and He is the only God, then He is the only way to be saved.

2. The foundational truth of Christianity

a) The premise

Paul says, "Is he the God of the Jews only?" (Rom. 3:29a).

103

The Jewish people would have to say no because there is only one God—they know that from the articles of their faith. He is the God over everyone. Then Paul says, "Is he not also of the Gentiles?" And he answers as if he were answering for the Jewish people, "Yes, of the Gentiles also, seeing it is one God" (Rom. 3:29b-30). There is only one God, and He is everybody's God. There are no other gods. That was basic to the understanding of the Jewish people. First Corinthians 8:5 says, "For though there be that are called gods, whether in heaven or in earth (as there are gods many, and lords many), but to us there is but one God, the Father, of whom are all things" (vv. 5-6a).

b) The principle

If there is only one God (and all of Israel would have to affirm that), then He must be the God of the Jewish person and the Gentile. That was very hard for the Jewish people to understand because they didn't like to think that the Gentiles could be blessed by their God.

(1) Illustrations from the Old Testament

(*a*) Jonah

Jonah had the same problem. God told him to go to Nineveh and preach. Now he wasn't afraid to preach, he wasn't lazy, and he wasn't concerned about receiving a big enough love offering, but he didn't want to go because he didn't want Gentiles becoming converted and making claims on his God. That is how narrow the Jewish perspective had become. He ran away because he didn't want to see Gentile salvation. Jonah 4:2 says, "And he prayed unto the Lord, and said, I pray thee, O Lord, was not this my saying, when I was yet in my country? Therefore, I fled before unto Tarshish; for I knew that thou art a gracious God, and merciful, slow to anger, and of great kindness, and repentest thee of the evil." He is saying, "I knew if I went there that You would save those Gentiles. I couldn't deal with that." It was a hard truth to admit, but he knew that God was the God of the Gentiles—the God of all.

(*b*) Ruth

Ruth said, "Entreat me not to leave thee, or to turn away from following after thee; for where thou goest, I will go; and where thou lodgest, I will lodge; thy people shall be my people, and thy God, my God" (Ruth 1:16). Ruth was a Gentile. God has always been the God of the Gentiles.

    (c) Naaman, the Syrian

        Naaman, the Syrian general, was relieved of his leprosy and came to worship the true God (2 Kings 5).

  (2) Illustrations from the New Testament

    If God is the God of the Jewish person and the Gentile, then He has a mode of salvation that is the same for both. It couldn't be law-keeping, because the Gentiles didn't have the law. If God was going to justify the circumcision and the uncircumcision the same way, it had to be by faith.

    If there were many gods, there could be many religions; but there is only one God, so there can only be one way to approach Him.

    (a) Mark 16:15—"Go ye into all the world, and preach the gospel to every creature." The same gospel is preached to every creature.

    (b) Acts 4:12—"Neither is there salvation in any other; for there is no other name under heaven given among men, whereby we must be saved."

    (c) John 14:6—"No man cometh unto the Father, but by me."

    There is only one way, one God, and one mode of approach. God is the God of all. He doesn't have a works system for the Jewish people and a faith system for the Gentiles. That may have been what the Jewish people began to believe: "Maybe He does save some of those people by their faith. Maybe they can trust in whatever limited perceptions they have. But we have the law." Paul is saying, "No, there are not two ways. There is one God, and that is basic to your faith. Justification by faith is granted to those who come to God, whether they be Jewish or Gentile."

    Salvation must be apart from keeping the law. It must be apart from works for God to be consistent. Heathen and religionist alike are saved by faith in Christ. That same principle is found throughout the New Testament. There is no other way to be saved than by faith in Jesus Christ. Whether you are a religious Jewish person or a heathen bushman, "There is one God, and one mediator between God and men, the man, Christ Jesus, who gave himself a ransom for all" (1 Tim. 2:5-6).

B. One Salvation for All (v. 30b)

    "[God] shall [continue to] justify the circumcision [the Jewish people] by faith, and uncircumcision [the Gentiles] through faith."

1. One level of humanity

   John Murray calls this "the ethnic universalism of the gospel" (*The Epistle to the Romans* [Grand Rapids: Eerdmans, 1965], p. 124). The entire human race is reduced to the same level in Romans 3:19—The whole world is guilty of sin. That is what Paul meant in Romans 1:16, "For I am not ashamed of the gospel of Christ; for it is the power of God unto salvation to everyone that believeth; to the Jew first, and also to the Greek." It is the same for both. God is utterly consistent. He is glorified by the revelation of His absolute, unwavering consistency. God is on display at the cross.

2. One way of salvation

   The mass of religions all over the world are very complex, but Christianity is simple. Ephesians 4:5-6 says, "One Lord, one faith, one baptism, one God and Father of all." There is only one way to Him, and it is direct and clear. How that glorifies God! He never changes.

   a) In the Old Testament

   People say, "Were people saved by faith in the Old Testament?" That is the only way anybody has ever been saved. God has never altered His method. You say, "Weren't they saved by works in the Old Testament?" No. No one could ever be saved by works. They were responsible to live a life of righteousness just as we are, but they were brought into the capacity to do that by believing God. For example:

   (1) Before the national theocracy

      (*a*) Noah

         People often say, "We are in the dispensation of grace. Grace didn't begin until the New Testament." Genesis 6:8 says, "But Noah found grace in the eyes of the Lord." If he hadn't found grace, he would have been drowned like everybody else.

      (*b*) Moses

         In Exodus 33:12, Moses found grace in the sight of the Lord.

      (*c*) Abraham

         Romans 4:3 says that Abraham was saved by faith.

   (2) During the national theocracy

      People were saved by grace during the period of national theocracy. Habakkuk said, "But the just shall live by his faith" (Hab. 2:4*b*).

   b) In the New Testament

   Hebrews 11 begins with the faith of Enoch and discusses

the faith of many heroes. Then Hebrews 12:1 says, "Wherefore, seeing we also are compassed about with so great a cloud of witnesses." Those people witnessed to the beauty and reality of a life of faith. If so many people testify to the reality of faith as the only way to God, then we ought to live by faith.

Men are always redeemed by believing God. People in the Old Testament had to believe all that God had revealed, and now we are to do the same. In the age we now live in, we are redeemed by faith. James says that saving faith will manifest fruitfulness (James 2:14-26).

You say, "If you're not saved by works, and you're not saved by keeping the law, doesn't that mean that the law is useless?" That is the last argument Paul deals with. The cross of Jesus Christ declares God's righteousness, exalts God's grace, reveals God's consistency, and finally:

IV. CONFIRMS GOD'S LAW (v. 31)

"Do we then make void the law through faith? God forbid [Gk., *mē genoito*]; yea, we establish the law."

A. Questioning the Law

You say, "That's a legitimate question. If you can't get saved by keeping the law, then what good is it?"

1. Psalm 119:126—"They have made void thy law."

2. Jeremiah 8:8—"How do ye say, We are wise, and the law of the Lord is with us? Lo, certainly in vain made he it; the pen of the scribes is in vain."

This opinion had been stated in the Old Testament: "The law is void; it's useless. If the law can't save us, then it's useless."

B. Establishing the Law

Paul says, "No. The law has been established." How can that be so? Because is was never given to save you. You say, "What was it given for?" It shows you that you need to be saved. It demonstrates your sinfulness; it doesn't save you from it. The law drives you to God in faith—it drives you to the point where you say, "I can't live up to Your standards, God. What will I do?" At that point, God intervenes in His mercy and grace, and says, "I see your sin. Because you are broken over your sin, I offer you grace, forgiveness, and healing through faith." The death of Christ on the cross doesn't make void the law. Rather, it establishes the law in three simple ways.

1. By the penalty

The law was valid because it had to be exacted. Jesus had to die. The law said that sin brings death, and somebody had to die. When Jesus died, He was saying, "The law is in effect. It must have its demands met." In Matthew 5:17 Jesus says, "Think not that I am come to destroy the law, or the prophets; I am not come to destroy, but to fulfill." I believe He was looking to the cross, and saying, "I'm coming to verify the law by showing you that its penalty must be met." In the death of Jesus Christ, the penalty of the law was paid, and the validity of the law was established.

2. By the purpose

The law had only one purpose, and that was to bring us to Christ.

a) Stirring up sin

Romans 3:20 says, "By the law is the knowledge of sin." In Romans 7:13, Paul says, "When I saw the law, I saw my sin and my death as a result." In other words, if I didn't know the rules, then I wouldn't know I was breaking them. That is what Galatians 3:24 says: "The law was our schoolmaster to bring us unto Christ." In other words, the law is your disciplinarian. It strikes blows against you to show you your inadequacy and your inability. The law worked in Paul and stirred up sin. The law can't cure sin—it just makes it manifest. But it starts the process of salvation at that point. You say, "Why can't the law save you?" James 2:10 says, "For whosoever shall keep the whole law, and yet offend in one point, he is guilty of all."

b) Signifying a Savior

When Jesus lays down His law in the Sermon on the Mount, He says, "Here is what you ought to do, but you don't do any of it." In Matthew 5:48 He says, "Be ye, therefore, perfect, even as your Father, who is in heaven, is perfect." In Matthew 5:20 He says, "Except your righteousness shall exceed the righteousness of the scribes and Pharisees, ye shall in no case enter into the kingdom of heaven." Why did He say that to the crowd? Some people will say, "That is how it's going to be in the future." No. He wanted the crowd to see the impossibility of obeying God's law. When God first gave the law, the people said that they would keep the whole law (Ex. 19:8). So the Lord kept piling laws on them until they couldn't even figure them out, let alone keep them. People ask me, "Why are there so many laws in the Old Testament?" I think some of them are there in order to show the people the absolute impossibility of keeping them. The whole point of the law is to drive people to the Savior.

3. By the potential

When you put your faith in Jesus Christ, then you can fulfill the law. Romans 8:3-4 says, "For what the law could not do, in that it was weak through the flesh, God sending his own Son, in the likeness of sinful flesh and for sin, condemned sin in the flesh, that the righteousness of the law might be fulfilled in us, who walk not after the flesh, but after the Spirit."

Justification by faith does not make void the law; it makes keeping the law a possibility. The law is not useless. I had to be fulfilled, so Christ died. It was given to drive us to Christ. And it can be fulfilled in the energy and power of the blessed Holy Spirit. The law is confirmed. When you see Christ's death on the cross, you see the exaltation of God's law. His righteous wrath was poured out on Christ because His law demanded it. You also see that the law will drive you to see your sinfulness. And then you see the sufficiency of Jesus Christ as He grants you His Holy Spirit and gives you a new ability to keep the law.

The cross exalts God's righteousness, grace, consistency, and law.

You may have heard it said that if you work in a barnyard, you smell like a pig. God worked His salvation in the muck of a barnyard called earth. He came in human flesh and rubbed shoulders with pigs. But He went away without a stench, only with spotless glory for Himself. The Reformers said that salvation is *sola gratia*—by grace alone, *sola fide*—by faith alone, and *sola deo gloria*—for God's glory alone.

Focusing on the Facts

1. What two things does justification by faith encompass? Explain each (see pp. 97-98).

2. How do we know that God makes a believer righteous (see 2 Cor. 5:21; p. 98)?

3. Whose offense brought death upon every person? According to Romans 5:17, are we simply declared sinners, or are we really sinners? Explain the parallelism of that verse (see pp. 98-99).

4. Why can God declare that a Christian is righteous? What excuse can be presented if Christians aren't made righteous but only declared to be righteous (see p. 99)?

5. What four things does the reality of justification by faith involve (see pp. 99-100)?

6. How does Galatians 3:26 support the fact that righteousness is a reality in the life of a believer (see p. 99)?

7. How does Galatians 3:27 support the fact that righteousness is a reality in the life of a believer (see p. 100)?

8. Explain Paul's possible usage of the *toga virilis* in Galatians 3:27 (see p. 100).

9. What does "heirs according to the promise" mean in Galatians 3:29? Explain (see p. 100).

10. What are the results of the Christian's justification? Support your answer with Scripture (see p. 101).

11. What restricts the full manifestation and development of the Christian's righteousness? Why (see p. 102)?

12. How can the Christian have victory over his sinfulness (see Rom. 8:2; p. 102)?

13. What is the only kind of religion that means anything (see p. 102)?

14. What does Romans 3:29-30a attack (see p. 103)?

15. What is the fundamental truth of Judaism? Support your answer with Scripture (see p. 103).

16. What does Paul conclude in Romans 3:29-30 (see p. 104)?

17. Why did the Jewish people have a problem with the fact that God was also the God of the Gentiles? How do we know that Jonah had that problem (see p. 104)?

18. Does God have a works system of salvation for Jewish people and a faith system for Gentiles? Explain (see 1 Tim. 2:5-6; p. 105).

19. Why is Christianity simple (see Eph. 4:5-6; p. 106)?

20. How were people saved in the Old Testament? Give some examples (see p. 106).

21. What is the purpose of the law if it doesn't save anyone (see p. 107)?

22. In what three ways does justification by faith establish the law? Explain how each one establishes the law (see pp. 107-9).

Pondering the Principles

1. Review the four aspects of justification (see pp. 99-100). Look up the following verses: John 15:26; Romans 4:13-14, 16-21; 5:5; 8:14-17; 13:14; Ephesians 4:24; Philippians 2:14-16; James 2:5. What does each of those verses teach about the benefits of our righteousness? Meditate on those truths. Which ones have the most meaning for you? Why? Praise God for everything He has given you in Christ.

2. Read Romans 7:7-25. How did Paul know he was not perfect? What did he teach in those verses about the law? What did he teach about sin? Do you experience the same battle he talked about with your sin? Give some examples. Do you truly want to be delivered from sin's power over your life? Read Romans 8:1-17. What did Paul discover as the resource in his fight against the flesh? What do you have to do in order to overpower the dominance of the flesh in your life?

3. Read James 2:14-26. What terminology does James use to explain that true saving faith will manifest fruitfulness? What is James's definition of living by faith? What should your faith result in? How do you manifest the reality of your faith in Christ to the world? Can people in the world conclude that there is something different about you based

on your behavior? What changes do you need to make in your life as a result of that passage? What do you have to begin to do in order to manifest the reality of your faith to the world?

7
Abraham—Justified by Faith—Part 1

Outline

Introduction
A. Abraham as an Illustration of Faith
  1. The reasons for Paul's illustration
    a) He is proof of righteousness by faith
    b) He is the supreme example of faith
      (1) The teaching of the New Testament
      (2) The teaching of the rabbis
        (a) Describing the myth
        (b) Destroying the myth
    c) He is a concrete example
  2. The rationale of Paul's illustration
B. Abraham as Identified by the Religious Leaders
  1. Twisting Abraham's righteousness
    a) From Scripture
    b) From tradition
  2. Twisting Abraham's faithfulness

Lesson
I. The Negative Perspective
  A. The Questions
    1. What do we learn from Abraham?
    2. What do we find that Abraham attained?
  B. The Answer
II. The Positive Perspective
  A. Abraham's Demonstration of Faith
    1. The appointment of Abraham
      a) As the father to the faithful
      b) As a witness to faithfulness
        (1) Abraham had obedient faith
        (2) Abraham had patient faith
        (3) Abraham had trusting faith
    2. The accounting of righteousness
      a) Crediting righteousness to the Christian's account
      b) Crediting sin to Christ's account
        (1) The cross of Christ
        (2) The cry of salvation

(*a*) Micah 6:6-7
(*b*) Job 25:4

Introduction

Romans 4 is the story of Abraham. Paul uses him as an illustration of the truth that salvation is by faith, not works. Bill Gold, in the Washington Post, told a story about a little girl who had saved enough money to buy her father a present for Father's Day. But she was concerned about one thing. She said to her mother, "I can't be going downtown every month to make payments. Is there a store where they'll let you pay for the whole thing at once?"

We understand that perspective. Men have always thought they they could buy salvation on the installment plan by earning their way, as if God looks at the good works this month, next month, and the month after that. But Paul says that is not true. The debt was paid once on the cross of Jesus Christ. He paid the full price, once for all. Therefore, salvation is a gift that has been paid for; it is not something earned on the installment plan.

A. Abraham as an Illustration of Faith

Paul's message in Romans 3:21-8:39 is that God provided salvation: a deliverance from sin, death, and hell. Salvation is provided through the work of Christ as a free gift to those who believe, not to those who work for it. Paul was very much aware that that doctrine would be foreign to the ears of the Jewish people, who believed you earned your way into heaven. It was even foreign to the pagans. Their systems of religion had always been based on human achievement. But he particularly had the Jewish people in mind as he argued through Romans. He realized that saying God saves by grace through faith was going to run contrary to what they had always been taught. Consequently, having talked about salvation in Romans 3:21-31, he selected Abraham as his illustration. That man is the classic proof—the classic model and illustration—of salvation by grace through faith.

Paul told us that a man can be right with God not by what he does, but by believing in Jesus Christ and His perfect work. It is very important that he chose Abraham as his illustration because his teaching in Romans 3:21-31 would have otherwise been unacceptable to the Jewish mind.

1. The reasons for Paul's illustration

There are several reasons why Paul selects Abraham.

a) He is proof of righteousness by faith

Abraham was an Old Testament character, and by using Him, Paul is saying that justification by faith is not new. Abraham even preceded Moses and the identity of Israel as a nation. Abraham belonged to the period of the patriarchs—a very primitive time. His appearance takes place

113

early in the book of Genesis. If Paul can establish that a man in Genesis was saved by grace through faith, and not by works, then he has given us a timeless truth that is not new at all.

b) He is the supreme example of faith

Nobody in the Old Testament exercised more faith than Abraham.

(1) The teaching of the New Testament

The New Testament tells us that Abraham is the father of all who believe (Gal. 3:7). All who come to God by faith are children of Abraham—they believe God.

(2) The teaching of the rabbis

The teaching of the New Testament ran contrary to the rabbis' teaching.

(*a*) Describing the myth

The majority of rabbis who lived during the time of our Lord believed that Abraham was made right with God—was saved, forgiven of his sin, received eternal life, and chosen by God for salvation—because of his character. (That is what the majority of the orthodox rabbis today believe.) They thought Abraham was the best man in the world during his generation. Therefore he was chosen by God to be the father of His people, Israel. They say that God chose Abraham because he was a righteous man.

We have to ask two questions: One, how could any man be righteous according to God's standards? Second, how could a man keep God's righteous standards when they hadn't been given yet? The rabbis answered that Abraham kept God's standard by intuition and anticipation—that he sensed the law of God in his conscience and kept it intuitively. So the rabbis said that God chose him because of his own righteousness.

(*b*) Destroying the myth

Paul selects Abraham in order to destroy the myth taught by the rabbis: He wants to establish the fact that Abraham is not an example of a righteous man whom God chose, but an example of an unrighteous man whom God chose. He is not a man who earned salvation by his good works. Rather, he is a man who received salvation by grace through believing in God. In simple child-like trust, in complete yieldedness to God, he took God's word at face value. He believed God, and by that act of faith received righteousness.

It was very important to the Jewish religious leaders that Abraham be an example of a righteous man whom God chose, because they believed that God chose them on the basis of their own self-righteousness. But Paul wants them, and us, to realize that the supreme discovery of life is to find that you don't need to torture yourself in a losing battle to gain acceptance with God by your own good works. You don't need to try to buy salvation on the installment plan.

   c) He is a concrete example

Paul's teaching in Romans 3:21-31 has consisted of theological theory and truth, but now he needs a flesh and blood example to make his teaching concrete. So he gives the example of Abraham.

2. The rationale of Paul's illustration

When Paul attacks the opponents of justification, or salvation by faith with the illustration of Abraham, he is storming the very fortress of Judaism and smashing down the walls of its strongest arsenal. If Abraham could not be justified by works, then nobody could because the rabbis thought he was the most righteous man of all. Conversely, if it could be demonstrated that Abraham was justified by faith, then everyone must be justified by faith because Abraham is the standard.

B. Abraham as Identified by the Religious Leaders

1. Twisting Abraham's righteousness

   a) From Scripture

The Jewish religious leaders thought that Abraham was righteous because they twisted certain Scriptures to come to that conclusion.

   (1) Genesis 26:5—"Abraham obeyed my voice, and kept my charge, my commandments, my statues, and my laws." The religious leaders note that Abraham obeyed God. What they don't notice is that God saved him and made him righteous first; then he obeyed God.

   (2) Isaiah 41:8—The religious leaders liked to point out that God spoke of Abraham as "my friend."

   b) From tradition

They also drew their conclusions from non-biblical sources.

   (1) The apocryphal book of *Ecclesiasticus* taught that Abraham was given justification and circumcision because he earned it by keeping the law (44:19-21).

(2) The rabbis taught that Abraham was one of seven men who, by his merit and his personal righteousness, had the privilege of bringing back the Shekinah glory to dwell in the tabernacle.

(3) The rabbis also taught that Abraham was so righteous that he began to serve God when he was only three years old.

(4) The following is from *The Prayer of Manasseh* (another non-biblical writing): "Therefore Thou, O Lord, God of the righteous, hast not appointed repentance for the righteous, for Abraham and Isaac and Jacob, who did not sin against Thee, but Thou hast appointed repentance for me, who am a sinner" (v. 8). But you would have to read through Genesis with blinders on to come to the conclusion that Abraham, Isaac, and Jacob didn't sin.

(5) *The Book of Jubilees* (another historic, traditional, non-biblical Jewish book, probably dating from the second century before Christ) said, "Abraham was perfect in all his deeds with the Lord, and well pleasing in righteousness all the days of his life" (23:10).

The rabbis concluded that Abraham was perfect and righteous. Therefore God chose him and made him the head of the nation. He was their standard. If you wanted to be righteous, if you wanted to be right with God, if you wanted your sins forgiven, and if you wanted to be saved and brought into the kingdom, you would have to be like Abraham and become righteous by your own good works.

2. Twisting Abraham's faithfulness

The Jewish leaders used Abraham as a support for their ugly pride. Some even twisted the issue of faith.

a) Paul quotes Habakkuk 2:4 in Romans 1:17, "The just shall live by faith." The rabbis changed it to say, "The just shall live by his faithfulness." Do you see the difference? Instead of teaching us to live before God in a right relationship of faith in Him, the verse tells us to live by being faithful to God's law. They twisted the Scripture to fit their own desires.

b) One ancient rabbinical commentary says, "Our father Abraham became the heir of this and of the coming world simply by the merit of the faith with which he believed in the Lord." The rabbis are saying that Abraham was saved by the *merit* of his own faith—that he earned salvation with his own faith. But that isn't right.

Paul had to attack that interpretation of Abraham's faith. Abraham became the standard of the Jewish people for the wrong

116

reason. They believed that they could gain righteousness by living like Abraham, in perfect obedience to the rules. They tried to keep the law on their own. And it is for that reason that the nature of Abraham's faith had to be made clear.

Romans 4 has been analyzed and divided in many ways, but let me give you what I think is a very simple way of dividing that chapter. Abraham's life is an example, model, and pattern of saving faith in three key ways. First, Abraham was justified by faith, not by works (vv. 1-8); second, he was justified by grace, not by law (vv. 9-17); third, he was justified by divine power, not by human effort (vv. 18-25). In all three cases there are both negative and positive perspectives. First of all, Abraham was made right with God by faith, not by works. Romans 4:1-8 says, "What shall we say, then, that Abraham, our father, as pertaining to the flesh, hath found? For if Abraham were justified by works, he hath something of which to glory, but not before God. For what saith the scripture? Abraham believed God, and it was counted unto him for righteousness. Now to him that worketh is the reward not reckoned of grace, but of debt. But to him that worketh not, but believeth on him that justifieth the ungodly, his faith is counted for righteousness. Even as David also describeth the blessedness of the man unto whom God imputeth righteousness apart from works, saying, Blessed are they whose iniquities are forgiven, and whose sins are covered. Blessed is the man to whom the Lord will not impute sin."

Lesson

I. THE NEGATIVE PERSPECTIVE (vv. 1-2)

A. The Questions (v. 1)

"What shall we say, then, that Abraham, our father, as pertaining to the flesh, hath found?"

1. What do we learn from Abraham?

When Paul says, "What . . . then," he is referring to the force of the statement from the previous passage. He is saying, "Since we have been talking about justification by grace through faith, then what do we say about our father Abraham? What do we say about the one we have always said was righteous based on his own self-righteousness, and therefore was our standard?"

Then Paul says, "What did he discover 'as pertaining to the flesh?' " In other words, what do we learn from him? Is his case a contradiction? He is the father of the nation, the father of the Abrahamic covenant, the supreme one of all God's people. The whole nation of Israel came out of his loins. Therefore, whatever is true of him must be true of all of those who are descended from him. If he was the progenitor, then whatever was true of him must be true of all Israel.

2. What do we find that Abraham attained?

What does the phrase "pertaining to the flesh" mean? It means "his natural unaided powers and human abilities." What did he discover? What did he find? What did he attain? What did he appropriate on his own? Did Abraham gain something on his own with his natural unaided human ability? Does he contradict what has been said in Romans 3:21-31?

B. The Answer (v. 2)

"For if Abraham were justified by works [those things which he did by his natural unaided powers], he hath something of which to glory, but not before God."

That is Paul's way of saying, "Not so. He can't open his mouth before God." Another way of translating verse 2 is, "If Abraham were justified by works, then he has something to boast about." If I save myself by being good, then I have a right to say, "I'm so good that I saved myself." But from God's viewpoint, Abraham had no right to boast—he had no basis for pride. And Paul is going to prove that in the remainder of chapter 4. Abraham was not justified by his works.

Men are never made right with God based on what they do. You can light all the candles you want, pray all the prayers you want, go to all the religious meetings you want, get baptized, buy a Bible, take communion, feel religious, perform religious exercises, and even be a very good person, but you still cannot attain God's standard of righteousness. That is why Romans 3:27 says that boasting is excluded. No one can boast. Ephesians 2:8-9 says, "For by grace are ye saved through faith; and that not of yourselves, it is the gift of God—not of works, lest any man should boast." Salvation is designed to give glory to God, not glory to man. So Abraham had nothing he could boast about.

Paul's Hypothetical Syllogism

In Romans 4:1-5, Paul presents what is known as a hypothetical syllogism, which is made up of a major premise, a minor premise, and a conclusion. The major premise is: If a man is justified by works, he has grounds for boasting. The minor premise is: Abraham was justified by works. The conclusion is: Therefore, Abraham has a right to boast. But God says that Abraham does not have a right to boast. So if the conclusion isn't true, then one of the premises is not true. The major premise is: If a man is justified by works, he has grounds for boasting. Is that true? Yes. If you were justified by works you would have grounds for boasting. The minor premise is: Abraham was justified by works. Is that true? No. We cannot grant the minor premise; therefore, the syllogism doesn't work. The minor premise is false. Abraham was not justified by works before God.

118

II. THE POSITIVE PERSPECTIVE (vv. 3-8)

A. Abraham's Demonstration of Faith (v. 3)

"For what saith the scripture? Abraham believed God, and it was counted unto him for righteousness."

That is a quote from Genesis 15:6. How did he gain righteousness? How did he become right with God? It wasn't because he was so good on his own that God had to accept him. Rather, he believed God and that was counted to him for righteousness. Abraham was justified by faith—he believed God.

1. The appointment of Abraham

   a) As the father to the faithful

   Galatians 3:6-9 says, "Even as Abraham believed God, and it was accounted to him for righteousness. Know ye, therefore, that they who are of faith, the same are the sons of Abraham. And the scripture, foreseeing that God would justify the Gentiles through faith, preached before the gospel unto Abraham, saying, In thee shall all nations be blessed. So, then, they who are of faith are blessed with faithful Abraham." Abraham was saved by faith, not by works. And in a very real sense, all who are saved by faith since Abraham are the children of Abraham. He is the father of all who exercise faith. Galatians 3:26 says, "For ye are all the sons of God by faith in Christ Jesus." To Paul and the Holy Spirit, the essence of Abraham's greatness lies in the fact that God chose him.

   b) As a witness to faithfulness

   What were the incidents in Abraham's life when he exercised faith? Hebrews 11 is a tremendous text that reveals what Abraham believed. He took God at His word with no debate, no hesitation, and no argument.

   (1) Abraham had obedient faith

   Hebrews 11:8 says, "By faith Abraham, when he was called to go out into a place which he should after receive for an inheritance, obeyed; and he went out, not knowing where he went." He lived in the city called Ur—a city of the Chaldees. His family, his possessions, his reputation, his business, and his life were there. The nation of Israel did not yet exist. There was no promised land. There was not a special people of God. Yet God called Abraham (present participle, indicating he was being called). When he was being called, he also obeyed. That was a great act of faith. God said, "Get out of Ur of the Chaldees. I want you to go somewhere else. I'm not going to tell you where you're going; just abandon everything" (Gen. 12:1). So Abraham left the land of his birth, forsook his home and his estate, severed ties with those he loved, and abandoned present security for future uncertainty (Gen. 12:4). Why did he do it? Because he believed God. He believed that God would take him to a good place and that He would bless his life. He believed, and that's all God wanted.

(2) Abraham had patient faith

Hebrews 11:9 says, "By faith he sojourned in the land of promise, as in a foreign country, dwelling in tents with Isaac and Jacob, the heirs with him of the same promise." To God, Abraham was the chosen man. Yet Abraham never saw the fulfillment of the promise. He never saw God's people possess the land. He never owned any land that he lived on; he spent his life as a tent dweller, wandering throughout the land like Isaac and Jacob. He never saw the fulfillment of his dreams. It was to be another generation from out of his loins that would see that fulfillment. Yet be believed. Verse 10 says, "For he looked for a city which hath foundations, whose builder and maker is God." He had his eyes on God: He had a heavenly perspective and a heavenly vision.

(3) Abraham had trusting faith

A time of great testing came for Abraham when he had to offer up his son Isaac to God. The Lord finally gave him a son through whom the blessings would come, but he told Abraham to slaughter him on the altar. Abraham obeyed. He put him on the altar and was ready to plunge the knife. Why did he do it? Hebrews 11:17-18 says, "By faith Abraham, when he was tested, offered up Isaac; and he that had received the promises offered up his only begotten son, of whom it was said, in Isaac shall thy seed be called." In other words, he would be killing the very fulfillment of God's promises. Why? Verse 19 says that he was "accounting that God was able to raise him up, even from the dead." Abraham thought, "If God says that I'm going to have a nation out of my child, but He wants me to kill him, then I will kill him in confidence that God will raise him up." Now that is great faith! Had Abraham ever seen a resurrection? Never! What faith Abraham must have had to go to a land he had never seen, have a child he could not have, and kill the child who was the hope of all God's promises! And he would have done it all, so great was his faith. He is a model of faith. What does the Scripture say in Genesis 15:6? "Abraham believed God, and it was counted unto him for righteousness" (Rom. 4:3). How did he gain righteousness? How did he become acceptable to God? Was it through his perfection? No, it was through his faith, because he believed God enough to leave his country, to trust God to give him a son, and to kill that son if God said so and believe that God would raise him from the dead.

2. The accounting of righteousness

The word "counted" is *logizomai* in the Greek. That word is used eleven times in Romans 4. What does it mean? It means, "to credit or put to one's account, to reckon, to impute to someone." When Abraham believed, God imputed to him—put to his account—a righteousness that Abraham did not possess on his own.

a) Crediting righteousness to the Christian's account

When you believe God—when you believe the Word of God and the promises of God—then the Lord puts a righteousness you don't have into your account. That is a legal act. Righteousness is credited to your account. It is as if you were a beggar or a pauper, but the world's richest person put a fortune into your bank account. You are credited with a righteousness by faith. That is the heart of Christian theology.

John Murray, in his book *Redemption Accomplished and Applied,* says, "God's judgment is according to the truth here as elsewhere. . . . He constitutes the ungodly righteous and consequently can declare them to be righteous" ([Grand Rapids: Eerdmans, 1955], p. 127). God actually credits righteousness to our account. He imputes righteousness to us; He infuses divine life into us. He regenerates and sanctifies us. He makes the unholy holy, and therefore declares that we are righteous. There is an ontological as well as a forensic declaration. There is a reality—God gives us righteousness, and thus He can declare that we are righteous. But how can that be? How can God look at Abraham with all of his sin and declare him righteous?

b) Crediting sin to Christ's account

(1) The cross of Christ

Isaiah 53:4-5 gives a description of Christ, "Surely he hath borne our griefs, and carried our sorrows; yet we did esteem him stricken, smitten of God, and afflicted. But he was wounded for our transgressions, he was bruised for our iniquities; the chastisement [the punishment] for our peace was upon him, and with his stripes we are healed." Do you know why God can credit righteousness to your account? Because he credited your sin to Christ's account. Christ paid the price for your sin on the cross. That satisfied God's requirement and allowed Him to credit His righteousness to your account and mine. That is the heart of the Christian faith. God never could have credited righteousness to Abraham's account had Abraham's sin not been paid for. And it was paid for on the cross of Jesus Christ even though Christ had not yet come into the world. That is no more difficult to understand than the fact that our sin should be credited to Christ, who came two thousand years ago. Jesus Christ is the apex of redemptive history.

The believing sinner is justified by righteousness infused into him. Arthur Pink says, "It is called 'the righteousness of God' (Rom. 1:17; 3:21) because He is the appointer, approver, and imputer of it. It is called 'the righteousness of God and our Savior Jesus Christ' (II Peter 1:1) because He wrought it out and presented it unto God. It is called 'the righteousness of faith' (Rom. 4:13) because faith is the apprehender and receiver of it. It is called man's righteousness (Job 33:26) because it was paid for him and imputed to him. All these varied expressions refer to so many aspects of that one perfect obedience unto death which the Savior performed for His people" (*The Doctrines of Election and Justification* [Grand Rapids: Baker, 1974], p. 188). And may I add to Pink's list? Daniel calls it "everlasting righteousness" (Dan. 9:24).

(2) The cry of salvation

What joy it is for a person who is deeply convinced that he's lost, who knows he's a rebel against God and as a lawbreaker condemned to hell, to discover that God will credit righteousness to his account because his sin has been credited to Christ's account on the cross! All he has to do is believe. When a sinner is alerted to the holy majesty, unbending justice, and sovereign power of God, there is a terrorizing sense of lostness and a great feeling of depravity. The foul character of sin and the inevitable deserved judgment become frontal in the mind and awaken the soul to cry out for a salvation that can't be earned.

(a) Micah 6:6-7—"With what shall I come before the Lord, and bow myself before the High God? Shall I come before him with burnt offerings, with calves of a year old? Will the Lord be pleased with thousands of rams, or with ten thousands of rivers of oil? Shall I give my firstborn for my transgression, the fruit of my body for the sin of my soul?" What am I going to do? What am I going to offer to God? How many religious rites does it take?

(b) Job 25:4—"How then can man be justified with God? Or how can he be clean that is born of a woman?"

And then comes this blessed answer: faith. Righteousness is credited to your account by faith. What a great reality!

Focusing on the Facts

1. Why is "Justified by Faith" an appropriate title for Romans 4 (see p. 113)?

2. What is the "installment plan" of salvation? How does God's method of salvation bypass the installment plan (see p. 113)?

3. What effect did Paul realize his teaching in Romans 3:21-31 would have on the Jewish mind? How did he decide to support his teaching (see p. 113)?

4. Why did Paul choose Abraham as his illustration of justification by faith? Explain the significance of each reason (see pp. 113-15).

5. What does Galatians 3:7 teach about Abraham (see p. 114)?

6. What myth did the Jewish rabbis believe and teach regarding Abraham? How did they think Abraham kept God's law (see p. 114)?

7. What conclusion can be made if Abraham was not justified by works? What conclusion can be made if Abraham was justified by faith (see p. 115)?

8. What are some of the ways that the rabbis had twisted truths about Abraham to make him fit their definition of salvation (see pp. 115-16)?

9. Interpret the meaning of Paul's question in Romans 4:1 (see p. 117).

10. What would Abraham need in order to boast? Why couldn't Abraham boast before God (see p. 118)?

11. What is a hypothetical syllogism? Explain how Paul uses one to show that Abraham was not justified by works (see p. 118).

12. How does Paul support the fact that Abraham became righteous through faith (see Rom. 4:3; pp. 119-20)?

13. According to Hebrews 11, how did Abraham exercise great faith (see pp. 119-20)?

14. What kind of perspective did Abraham have? Give a verse that would support your answer (see p. 120).

15. Why was Abraham willing to kill Isaac as a sacrifice to God (see Heb. 11:17-19; p. 120)?

16. What does the Greek word *logizomai* mean? What did God do for Abraham when he believed? What does God do for anyone who comes to Him in faith (see p. 121)?

17. How could God declare Abraham righteous in spite of his sin? What does God credit to Christ's account (see pp. 121-22)?

Pondering the Principles

1. By using Abraham as an example, Paul shows that salvation cannot be gained by human effort. In John 15:1-11, Jesus uses a different kind of illustration to show that a Christian can't do a certain thing by human effort. What is that certain thing, according to verse 5? What can Christians accomplish on their own? What does Jesus say is the only way to accomplish what He desires for you? Look up the following verses: 1 Corinthians 16:15; Galatians 5:22-23; Colossians 1:10; Hebrews 13:15. According to those verses, what are you able to produce when you depend on God instead of yourself? Meditate on John 15:1-11. Begin to make those truths a part of your life. Memorize Philippians 4:13, "I can do all things through Him who strengthens me" (NASB).

2. According to Hebrews 11:8-10, 17-19, Abraham exercised obedient, patient, and trusting faith. On a scale of 1-10, how would you rate your faith in each of those areas? What was the occasion when you last exercised obedient faith? patient faith? trusting faith? What improvements do you need to make in your obedience to God's plan for your life? Would you be willing to leave everything to follow God like Abraham did? What improvements do you need to make in your patience towards the revelation of God's plan in your life? What improvements do you need to make in your trust of God's leadership? Commit those desired improvements to God.

3. Hebrews 11:10 says this about Abraham: "He looked for a city which hath foundations, whose builder and maker is God." Abraham had a heavenly perspective. Do you have a heavenly or a worldly perspective? Do you gain great satisfaction from things of this world or from spiritual things? Look up the following verses: Matthew 6:19-21; James 4:4; 1 John 2:15-17. According to those verses, what will be the result of a worldly perspective? What will be the result of a heavenly perspective? Read James 4:5-10. In order to have a heavenly perspective, what kind of attitude do you need to have? What will be the results of that attitude? Which perspective do you want to maintain? Make a commitment to maintain a godly perspective.

8
Abraham—Justified by Faith—Part 2

Outline

Introduction
A. Abraham's Designation
B. Abraham's Destiny
  1. His sinful upbringing
  2. His sovereign call
  3. His specific responses
    a) His immediate obedience
    b) His incomplete obedience
    c) His improving obedience
    d) His imperfect obedience
      (1) He compromised the truth (Gen. 12:10-20)
      (2) He disobeyed God's command (Gen. 12:4-5)
      (3) He committed adultery (Gen. 16:1-16)
  4. His significant epitaph
    a) Died in faith
    b) Remained a stranger

Review
  I. The Negative Perspective
  A. The Questions
  B. The Answer
 II. The Positive Perspective
  A. Abraham's Demonstration of Faith
    1. The appointment of Abraham
    2. The accounting of righteousness

Lesson
    3. The action of God
    a) 2 Corinthians 5:17
    b) Titus 3:5
    4. The analysis of faith
    a) The error
      (1) Faith is not a work
      (2) Faith is a channel
    b) The elements
      (1) Facts

(*a*) The faith in the gospel
(*b*) The facts of the gospel
(2) Agreement
(3) Internalization
    (*a*) John 1:11-13
    (*b*) John 8:31
(4) Trust
    (*a*) 1 Peter 2:25
    (*b*) 1 Thessalonians 1:9
(5) Hope
    (*a*) The commitment of eternal destiny
    (*b*) The confidence in eternal destiny
        i) 2 Thessalonians 2:13-16
        ii) 1 Thessalonians 5:8

Introduction

If there is one doctrine the Enemy desires to attack, it is the doctrine of salvation. If Satan can foul us up on how we can be saved, then he has damned our souls. Romans 3 and 4 has been the personal study of Bible teachers and commentators for centuries since it was written, and it still yields fresh insight to those who study it.

The primary illustration of salvation by grace through faith is Abraham—the father of the nation Israel. There are many reasons why Paul chose him as that illustration. He was God's specially chosen man. Through his loins would come the Messiah. He is the model of faith. He is the model of the right kind of approach to God. He is the model of true salvation. Abraham could demand our study for months and years. Here are a few things that will help our perspective of Abraham.

A. Abraham's Designation

Abraham is frequently called the "friend" of God in the Bible (2 Chron. 20:7; Isa. 41:8; James 2:23). Several times in Scripture, God—the Creator of the universe—is called "the God of Abraham" (eg. Ex. 3:16; 1 Kings 18:36). More than twelve chapters in Genesis are devoted to the life of that man. In the New Testament, the apostle Paul, James, and the writer of Hebrews all use Abraham as an illustration of salvation by grace through faith.

B. Abraham's Destiny

Abraham's story begins in Genesis 12.

1. His sinful upbringing

Abraham lived in a city called Ur. It was a busy city. As best archaeologists can determine, the city probably had about 300,000 inhabitants. The majority of the people were polytheistic—they believed in many gods, the foremost of which was the god Nanna, the moon god.

Abraham's father was Terah. According to Joshua 24:2, he was an idolatrous man. Abraham was raised in a pagan environment, yet Ur was an important educational center as well. It also may have been an effective trading center and a splendid agricultural city. But Abraham was still raised in a family that worshiped idols.

2. His sovereign call

God came to Abraham in the midst of his pagan environment and called him to follow a new path. God said, "Abraham, I want you to leave everything." Genesis 12:1-3 says, "Now the Lord had said unto Abram, Get thee out of thy country, and from thy kindred, and from thy father's house, unto a land that I will show thee; and I will make of thee a great nation, and I will bless thee, and make thy name great; and thou shalt be a blessing. And I will bless them that bless thee, and curse him that curseth thee: and in thee shall all families of the earth be blessed." That is a sovereign call. At that point in Genesis, we don't know much about Abraham except that he was begotten by Terah (Gen. 11:27), but God called him. People have often wondered why God called him, and the answer is: God is God, and He calls whomever He wants to call.

The Lord promised Abraham three things: land (v. 1), seed (or a nation, v. 2), and blessing (v. 3). God said that through Abraham would come the hope of salvation for the world. Through Abraham's loins all families of the earth would be blessed. Today, those of us who are saved—those who know salvation in Jesus Christ—are blessed with Abraham the believer, according to Galatians 3:9. We have been blessed because the seed came through his loins.

3. His specific responses

What was Abraham's response to the call?

a) His immediate obedience

Genesis 12:4 says, "So Abram departed." He packed up and left—instantaneous obedience. He responded to the sovereign call of God. When God first called, Abraham may have been about sixty years of age. He was going to make a complete break with his lifestyle, his career, his possessions, his friends, his relatives, and his religion. In verse 1 God says, "Get thee out of thy country, and from thy kindred, and from thy father's house." That is a very far-reaching directive. Verse 4 says, "So Abram departed, as the Lord had spoken unto him."

b) His incomplete obedience

But Genesis 12:4 also says, "And Lot went with him." I believe that was a hedge against the will of God. God told Abraham to leave his kindred, but Lot went with his uncle and became a serious problem later.

When Abraham left Ur, he did not fully obey God. Genesis 11:31-32 says, "And Terah took Abram, his son, and Lot, the son of Haran, his son's son, and Sarai, his daugher-in-law, his son Abram's wife; and they went forth with them from Ur of the Chaldeans, to go into the land of Canaan; and they came unto Haran, and dwelt there. And the days of Terah were two hundred and five years: and Terah died in Haran." Then Genesis 12:4 says, "And Abram was seventy and five years old when he departed out of Haran." God said to Abraham, "Leave your father's house and your kindred and go to the land that I will show you." But Abraham did not separate himself from Lot and his father. They didn't travel any farther than Haran. And Abraham may have stayed there for as long as fifteen years. That was not complete obedience. Many years were wasted in the idolatrous city of Haran. Instead of making a clean break, Abraham dragged along his relatives.

c) His improving obedience

When Terah died in Haran at the age of 205, then Abram decided to leave (Gen. 12:4). It appears that once he was rid of the tremendous power and pressure of his father, he could get on with obeying God. That is not an uncommon situation. Many people are reluctant to obey the call of God when there is pressure from some other source. But after the death of his father, Abraham began to move. Verse 5 says, "And Abram took Sarai, his wife, and Lot, his brother's son, and all their substance that they had gathered, and the souls they had gotten in Haran; and they went forth to go into the land of Canaan; and into the land of Canaan they came." I believe that Abraham's obedience was still not complete yet, but it was improving. At least he was finally leaving Haran. He crossed the hot, burning desert to a place that was unknown to him.

At this point, Abraham's faith was sufficient to be honored by God. Verses 6-7 say, "And Abram passed through the land unto the place of Shechem, unto the oak of Moreh. And the Canaanite was then in the land. And the Lord appeared unto Abram, and said, Unto thy seed will I give this land: and there builded he an altar unto the Lord, who appeared unto him." That is the appropriate response of a sovereignly chosen man—he worships the true God. It appears as if he couldn't bring himself to worship God until he had been removed from his idolatrous father. Verse 8 says, "And he removed from there unto a mountain on the east of Bethel, and pitched his tent, having Bethel on the west, and Hai on the east: and there he builded an altar unto the Lord, and called upon the name of the Lord." Abraham jettisoned his past idolatry and began to worship the true God. He became the model of faith.

d) His imperfect obedience

Abraham was not perfect.

(1) He compromised the truth (Gen. 12:10-20)

The first test Abraham had to face in Canaan was a famine. But instead of seeking help from God, he decided to seek it from the Egyptians. He found himself in a compromising situation, and lied to Pharaoh. If he had trusted God to meet his needs in the midst of the famine instead of trusting Egypt (which became a common problem for the Jewish people), he could have avoided that sin.

(2) He disobeyed God's command (Gen. 12:4-5)

Abraham also maintained an alliance with Lot that resulted in dire consequences. The greatest consequence occurred when Lot's wife was turned into a pillar of salt (Gen. 19:26).

(3) He committed adultery (Gen. 16:1-16)

Abraham, the model of faith, committed adultery in a stupid effort to produce the seed that he wasn't sure God could produce. As a result of the adultery he committed with Sarah's handmaiden Hagar, he produced a nation of enemies towards Israel.

But in spite of his imperfection, Abraham recovered from his lack of faith and sin to be known as a man who believed God. No man believes God perfectly, but Abraham is a model of belief despite his imperfection. He left his city, his environment, and his idols to go to a place that was unknown to him. He believed God for a child, even when his wife was barren her whole life. And thus he became the pattern of faith.

4. His significant epitaph

a) Died in faith

An amazing epitaph to the life of Abraham is found in Hebrews 11:13. It says, "These all died in faith, not having received the promises." Abraham never saw the fulfillment of the promise—he never saw the land in his possession, he never saw the nation, and he never saw the blessing. But he died believing that God would keep His word. That's what faith is all about.

b) Remained a stranger

Even the pagans were in awe of Abraham. In Genesis 23:6 the Hittites said, "Thou art a mighty prince." They could see a quality about him that made him stand out. When Sarah died, they wanted to give Abraham the grave site that he wanted to buy. But Abraham insisted on paying for it because he did not want to be obligated to the world and its people. When it was time to find a wife for Isaac, he did not want him to have a wife from among the Canaanites, but from the people he trusted.

Genesis 23:4 says that Abraham was a stranger and a sojourner in the land. He never returned to the lush green land of his home in Mesopotamia. Why? Hebrews 11:10 says, "He looked for a city which hath foundations, whose builder and maker is God." He had a divine perspective. In overcoming his human weaknesses, his periods of doubt, and his acts of stupidity, Abraham maintained a life of faith. He looked for that city whose builder and maker was God. He stepped out of his comfortable environment to go to a new land, build a nation, and receive a blessing; none of which he ever saw. But he died with the faith that God would fulfill His promises. Abraham is a classic illustration of the definition of faith given in Hebrews 11:1, "Now faith is the substance of things hoped for, the evidence of things not seen."

Abraham became the model of faith because he believed what he couldn't see, and died believing. That is what the perspective of life should be for every Christian. We believe in One whom we have never seen. We believe that we are going to a city whose builder and maker is God. Right up to the moment of our last breath, we are hoping for an eternity we have never seen. We believe in a salvation we cannot see, a Savior we cannot see, a heaven we cannot see, and an eternal blessedness we cannot see. In that sense, we are the children of Abraham. We have a faith that is like the faith of Abraham. In spite of all our human imperfections, we are saved by God through faith.

Review

In Romans 4, Paul uses Abraham to illustrate three points. First, Abraham was justified by faith, not works (vv. 1-8); second, by grace, not law (vv. 9-17); and third, by divine power, not human effort (vv. 18-25). We are presently looking at the first point: Abraham was justified by faith, not works. Paul gives us both a negative and a positive perspective.

I. THE NEGATIVE PERSPECTIVE (vv. 1-2; see pp. 117-18)

   A. The Questions (v. 1; see pp. 117-18)

   "What shall we say, then, that Abraham, our father, as pertaining to the flesh, hath found?"

   B. The Answer (v. 2; see p. 118)

   "For if Abraham were justified by works, he hath something of which to glory, but not before God."

   What did Abraham gain through his own flesh? First, if he gained righteousness with God because of his own effort, then he should be glorified, not God. But Abraham couldn't claim righteousness apart from God. Second, if Abraham was justified by works, he could boast. But from God's viewpoint he was not made right by his works. You cannot do anything on your own effort to gain acceptance with God. Romans 3:20 says, "By the deeds of the law [keeping God's law by your own good works] there shall no flesh be justified in his sight." Nobody can approach God on those terms. Romans 3:27 says, "Where is boasting then? It is excluded. By what law? Of works? Nay, but by the law of faith." In other words, if you were saved because of what you did, then you can receive the glory. If you can say, "I had the intelligence, foresight, insight, cleverness, and righteousness to do good works and come to God on my own," then you can receive the glory and credit. But that is not true. God is not in the business of glorifying men; He is in the business of glorifying Himself. What had Abraham gained by a manure pile of human works apart from God (cf. Phil. 3:7)? Nothing but a sickening stench in the nostrils of holy God. That is the best man can do. That a man is made right with God by works is absolutely contrary to everything the Bible teaches.

II. THE POSITIVE PERSPECTIVE (vv. 3-8; see pp. 119-22)

Romans 4:1-2 says that Abraham was not justified by works; Romans 4:3-8 says he was justified by faith.

A. Abraham's Demonstration of Faith (v. 3; see pp. 119-22)

"For what saith the scripture? Abraham believed God, and it was counted unto him for righteousness."

Abraham's salvation wasn't based on what he did, but what he believed. Ephesians 2:8-9 says, "For by grace are ye saved through faith; and that not of yourselves, it is the gift of God—not of works, lest any man should boast."

1. The appointment of Abraham (see pp. 119-21)

The essence of Abraham's greatness was his belief in God. And God sovereignly chose him. That was the elective purpose of God. Abraham responded to that call in faith. He took God at His word and left his home. With all of his human frailties, he lived a life of trusting God.

2. The accounting of righteousness (see pp. 121-22)

Abraham's faith was credited to his account as righteousness. That is the basic doctrine of salvation. How can a man be made right with God? How can his sin be forgiven? How can he receive entrance into God's kingdom? He is made right by what he believes, not by what he does. The righteousness of Christ is credited to his account.

Lesson

3. The action of God

The word *justification* is a technical term that refers to our legal standing before God: We have been declared to be just because of our faith. But the word also embraces a radical and real transformation. Our moral character has been altered eternally through regeneration. Justification by faith means that God has both declared us righteous and made us righteous. We have been regenerated—made new by faith. That regeneration by God is wonderfully described in the Bible in many places.

a) 2 Corinthians 5:17—"Therefore, if any man be in Christ, he is a new creation."

b) Titus 3:5—"Not by works of righteousness which we have done, but according to his mercy he saved us, by the washing of regeneration, and renewing of the Holy Spirit."

Justification is not only a state of being righteous; it is an actual regeneration. We are made righteous by faith.

4. The analysis of faith

a) The error

(1) Faith is not a work

There are people who say, "If you're saved by faith, then faith is a work. So salvation is by works." But the Bible says you can't be saved by works; you are saved by faith. Therefore, faith can't be a work. So what may appear to be very logical is unbiblical.

(2) Faith is a channel

Faith is never the basis or the reason for justification; it is only the channel that justification is received through. Faith is not what I do to earn salvation. God does not say, "Look at that wonderful faith." James 1:18 says, "Of his own will begot he us with the word of truth." James 1:17 says, "Every good gift and every perfect gift is from above, and cometh down from the Father." All faith does is accept that perfect gift.

I believe that within the saving work of God there is the creation of the faith necessary to believe in that work. We are not saved because of the value and worth of our faith; we are saved because our convicted hearts respond to the gift of salvation. Don't believe that faith is a work you do that you are rewarded for; it is only a channel—a response to God. One writer said, "God does not justify the believing person because of the worthiness of his belief, but because of the worthiness of the One who is believed." Our faith is not meritor-

132

ious; it is only the empty hand that takes the gift.

b) The elements

If saving faith is not a meritorious work, if God doesn't say, "That person has such virtuous faith. I think I will redeem him for it," then what is saving faith? There are many people who believe they have faith in God and Christ, but if they are hoping in their works, they are lost no matter what they may believe about the quality of their faith. So, what is saving faith? The following five elements should help you understand saving faith.

(1) Facts

When we say we believe, what do we believe in? Many people might say, "I believe in God," "I believe in goodness," "I believe that all is well with the world," "I believe in religion," "I believe in going to church," or "I believe in Jesus," but that doesn't do them any good. The issue is: What facts do they believe about God? Saving faith begins with facts. It is not a blind leap. Liberal theologians talk about a "leap of faith." That leap might include a belief in generalities about God, Jesus, and the Bible, but that isn't saving faith. Saving faith is based on facts.

(*a*) The faith in the gospel

First Corinthians 15:1-2 says, "I declare unto you the gospel which I preached unto you, which also ye have received, and in which ye stand; by which also ye are saved, if ye keep in memory what I preached unto you, unless ye have believed in vain." Another word for "vain" is nothing. If your faith is legitimate faith, you are saved. And that is based on keeping in mind what Paul preached—the facts.

(*b*) The facts of the gospel

The first fact is found in 1 Corinthians 15:3, which says, "That Christ died for our sins according to the scriptures." Christ died as a substitutionary atonement for our sins, according to the fulfillment of Old Testament prophecies. Verses 4-8 say, "That he was buried, and that he rose again the third day according to the scriptures; and that he was seen of Cephas, then of the twelve. After that, he was seen of above five hundred brethren at once, of whom the greater part remain unto this present time, but some are fallen asleep. After that, he was seen of James; then, of all the apostles. And last of all he was seen of me also, as of one born out of due time." Those are the facts. Jesus Christ died a substitutionary death for sin on the cross according

133

to the Old Testament prophets. He was buried and three days later rose in triumph. His bodily resurrection was literal as evidenced by the testimony of over five hundred eyewitnesses, the last of which was Paul. Those are the facts.

Saving faith starts with the facts. It is not enough to believe without the right facts. Galatians 1:8 says, "Though we, or an angel of heaven, preach any other gospel unto you than that which we have preached unto you, let him be accursed." You cannot alter the facts. They are essential to the matter of believing. Second John 10-11 says that if anybody talks about some other doctrine, don't let him into your house—don't even bid him Godspeed—or you will be a partaker of his evil deeds.

(2) Agreement

It is one thing to know the facts; it is another thing to believe them. Having been exposed to an understanding of the facts, you can believe they are true. First, you need to know the facts, and then you need to agree with them, which is to affirm them in your heart.

Are there people who know the facts but aren't saved? Sure. Are there people who believe the facts but aren't saved? Yes. Many people. I've been witnessing to a man for over twenty years who believes the facts I've mentioned, but never affirms them in his heart.

(3) Internalization

First, you know the facts. The Bible is a literal historical book. That's why we preach the reality of the Scripture. People have to be convinced of the facts. What follows is internalization—the desire to make their beliefs personal. That involves personal appropriation.

(a) John 1:11-13—"He came unto his own, and his own received him not. But as many as received him, to them gave he power to become the children of God, even to them that believe on his name; who were born, not of blood, nor of the will of the flesh, nor of the will of man, but of God." Men are given eternal life by an act of God, not by their will, flesh, or power. They need to respond to the facts by believing and receiving them. Knowing the facts, and agreeing with them can't make salvation a reality by themselves.

(b) John 8:31—"Then said Jesus . . . If ye continue in my word, then are ye my disciples indeed." There has to be an internalization—a desire for personal appropriation.

134

Yet even with that, a person could still fall short of being saved. There are people who know the facts and believe them, and desire to appropriate them into their lives, but they can't let go of something.

(4) Trust

Saving faith does not merely involve intellectual knowledge, agreement with the facts, and a personal desire to apply those facts. It involves a trust that says, "I give you my life." I call that total commitment. That means that I repent of my sin, affirm the lordship of Jesus Christ, and put my life in His care. When you are saved, you exchange all that you are for all that He is. You exchange all that you possess for all that He possesses. That involves turning from your sin, affirming His lordship, and giving Him your life.

(a) 1 Peter 2:25—Peter describes salvation as a return to God after being led astray. Salvation is not adding God to your activities, but turning from sin to God.

(b) 1 Thessalonians 1:9—The Thessalonians gained salvation because they "turned to God from idols." They knew the facts, agreed with them, internalized them, and then entrusted themselves to them. That's full commitment.

When you come to Christ there is a turning from idols and sin to God, a repenting of the past to move toward God. Don't ever let anybody ever tell you that salvation is apart from repentance. Salvation incorporates the aspect of trust—you drop all you possess and receive all that God has to give.

(5) Hope

When you were saved, you were saved in hope because you have not yet seen the ultimate provision of your salvation. You believe with all your heart that you're going to go to heaven, but you haven't seen heaven yet. You believe with all your heart that you're going to dwell in the presence of the eternal God, but you haven't seen Him yet. You believe with all your heart that you're going to be in a place where Jesus Christ will be, in the presence of the redeemed saints forever, but you are not there yet. And you believe there will be a time when you will be perfect and won't have your human frailties and the propensity to sin, but you haven't seen that yet. But still you believe all of those things, and that means you are saved in hope.

135

(*a*) The commitment of eternal destiny

True salvation is not a momentary thing; it is a commitment of my entire temporal and eternal destiny to God. How many people have you known who knew the facts, believed the facts, wanted to appropriate the facts, and committed their lives to the Lord, but when their lives improved, wanted their old lives back? True saving faith gives God not only the moment, but the destiny. It does not provide for momentary escapism or satisfaction; it places my eternal destiny in the Lord's control. But Christians live with unfulfilled hope for now.

(*b*) The confidence in eternal destiny

I know how my future will turn out. I know what the Word of God says, and I have the confirmation of the witness of the Spirit in my heart.

i) 2 Thessalonians 2:13-16—"But we are bound to give thanks always to God for you, brethren beloved of the Lord, because God hath from the beginning chosen you to salvation through sanctification of the Spirit and belief of the truth" (v. 13). Salvation involves believing the truth; the sanctifying work (the regenerating, transforming work of the Spirit) follows. Verse 14 says, "He called you by our gospel, to the obtaining of the glory of our Lord Jesus Christ. Therefore, brethren, stand fast, and hold the traditions which ye have been taught, whether by word or our epistle. Now our Lord Jesus Christ himself, and God, even our Father, who hath loved us, and hath given us everlasting consolation and good hope through grace" (vv. 14-16). We are saved in hope.

ii) 1 Thessalonians 5:8—We are to be "putting on the . . . helmet, the hope of salvation."

Saving faith includes knowing the facts and agreeing with them (that is, believing the facts), desiring to make them personal (appropriating the death of Christ on your behalf), and entrusting all you are to the Lord—turning from idols to God—not just for the moment but forever. That is saving faith, and that is the kind of faith that Abraham had. He believed what God said—he heard the facts and agreed with them. He wanted to appropriate those facts, so he entrusted everything to God. And it was all done in hope because he never saw the fulfillment, but he believed God to his dying day. Abraham is a perfect illustration of saving faith. And Romans 4:3 says that his faith "was counted unto him for righteousness."

Focusing on the Facts

1. What is one doctrine that Satan desires to attack? Why (see p. 126)?

2. Why did Paul choose Abraham as his illustration of salvation by grace through faith (see p. 126)?

3. What is Abraham frequently called in the Bible? List some verses where he is so called (see p. 126).

4. Describe the environment that Abraham was raised in (see pp. 126-27).

5. When God called Abraham, what did he promise to give him (Gen. 12:1-3; see p. 127)?

6. Detail Abraham's varied responses to the call of God (Gen. 11:31-32; 12:4; see pp. 127-29).

7. When was Abraham's faith sufficient to be honored by God (see p. 128)?

8. Give some examples of Abraham's imperfect obedience (see p. 129).

9. What verse is a fitting epitaph to Abraham's life? Why (see p. 129)?

10. Why did Abraham remain a stranger and a sojourner in the land of Canaan (Heb. 11:10; see pp. 129-30)?

11. Describe the meaning of the word *justification* (see p. 132).

12. Some people say, "If you are saved by faith, then faith is a work." How would you respond to that statement (see p. 132)?

13. Discuss faith as a channel for justification (see p. 132).

14. What five elements does saving faith incorporate (see pp. 133-35)?

15. According to 1 Corinthians 15:1-8, what is saving faith based on? Be specific (see p. 133).

16. Once someone is exposed to the facts of the gospel, what must follow for saving faith to be real (see p. 134)?

17. Jesus said, "If ye _____ in my word, then are ye my disciples indeed." What element of saving faith does that Scripture help explain (John 8:31; see p. 134)?

18. What does trust in God require from the believer (see p. 135)?

19. Why is the Christian saved in hope (see p. 135)?

20. Fill in the blanks: True saving faith gives God not only the _____ _____ but the _____ (see p. 136).

Pondering the Principles

1. What has God called you to do? How would you characterize your obedience to God's call? Has it been immediate, or is it still incomplete? If it is incomplete, is it at least improving? In what ways

does your obedience to God's call parallel Abraham's? In what ways is it different? If you were put in Abraham's situation, how do you think you would respond, based on your present pattern of obedience? If your obedience is incomplete and not improving, what must you do to begin to obey again? What lessons can you learn from Abraham?

2. What would you like to be your epitaph? Spend some time and write it down. Now, what are you presently doing in your life that would cause someone to agree with your analysis of your life? What are the things that you need to be doing in your life that would make that epitaph true? Make the commitment to begin to do those things.

3. What is your hope as a Christian? Look up the following verses: Psalm 31:24; 33:22; 130:7; Proverbs 10:28; Romans 5:2-5; 8:24-25; Colossians 1:5, 23, 27; 1 Thessalonians 1:3; 2 Thessalonians 2:16; Titus 2:13; 3:7; Hebrews 11:1; 1 Peter 1:3. What are the different ways those verses describe the Christian's hope? What are the benefits of that hope? Spend this time in prayer. Thank God for giving you what you are hoping for. Ask Him to help you wait for your eternal destiny with patient hope.

9
Abraham—Justified by Faith—Part 3

Outline

Introduction
A. The Promise of God
  1. A physical father
  2. A spiritual father
B. The Belief of Abraham
  1. For a new country
  2. For a child
  3. For a Redeemer
    a) Galatians 3:16
    b) John 8:56

Review
 I. The Negative Perspective
II. The Positive Perspective
A. Abraham's Demonstration of Faith

Lesson
B. Paul's Depiction of Justification
  1. The one who works
    a) His effort is unrewarded
      (1) Romans 3:12
      (2) Romans 3:20
      (3) Isaiah 64:6
    b) His purpose is unfulfilled
  2. The one who doesn't work
    a) Justification for the ungodly
      (1) The affirmation
      (2) The attitudes
        (*a*) The wrong attitude
        (*b*) The right attitude
    b) Judgment on the ungodly
C. David's Description of Blessedness
  1. The relationship of blessedness
    a) The illustration of imputed righteousness
    b) The impact of imputed righteousness
  2. The reasons for blessedness

a) Sins are forgiven
   (1) The symbol of forgiveness
   (2) The scope of forgiveness
b) Sins are covered
   (1) The motive of the cross
   (2) The message of Hebrews 9-10
      (*a*) The imperfect picture
      (*b*) The perfect priest
c) Sins are disregarded
   (1) Isaiah 53:5, 10
   (2) Psalm 130:3-4
   (3) Exodus 34:6-7

Introduction

In Romans 4, Abraham is Paul's great illustration of the doctrine of justification by faith, which the apostle so marvelously and masterfully presented under the inspiration of the Holy Spirit in Romans 3:21-31. Abraham is a good choice because he was the man the Jewish leaders were using as proof of justification by law, or legalism. Paul demolishes their proof by showing that Abraham was justified by faith.

A. The Promise of God

Abraham's name at first was *Abram,* and it means, "exalted father." God later changed his name to *Abraham* (Gen. 17:5), which means "the father of many nations," for God gave Abraham that very promise. The promise was twofold. God promised that Abraham would be:

1. A physical father

From the loins of Abraham would come multitudes of people (Gen. 17:1-8). The Semitic world descended from Abraham. God said that Abraham would produce generations of people that could be numbered as the sand of the sea, or the stars of the heavens (Gen. 22:17). God also said that Abraham would be:

2. A spiritual father

Abraham is the father of all those who are the faithful. He established the pattern, and all who put their faith in God follow the pattern of their father, Abraham. In Galatians 3:6-9 Paul says, "Even as Abraham believed God, and it was accounted to him for righteousness. Know ye, therefore, that they who are of faith, the same are the sons of Abraham. And the scripture, forseeing that God would justify the Gentiles through faith, preached before the gospel unto Abraham, saying. In thee shall all nations be blessed. So, then, they who are of faith are blessed with faithful Abraham.

So Abraham did not only produce physical seed; he set the standard for spirituality as well. Millions follow his pattern of faith, occupying a position uniquely identified in the Scripture as "chil-

140

dren of Abraham." He is the example of justification by faith.

B. The Belief of Abraham

There are three key things that summarize the faith of Abraham.

1. For a new country

He left the city of Ur and journeyed to Canaan.

2. For a child

A child was born to him and Sarah when she was barren and they both were very old.

As important as those two elements of his faith were, they stand in secondary importance to his belief in God.

3. For a Redeemer

Today, we look back in time to Christ. Abraham looked forward in time to Christ. He didn't know His name, and didn't know any historical information about Him, but he looked for a Redeemer.

a) Galatians 3:16— "Now to Abraham and his seed were the promises made. He saith not, And to seeds, as of many; but as of one, And to thy seed, which is Christ." In other words, when the Lord gave the promise to Abraham, He didn't give the promise to many seeds, but to one seed. Abraham must have understood that the one seed was the key to the promise.

b) John 8:56—Jesus said, "Your father, Abraham, rejoiced to see my day; and he saw it, and was glad."

Abraham believed God for a new country, a son, and a Redeemer. Then he put his faith in that promised Redeemer. Thus, Abraham becomes the pattern for all who put their faith in God's promised Redeemer. When the promise concerning a son came to Abraham, he believed beyond that promise to the blessed Seed. And it is very likely that he understood the significance of Genesis 3:15, that the seed of the woman would bruise the serpent's head.

Abraham lived and died in faith that included belief in God's promised Redeemer. And that faith was credited to his account as righteousness. He becomes the pattern. He is our father, maybe not in terms of racial genealogy, but in terms of ethical similarity. He is the perfect illustration of Romans 3.

Review

There are basically three angles to Paul's presentation in Romans 4. First, Abraham was justified by faith, not works (vv. 1-8); second, he was justified by grace, not law (vv. 9-17); and third, he was justified by divine effort, not human effort (vv. 18-25). We are currently looking at the first angle. Abraham was justified by faith, not works.

I. THE NEGATIVE PERSPECTIVE (vv. 1-2; see pp. 117-18)

"What shall we say, then, that Abraham, our father, as pertaining to the flesh, hath found? For if Abraham were justified by works, he hath something of which to glory, but not before God."

II. THE POSITIVE PERSPECTIVE (vv. 3-8; see pp. 119-22, 131-36)

A. Abraham's Demonstration of Faith (v. 3; see pp. 119-22, 131-36)

"For what saith the scripture? Abraham believed God, and it was counted unto him for righteousness."

Lesson

B. Paul's Depiction of Justification (vv. 4-5)

"Now to him that worketh is the reward not reckoned of grace, but of debt. But to him that worketh not, but believeth on Him that justifieth the ungodly, his faith is counted for righteousness."

Abraham's faith was genuine. He heard the facts, believed them, and entrusted his life to the living Lord in the hope of eternal fulfillment. He manifested genuine faith by his obedience and worship. His faith was not the result of his own effort, but of grace. Romans 11:6 says, "And if by grace, then is it no more of works; otherwise grace is no more grace." Salvation is either of grace or works; it can't be both.

1. The one who works (v. 4)

"Now to him that worketh is the reward not reckoned of grace, but of debt."

a) His effort is unrewarded

If you did something to earn your salvation, you wouldn't be given grace; you would be given wages. If you worked for salvation, God would owe it to you. But salvation comes by grace, which is free favor on the part of God. Abraham did not earn salvation; he was given it by grace.

Romans 4:5 says, "But to him that worketh not, but believeth on him that justifieth the ungodly, his faith is counted for righteousness." The faith of Abraham agrees with the doctrine of Paul. Faith is not a work that deserves to be rewarded; it is merely a channel that receives the work that God has done. It is an empty hand that reaches out. God doesn't say, "That person is worthy because of his marvelous faith, so I'll redeem him." Man cannot do meritorious good works to make himself right with God.

The Four Kinds of Works

Theologian John Gerstner lists four kinds of human deeds.

1. Bad-bad works

142

Unregenerate people can't do anything morally or ethically that can bring them into a right relationship with God. But some of the things they do are evil. Those are bad-bad works. Those are the evil activities of non-Christians.

2. Good-bad works

Good-bad works are bad works in the sense that they cannot earn salvation, but they are good in the sense that they are philanthropic. Those works could be called unregenerate niceness. So there are non-Christian bad works, and non-Christian good works. But neither kind will make people right with God.

3. Bad-good works

Bad-good works are the activities of hypocrites, who attempt to do good, religious works. But those kind of works won't earn them salvation.

4. Good-good works

Man can't do good-good works. He can do bad-bad works, good-bad works, and bad-good works. It is impossible for man to do the kind of works that can bring him into a redemptive relationship with God.

The following verses describe man's incapacity.

(1) Romans 3:12—"They are all gone out of the way, they are together become unprofitable; there is none that doeth good, no, not one."

(2) Romans 3:20—"By the deeds of the law there shall no flesh be justified."

(3) Isaiah 64:6—"All our righteousnesses are as filthy rags."

A person with true faith knows he cannot do good-good works to gain salvation; he acknowledges his bad-bad works, good-bad works, or bad-good works and desperately cries out to God for redemption. In the Beatitudes, Jesus said that a person should come to God with meekness, brokenness, and a begging spirit. Then he is to cry out for righteousness, and in faith embrace the work that Jesus did. Salvation is by grace. If it were by works, then grace would be unnecessary because salvation would be deserved. And if that were true then you would steal the glory from God. But God doesn't allow that to happen, for the Old Testament says, "My glory will I not give to another" (Isa. 42:8).

b) His purpose is unfulfilled

In Romans 4:4, the Greek word for "worketh" is *ergazomai,* which means, "to do that which brings results." If we received righteousness because of our work, then grace would not be involved. That's like going to work, putting in your eight hours, and collecting your check at the end of the week. You don't say to your boss, "I've given you a full week. Please be gracious and pay me." You don't want grace; you want pay for your works. Your boss is in debt to you. But God is not. He is in debt to no man. There is no such thing as saving wages. God owes you absolutely nothing, and that is abundantly clear in Scripture. The intended purpose of all creation is to give glory to God. If men were redeemed by works, the intended purpose of the universe would be violated. All things are made by Him and for Him (Col. 1:16).

Paul gives an excellent affirmation to that truth in Romans 11:36: "For of him, and through him, and to him, are all things: to whom be glory forever. Amen." According to Ephesians 1:14, everything that God does in redemption is to the praise of His glory. According to Ephesians 3:20-21, the work that God does in the church is done in the Spirit's power so that God might be glorified. Man earns no wage lest he steal the glory of God.

Works Can't Save People

1. Good works make no provision for past sin

   You can't be saved by your present righteousness because it doesn't affect your past sin. How can your past sins find atonement if you are redeemed by works?

2. Fallen creatures can't meet the divine standard

   The divine standard is, "Be ye, therefore, perfect" (Matt. 5:48a).

3. Christ's death would have been needless

4. God's glory would be eclipsed

2. The one who doesn't work (v. 5)

   "But to him that worketh not, but believeth on him that justifieth the ungodly, his faith is counted for righteousness."

   It is important that the one who is justified sees himself as ungodly. A man said to me, "I enjoy church and the fellowship of Christians, but I don't see myself as a sinner." I said, "That's your basic problem." If you don't see yourself as a sinner then salvation isn't available to you. Unless you believe in the One who justifies the ungodly, there is no accounting of righteousness to you. Initially, you must affirm that you are ungodly. Saving grace is available to the one who knows in his heart that he can't work his way into God's kingdom by his own self-effort—he knows he is unacceptable to God—but by faith he embraces the One who justifies the ungodly.

Illustrating Saving Grace

The concept of saving grace is very hard to understand. People often ask, "Aren't some people better than others? Does God accept anybody—the good along with the vile? Doesn't having more good works help?" Let me show you an illustration that answers those questions.

Matthew 20:1-16 contains a parable that is difficult to understand because most people don't understand grace; all they understand is reward, debt, and wages. Verse 1 begins, "For the kingdom of heaven is like a man that is an householder, who went out early in the morning to hire laborers into his vineyard." That probably happened about six o'clock in the morning because that is when a workday usually began during Christ's time. The parable continues: "And when he had agreed with the laborers for a denarius a day [the standard pay for a laborer], he sent them into his vineyard. And he went out about the third hour, and saw others standing idle in the market place, and said unto them, Go ye also into the vineyard, and whatever is right, I will give you. And they went their way. Again he went out about the sixth and ninth hour, and did the same. And about the eleventh hour he went out, and found others standing idle, and saith unto them, Why stand ye here all the day idle? They say unto him, Because no man hath hired us. He saith unto them, Go ye also into the vineyard, and whatever is right, that shall ye receive. So when evening was come [6:00 P.M.], the lord of the vineyard saith unto his steward, Call the laborers, and give them their hire, beginning from the last unto the first. And when they came that were hired about the eleventh hour, they received every man a denarius [a day's wage for one hour's work]. But when the first came, they supposed that they should have received more; and they likewise received every man a denarius. And when they had received it, they murmured against the householder, saying, These last have worked but one hour, and thou hast made them equal unto us, who have borne the burden and heat of the day. But he answered one of them, and said, Friend, I do thee no wrong. Didst not thou agree with me for a denarius? Take what is thine, and go thy way; I will give unto this last, even as unto thee. Is it not lawful for me to do what I will with mine own? Is thine eye evil, because I am good? So the last shall be first, and the first last; for many are called, but few chosen."

What is that teaching? God bestows the same benefits of grace on the people who barely get saved as much as those who have served their whole life. It is hard for us to understand that God's grace is equally bestowed on all. Whoever they are and whenever they come, God's grace is the same for all. In Romans 4:5 Paul says that their faith is accounted to them for righteousness. They are not righteous, but righteousness is credited to their account.

a) Justification for the ungodly

We cannot justify ourselves. That's why Job said, "If I justify myself, mine own mouth shall condemn me" (Job 9:20*b*). You can't justify yourself.

(1) The affirmation

If you want to be saved, you must affirm that you are ungodly. The Pharisees never admitted their ungodliness, so they were unredeemable. According to Romans 4:5, God only justifies the ungodly. The fact is that all people are ungodly, but not all of them are willing to admit it. When people think they are OK the way they are, then they are unredeemable because God only justifies those who know they are ungodly.

(2) The attitudes

(*a*) The wrong attitude

The Pharisees were never willing to accept the fact that they were ungodly. That's why they rejected Jesus Christ. In Matthew 9:12 Jesus said, "I haven't come for the people who are well; I've come for the people who are sick. Since you don't think you're sick, I can't help you."

(*b*) The right attitude

Anyone who ever comes to Jesus Christ must realize that he is a sinner. Paul said, "And I thank Christ Jesus, our Lord, who hath enabled me, in that he counted me faithful, putting me into the ministry, who was before a blasphemer, and a persecutor, and injurious; but I obtained mercy. . . . And the grace of our Lord was exceedingly abundant with faith and love which is in Christ Jesus. This is a faithful saying, and worthy of all acceptance, that Christ Jesus came into the world to save sinners, of whom I am chief" (1 Tim. 1:12-15). That's the right attitude.

b) Judgment on the ungodly

Man is ungodly. That truth is repeated throughout the New Testament (Rom. 5:6; 1 Tim. 1:9; 1 Pet. 4:18; 2 Pet. 2:5). One Scripture that stands out is Jude 14-15, "The Lord cometh with ten thousands of his saints, to execute judgment upon all, and to convict all that are ungodly among them of all their ungodly deeds which they have ungodly committed, and of all their hard speeches which ungodly sinners have spoken against him." Four times Jude says that men are ungodly. The only kind of people God saves are the ungodly. Until man faces the reality of his ungodliness, he is unredeemable.

You say, "How can a just and holy God simply forgive the ungodly?" God imputes righteousness to them because their sin has been imputed to Jesus Christ. When Christ died on the cross, He bore in His own body our sins that we might be the recipient of His righteousness. One writer said,

The best obedience of my hands,
Dares not appear before Thy throne;
But faith can answer Thy demands,
By pleading what my Lord has done!

It is not the worst of sinners that misses out on heaven, but the one that thinks himself the least of sinners. A right relationship with God is a gift appropriated by faith.

Abraham's experience was not isolated, so in addition, Paul uses David as an illustration.

C. David's Description of Blessedness (vv. 6-8)

"David also describeth the blessedness of the man unto whom God imputeth righteousness apart from works, saying, Blessed are they whose iniquities are forgiven, and whose sins are covered. Blessed is the man to whom the Lord will not impute sin."

In verse 7 a sinner is characterized by iniquity and sin, and in verse 8 he is characterized by sin alone. In both cases the Lord forgives and does not hold sin against a person. Those verses show us that salvation is not by works because the individual is defined as a sinner. How can a sinner be blessed? If he has been forgiven, the Lord does not credit sin to his account. The blessing is not a result of works, but of faith. The truly blessed man is forgiven of his sin.

Romans 4:7-8 is a quote from Psalm 32:1-2. When David wrote that Psalm, he was experiencing guilt. He had been involved in adultery. He had been involved in murder. He had desecrated his throne and the sanctity of his own virtue. He was a vile, wretched sinner. Psalm 51 reveals the agony and pain he endured. He felt as if God had abandoned him. He was experiencing horrible guilt. In Psalm 32:4 he said that his life's juices dried up. That's what happens when guilt occurs. Saliva dries up. Anxiety creates pressure in the head, and that restricts the flow of blood. The lymphatic and nervous systems are affected. He was getting old before his time. He began to ache in his joints (Ps. 32:3). Guilt does that. But in the midst of all that, he experienced the goodness of God. That is why he said, "Blessed are they whose iniquities are forgiven. . . . Blessed is the man to whom the Lord will not impute sin" (Rom. 4:7-8). The truly blessed man knows forgiveness.

Abraham was a pre-Mosaic figure; David was a Mosaic figure. Abraham pre-dates the clear definition of the Mosaic covenant. That shows us that God redeemed people in both the pre-Mosaic and Mosaic eras by faith. Redemption is always a matter of faith resulting in imputed righteousness.

1. The relationship of blessedness (v. 6)

"David also describeth the blessedness of the man unto whom God imputeth righteousness apart from works."

Verse 5 says that God justifies the ungodly, and counts his faith as righteousness. David said the same thing—the Lord imputes righteousness to a person whose faith is apart from works. The righteousness of Jesus Christ is imputed to the sinner who believes.

a) The illustration of imputed righteousness

Psalm 84:1-3 illustrates what it means to have a right relationship with God. Verses 1-2 say, "How amiable are thy tabernacles, O Lord of hosts! My soul longeth, yea, even fainteth for the courts of the Lord; my heart and my flesh cry out for the living God." Those verses describe an individual who has experienced intimacy with God. Such a person is known by God, and has been made right with Him; he continues to seek for fellowship with God. A marvelous picture of that relationship is found in verses 3-4, "Yea, the sparrow hath found an house, and the swallow a nest for herself, where she may lay her young, even thine altars, O Lord of hosts, my King and my God. Blessed are they who dwell in thy house."

What is that saying? A sparrow is the biblical symbol of worthlessness. Sparrows could be bought cheaply—five for two farthings (Luke 12:6). (A farthing was equal to one-fourth of a penny.) They were two for a farthing (Matt. 10:29), but if you wanted to buy two farthings-worth of sparrows, an extra sparrow would be thrown in. But in a right relationship with God, the one who is worthless becomes infinitely valuable. The sparrow has found a house. The swallow is also the biblical symbol of restlessness. But the swallow has found a nest in the presence of God. The worthless become infinitely valuable; the restless find rest.

b) The impact of imputed righteousness

A marvelous transformation takes place. When the ungodly sinner reaches out in faith to embrace the Redeemer—knowing that in God alone is his hope for salvation—God hears his cry and does not impute sin to him anymore. That sin is transferred to Jesus Christ, who bore it on the cross, and Christ's righteousness is transferred to the sinner. That is the divine transaction we know as salvation, which is a blessed thing because our sins are enough to damn us and send us to hell forever, to say nothing of the anxiety that results if those sins remain unforgiven. Mental hospitals are filled with people suffering from guilt—as much as ninety to ninety-five percent, according to some psychiatrists. Those people can't find release from the bondage of their unending sinfulness and fear of inevitable retribution.

2. The reasons for blessedness (vv. 7-8)

   a) Sins are forgiven (v. 7a)

   "Blessed are they whose iniquities [Gk., *anomia,* "lawlessness"] are forgiven."

   The word translated as "forgiven" is the main Greek word used in the New Testament for forgiveness; it means "to send away." You say, "Do you mean that the Lord simply sends our sins away? How far?" Psalm 103:12 says, "As far as the east is from the west, so far hath he removed our transgressions from us."

   (1) The symbol of forgiveness

   In Leviticus 16:21-22, the priest put his hands on a goat, symbolically transferred the people's sins to it, and sent the goat outside the camp.

   John the Baptist talked about the removal of sin when he said this of the Lord Jesus Christ, "Behold the Lamb of God, who taketh away the sin of the world" (John 1:29b).

   (2) The scope of forgiveness

   Forgiveness involves the removal of all our sins. First John 2:12 says, "Your sins are forgiven you for his name's sake." He has to forgive all of our sins; otherwise He wouldn't be a fully gracious God if He left some of the sins of those who come to Him unforgiven.

   b) Sins are covered (v. 7b)

   "Whose sins are covered."

   The word "covered" has Old Testament roots. Sacrifices covered sins. In those days, the sins were covered up and not fully dealt with. The symbol of the scapegoat in Leviticus 16:21-22 indicated that they were sent away.

   (1) The motive of the cross

   I believe that sins were uncovered and sent away for good at the cross. Jesus didn't just cover up our sin; He removed it. When Jesus died on the cross, He dealt with the sins of the people who would live after Him and those who lived before Him. Abraham's sin was dealt with on the cross. Sin was no longer covered; it was uncovered and sent away.

(2) The message of Hebrews 9-10

    (a) The imperfect picture

Hebrews 9:1-5 says, "The first covenant [the Old Testament] had also ordinances of divine service, and an earthly sanctuary. For there was a tabernacle made; the first, in which was the lampstand, and the table, and the showbread; which is called the sanctuary. And after the second veil, the tabernacle, which is called the Holiest of all, which had the golden censer, and the ark of the covenant . . . Aaron's rod that budded, and the tables of the covenant; and over it the cherubim of glory." Verses 6-7 describe the routine of the high priest. Verse 8 says, "The Holy Spirit thus signifying that the way into the holiest of all was not yet made manifest, while the first tabernacle was yet standing." That routine was just a picture—it didn't secure salvation. Verse 9 says, "[It] was a figure for the time then present, in which were offered both gifts and sacrifices that could not make him that did the service perfect, as pertaining to the conscience." In other words, those pictures and emblems couldn't make anybody right with God. Food, drink, and washings were fleshly ordinances that were imposed until the time of reformation.

    (b) The perfect priest

However, verses 11-15 say, "But Christ being come an high priest of good things to come, by a greater and more perfect tabernacle, not made with hands, that is to say, not of this building, neither by the blood of goats and calves, but by his own blood he entered in once into the holy place, having obtained eternal redemption for us. For if the blood of bulls and of goats, and the ashes of an heifer sprinkling the unclean, sanctifieth to the purifying of the flesh, how much more shall the blood of Christ, who through the eternal Spirit offered himself without spot to God, purge your conscience from dead works to serve the living God? And for this cause he is the mediator of the new testament, that by means of death, for the redemption of the transgressions that were under the first testament, they who are called might receive the promise of eternal inheritance."

Abraham was saved by the death of Jesus Christ on the cross. That death was just as much for the sin of Abraham, David, and all those who believed God and looked for a redeemer in the past, as it was for our sin. Verse 15 says, "He is the mediator of the new testament, that by means of death, for the redemption of the transgressions that were under the first testament, they who are called might receive the promise of eternal inheritance." Jesus' death took care of people under the first testament as well as those under the second. What a great reality!

Verses 24-26 say, "For Christ is not entered into the holy places made with hands, which are the figures of the true, but into heaven itself, now to appear in the presence of God for us; nor yet that he should offer himself often, as the high priest entereth into the holy place every year with blood of others; for then must he often have suffered since the foundation of the world. But now once, in the end of the ages, hath he appeared to put away sin by the sacrifice of himself." Jesus didn't just cover up sin; He put it away. Blessed is the man whose transgression is forgiven, whose sin is covered, and is now put away!

Hebrews 10:1 says that the law was a shadow of good things to come. Christ is the very image of those good things.

c) Sins are disregarded (v. 8)

"Blessed is the man to whom the Lord will not impute sin."

That verse makes me think of the following:

(1) Isaiah 53:5, 10—Verse 5 says that Christ "was wounded for our transgressions, he was bruised for our iniquities; the chastisement of our peace was upon him, and with his stripes we are healed." But verse 10 is the clincher, "Yet it pleased the Lord to bruise him. . . . When thou shalt make his soul an offering for sin." The only way that God could avoid imputing our sins to us was by imputing them to someone who would bear their penalty. And that's what He did. God then imputed His righteousness to us.

(2) Psalm 130:3-4—"If thou, Lord, shouldest mark iniquities, who shall stand? But there is forgiveness with thee, that thou mayest be feared." I suggest that the word *revered* replace "feared." If you have trouble giving God glory, you ought to be able to give Him glory for the fact that He doesn't put your sins to your ac-

count. God imputes righteousness to the undeserving, yet He imputes sin to the undeserving Christ. God manifests His great glory so that He might be revered. David committed gross sins; he knew the pain they caused, but he also knew the blessedness of forgiveness.

(3) Exodus 34:6-7—"The Lord God, merciful and gracious, long-suffering, and abundant in goodness and truth, keeping mercy for thousands, forgiving iniquity and transgression and sin, and who will by no means clear the guilty." If you maintain your guilt, you won't be cleared until you embrace Jesus Christ.

James Proctor wrote,

Nothing, either great or small,
Nothing, sinner, no.
Jesus died and paid it all,
Long, long ago.

When He, from His lofty throne,
Stooped in love to die,
Everything was fully done;
Hearken to His cry.

Weary, working, burdened one
Wherefore toil ye so?
Cease your doing, all was done,
Long, long ago.

'Till to Jesus' work you cling,
By a simple faith,
"Doing" is a deadly thing,
"Doing" ends in death.

Cast your deadly doing down
Down at Jesus' feet;
Stand "in Him," and Him alone,
Gloriously complete.

It is finished, yes indeed,
Finished every jot.
Sinner, this is all you need,
Tell me, is it not?

Focusing on the Facts

1. What was Abraham's name before God changed it? What did it mean? What does the name "Abraham" mean (see p. 140)?

2. Explain the twofold promise that God gave to Abraham (see p. 140).

3. What were the three things that Abraham believed God would provide (see p. 141)?

4. If a man could do something to earn his salvation, what would he deserve (see p. 142)?

5. According to John Gerstner, what are the four kinds of works? Explain each one. Which of those four kinds of works is man unable to do (see pp. 142-43)?

6. Does God allow another to steal the glory that He deserves? What verse supports your answer (see p. 143)?

7. What is God's intended purpose for all creation? Give a verse that supports your answer (see p. 144).

8. Give four reasons why works can't save people (see p. 144).

9. To whom is saving grace available (see p. 144)?

10. How does the parable in Matthew 20:1-16 illustrate God's saving grace (see pp. 145-46)?

11. Why were the Pharisees unredeemable? Why is anyone ever unredeemable (see p. 146)?

12. How does Paul demonstrate the attitude of a redeemable person (see 1 Tim. 1:12-15; p. 146)?

13. How can a just and holy God simply forgive the ungodly (see p. 147)?

14. How can a sinner be blessed (Rom. 4:6-8; see p. 147)?

15. Why could David relate so well the feelings of guilt when he wrote Psalm 32? What are some of the things that happen to the human body when guilt occurs (see Psalm 32:3-4; p. 147)?

16. Explain how Psalm 84:1-3 illustrates what it means to have a right relationship to God (see p. 148).

17. Fill in the blanks: In a right relationship with God, the _____ become infinitely _____; the _____ find _____ (see p. 148).

18. Describe the divine transaction known as salvation. What is transferred to Jesus Christ? What is tranferred to the sinner (see pp. 148-49)?

19. What does the word "forgiven" mean in the New Testament? According to Psalm 103:12, how far is the believers' sin sent away (see p. 149)?

20. What was an Old Testament symbol for the removal of sins (see Lev. 16:21-22; p. 149)?

21. Why must God provide for the forgiveness of all sins (see p. 149)?

22. Whose sins did Jesus deal with on the cross? What did He do with sin (see pp. 150-51)?

Pondering the Principles

1. As a Christian, you are a child of Abraham by faith (Gal. 3:7). Are you following his pattern of faith? Read Hebrews 11:8-19. List the different situations where Abraham applied his faith in God. List some situations where you have applied your faith in God. How did

they turn out? List some situations where you didn't exercise faith in God. How did those situations turn out? Did God remain faithful to you in spite of your unfaithfulness? What lessons do you still need to learn from Abraham's example?

2. Read Matthew 10:1-16 and 1 Timothy 1:12-15. What is your attitude toward your service to God? Are you like the laborers that were hired in the morning? Do you expect to be rewarded based on all the work you have done? Or are you like the apostle Paul, who saw himself as the chief of sinners? What attitude does God want you to have? Do you need to change your attitude? If so, make the commitment to do so.

3. Read Psalm 32:1-5 and Psalm 51. Why did David's sin cause him such agony? Has there been a time in your life when your sin caused you to feel the way that David did? How did you feel? According to Psalm 32:5 and Psalm 51:17, how did David learn to rid himself of the guilt of his sin? Perhaps you are harboring some sin in your life right now. What do you plan to do with it? Meditate on Psalm 51. Then read through it as a prayer to God. Confess your sin to God and praise Him for His gracious forgiveness. Now memorize Psalm 32:5 for those occasions when the burden of sin weighs on your heart, "I acknowledged my sin to Thee, and my iniquity I did not hide; I said, 'I will confess my transgressions to the Lord'; and Thou didst forgive the guilt of my sin" (NASB).

10
Abraham—Justified by Grace—Part 1

Outline

Introduction
A. Exalting God's Grace
　　1. Noah
　　2. Abraham
　　3. Hosea and Gomer
　　4. Jonah and the Ninevites
B. Questioning God's Grace
　　1. "What advantage, then, hath the Jew?"
　　2. "What profit is there of circumcision?"
　　　　a) The reactions of circumcision
　　　　　　(1) The interpretation of the rabbis
　　　　　　(2) The issue at the Jerusalem council
　　　　　　(3) The instruction of Paul
　　　　　　　　(*a*) Philippians 3:2
　　　　　　　　(*b*) Galatians 5:1-4, 6-7; 6:12-13
　　　　b) The relevance of circumcision
　　　　　　(1) The issue
　　　　　　(2) The illustration
　　　　　　　　(*a*) Defining the sacraments
　　　　　　　　(*b*) Describing the sacraments
　　　　　　　　　　i) Baptism
　　　　　　　　　　ii) Confirmation
　　　　　　　　　　iii) The Eucharist

Lesson
I. Abraham Was Not Justified by Circumcision
A. The Sequence of Abraham's Circumcision
　　1. Righteousness reckoned by faith
　　2. Righteousness reckoned in uncircumcision
　　　　a) The question
　　　　b) The answer
　　　　　　(1) Chronological proof
　　　　　　(2) Covenantal proof
B. The Sign of Abraham's Faith
　　1. The purpose of circumcision
　　　　a) The mark of God's physical people

155

      b) The mark of God's covenant
      c) The mark of righteousness
        (1) Authenticated by God
        (2) Affirmed in the Old Testament
          (*a*) Deuteronomy 30:6
          (*b*) Jeremiah 4:3-4
          (*c*) Jeremiah 9:24-26
        (3) Analyzed by Paul
  2. The paternity of Abraham
      a) The uncircumcised
      b) The circumcised

Introduction

Having established that righteousness in both a declaration and a reality, Paul uses Abraham as a classic illustration of the fact that God redeems the ungodly by their faith, not by their works. Abraham is the classic model of salvation by grace through faith. In Romans 4, Paul emphasizes three things: Abraham was saved by faith, not works (vv. 1-8), by grace, not law (vv. 9-17), and by divine power, not human effort (vv. 18-25).

A. Exalting God's Grace

In the section beginning at verse 9, Paul tells us that Abraham was justified by grace, not law. Verse 16 is the key of this section, "Therefore, it is of faith, that it might be by grace." God saves people to exalt His grace. Ephesians 2:8-9 says, "For by grace are ye saved through faith; and that not of yourselves, it is the gift of God—not of works, lest any man should boast." God has always saved people by grace.

1. Noah

Genesis 6:8 says that Noah found grace in God's sight.

2. Abraham

Romans 4:3 says that Abraham believed God and righteousness was put to his account on the basis of his faith, even though he was unworthy. God saves people on the basis of His grace—His free favor to undeserving sinners.

3. Hosea and Gomer

Hosea bought his adulterous wife in the marketplace when she was offered for sale as a prostitute (Hos. 3:1-2). He forgave her for everything and took her back to himself. That is an illustration of God's great grace.

4. Jonah and the Ninevites

When God sent Jonah to preach to the Ninevites, all the people repented. Jonah said, "I didn't want to come here because I knew you were a God of grace, and that You would forgive those Gentiles." God is gracious.

Salvation is a result of God's grace, not a result of keeping certain laws and ordinances.

If Abraham (one of the greatest men in the Old Testament) had to deny keeping the law as a way to be right with God and had to be saved by grace as an ungodly sinner, then justification by keeping the law must be impossible for all men. No Jewish person would think himself the equal of Abraham. So if Abraham was an ungodly sinner who had to be saved by God's free favor, then everyone must be saved that way. Men are not saved by their works; they are saved by faith. God's grace reaches out to men.

B. Questioning God's Grace

The concept that Abraham was not saved by works left important questions in the Jewish mind:

1. "What advantage, then, hath the Jew?" (v. 3:1a)

In Romans 1-2 Paul said that everyone was under condemnation, whether Jew or Gentile. In Romans 1 he dealt with the pagan world, and in Romans 2 he dealt with the Jewish people. In Romans 2:12 he told them both that they were the same in God's eyes whether they had the law or not.

2. "What profit is there of circumcision?" (v. 3:1b)

Circumcision was the major historical issue of the Jewish people because it identified them in terms of race. The question could be stated, What part do religious rites and ceremonies play in salvation? Paul had to deal with the issue of circumcision because the Jewish people could say, "If we are saved by faith then why did God tell us to be circumcised? What validity does circumcision have if it doesn't guarantee us entrance into the covenant of God?

a) The reactions to circumcision

(1) The interpretation of the rabbis

The Jewish people believed that when a male child was circumcised, he was placed into a covenant with God. They actually believed that a man was made right with God when the surgical act was performed on him when he was eight days old. For example, the rabbis taught that:

(a) An Israelite who practiced idolatry had to have his circumcision removed before he could enter into hell. An act of God had to remove that circumcision before the idolatrous Israelite entered the place of judgment (*The Book of Jubilees* [15:25ff]).

The Jewish people believed that circumcision was the way into the covenant—that salvation was imparted in that act of obedience. They got that understanding from Genesis 17:9-14, when God told Abraham to circumcise the male children when they were eight days old.

(b) Rabbi Menachem, in his Commentary on the Book of Moses, said, "Our rabbis have said that no circumcised man will ever see hell" (fol. 43, col. 3).

(c) A teaching in the Jalkut Rubem says, "Circumcision saves from hell" (num. 1).

(d) A teaching in the Midrash Tillim says, "God swore to Abraham that no one who was circumcised should be sent to hell" (fol. 7, col 2).

(e) The book Akedath Jizehak teaches that "Abraham sits before the gate of hell, and does not allow that any circumcised Israelite should enter there" (fol. 54, col. 2).

In other words, if you are circumcised, you have been prevented from going to hell.

(2) The issue at the Jerusalem council

In the New Testament, Paul frequently confronted the circumcision issue. In Acts 15 the Jerusalem council (the first church council) convened to try to solve the problems surrounding circumcision. Verse 1 says, "And certain men who came down from Judea taught the brethren, and said, Except ye be circumcised after the manner of Moses, ye cannot be saved." Those men believed in salvation by surgery—by circumcision. The early church evangelists were preaching salvation by grace through faith, but a group known as the Judaizers were following them and trying to impose the need for circumcision on the people who had been led to Christ. They believed that circumcision was a meritorious act of obedience to the law that saved man.

(3) The instruction of Paul

The apostle Paul came out of a background of boasting in his circumcision. In Philippians 3:4-5 he said, "If any other man thinketh that he hath reasons for which he might trust in the flesh, I more: circumcised the eighth day." Paul had credentials—he had his circumcision. For years he felt that circumcision was a securing reality in his life. But he learned enough to give these warnings.

(a) Philippians 3:2—"Beware of the concision." In other words, beware of the people saying that you can't be saved unless you are circumcised. The "concision" were Judaizers who claimed to be Christians. They constantly hounded Paul and the early church and tried to force Gentile Christians to

158

be circumcised.

(b) Galatians 5:1-4, 6-7; 6:12-13—"Stand fast, therefore, in the liberty with which Christ hath made us free, and be not entangled again with the yoke of bondage" (v. 1). In other words, you have been liberated in Christ; don't go back to the legal system. What does Paul mean? Verse 2 says, "Behold, I, Paul, say unto you, that if ye be circumcised, Christ shall profit you nothing." If you can be saved by circumcision, then what good is Christ? If you can be saved by surgery, then you don't need Him. Verse 3 says, "For I testify again to every man that is circumcised, that he is a debtor to do the whole law."

If you believe that you are saved by circumcision, two things result: one, you have nullified the work of Christ; two, you have put yourself under the law. If you are going to justify yourself by the law, then you have to keep all of it. You are a debtor to the whole law. Verse 4 says, "Christ is become of no effect unto you, whosoever of you are justified by the law; ye are fallen from grace." If you try to be justified by the law, you have fallen away from the grace principle of salvation and have acquiesced to a law principle of works righteousness. You have also forfeited true righteousness.

The sum of Paul's teaching is in verse 6, "For in Jesus Christ neither circumcision availeth anything, nor uncircumcision, but faith which worketh by love." It doesn't matter whether you are circumcised or uncircumcised; faith is the issue.

In verse 7 Paul asks the Galatians, "Who confused you with that teaching?" The Judaizers did. Galatians 6:12-13 says, "As many as desire to make a fair show in the flesh, they constrain you to be circumcised; only lest they should suffer persecution for the cross of Christ. For neither they themselves who are circumcised keep the law, but desire to have you circumcised, that they may glory in your flesh." That covers up their true sinfulness.

Based on what Paul said in Philippians and Galatians, circumcision was a major issue that he had to deal with. And he used Abraham as his weapon to strike a blow at the ceremonial salvationists. The Jewish people said that when Abraham was circumcised, God performed it. Abraham's circumcision became their model for salvation based on Genesis 17. But Paul used that belief to prove that the very opposite is true.

159

b) The relevance of circumcision

(1) The issue

You say, "What relevance does that have for us? After all, circumcision is strictly a normal medical operation today." Many people today are basing their salvation on infant baptism, confirmation, adult baptism, communion, or some other religious ceremony. There are many people who call themselves Christians in our society who believe that their children are eternally secured by infant baptism. Many are basing their salvation on religious rites. That is the same basic perspective as salvation through circumcision.

(2) The illustration

I want to provide you with some information on Roman Catholic theology from *Fundamentals of Catholic Dogma* by Dr. Ludwig Ott (St. Louis: B. Herder, 1962). Ott writes from a Catholic perspective. He crystalizes and categorizes the thoughts of Thomas Aquinas, one of the main theologians of Roman Catholicism.

(*a*) Defining the sacraments

A sacrament is defined as "a thing perceptible to the senses." In other words, it is something tangible—something visible that you can touch and feel. The definition continues, "on the ground of Divine institution [it] possesses the power both of effecting and signifying sanctity and righteousness" (p. 326). That definition is saying that sacraments are perceptible things that impart righteousness and grace and make people holy.

The following are some quotes that further define the sacraments.

"The sacraments confer grace immediately, that is, without the mediation of fiducial faith" (p. 329). In other words, when a sacrament is administered, grace and righteousness are immediately received whether there is faith or not.

"All the Sacraments of the New Covenant confer sanctifying grace on the receivers" (p. 332).

The book also states that sacramental rites confer regeneration, forgiveness, the Holy Spirit, and eternal life (p. 332). Catholic people go to mass and confession, and want extreme unction, penance, and infant baptism because they supposedly impart regeneration, forgiveness, the Holy Spirit, and eternal life whether there is a mediation of faith or not.

Ott also says, "For the valid dispensing of the Sacraments it is necessary that the minister accomplish the Sacramental Sign in the proper manner" (p. 343). In other words, the issue is not the heart of the individual, but the method of giving the sacrament.

Ott further says, "Neither orthodox belief nor moral worthiness is necessary for the validity of the Sacrament, on the part of the recipient" (p. 345). In other words, you receive righteousness whether you care about it or not.

(b) Describing the sacraments

 i) Baptism

Ott says, "Baptism confers the grace of justification" (p. 354). Justification occurs in the Roman Catholic church through baptism as an infant. The Council of Trent issued this decree on original sin, "If any one denies that by the grace of our Lord Jesus Christ which is conferred in Baptism, the guilt of original sin is remitted; or even asserts that the whole of that which has the true and proper nature of sin is not taken away . . . let him be anathema" (p. 354). In other words, if anyone denies that infant baptism takes away the guilt of original sin, he is cursed.

The Barnabas Letter says, "We descend into the water full of sins and filth and we arise from it bearing fruit as we have in our hearts the fear of God, and in our spirit hope in Jesus" (p. 355).

Another statement says, "According to the testimony of Holy Writ, Baptism has the power both of eradicating sin and of effecting inner sanctification" (p. 355). There is an entire section in Catholic theology that states that the material for baptism has to be "true and natural water" (p. 352).

Ott says, "Baptism effects the remission of all punishments of sin, both the eternal and the temporal" (p. 355).

"Baptism by water is . . . necessary for all men without exception, for salvation" (p. 356).

 ii) Confirmation

Confirmation occurs around the age of twelve. Roman Catholic theologians believe that through the sacrament of confirmation, the

Holy Spirit is imparted in fullness to a person. Their theology says, "Confirmation effects an increase of Sanctifying Grace" (p. 365). It also states, "A baptized person can achieve eternal salvation even without Confirmation" (p. 367). So Roman Catholic theology teaches that a person can still be saved without having the impartation of the fullness of the Spirit.

iii) The Eucharist

The Eucharist is the sacrament of administering the bread and the cup. Catholic theology states, "The chief fruit of the Eucharist is an intrinsic union of the recipient with Christ" (p. 394). That is one reason it can be confusing to ask Catholic people, "Have you received Christ?" Most of them are going to say, "Yes." Every time they go to mass and receive the Eucharist they believe they are entering into an intrinsic union with Christ. Catholic theology also says, "The Eucharist, as food for the soul, preserves and increases the supernatural life of the soul" (p. 395). It also says that the Eucharist purges "venial sins and the temporal punishments due to sin" (p. 395). Ott's book says, "The Eucharist increases the life of grace" (p. 395). It further states, "The reception of the Eucharist is necessary for salvation" (p. 396).

The remainder of the sacraments (such as penance, holy orders, marriage, and extreme unction) all say the same basic thing: If performed in the properly described method, those sacraments, according to tradition, impart redemption, salvation, righteousness, grace, and holiness to an individual. That is no different than the Jewish perspective of circumcision. That is why the issue of circumcision has relevance today.

Paul is dealing with a larger picture than we first thought—the fact that religious rites and ceremonies do not justify anyone. Paul shows that the religion of human achievement negates grace.

In Romans 4:9-17, Paul shows that Abraham was justified by grace not law.

Lesson

I. ABRAHAM WAS NOT JUSTIFIED BY CIRCUMCISION (vv. 9-12)

A. The Sequence of Abraham's Circumcision (vv. 9-10)

1. Righteousness reckoned by faith (v. 9)

162

"Cometh this blessedness, then, upon the circumcision only, or upon the uncircumcision also? For we say that faith was reckoned to Abraham for righteousness."

The blessedness Paul is talking about was stated in Romans 4:6-8: "The blessedness of the man unto whom God imputeth righteousness apart from works, saying, Blessed are they whose iniquities are forgiven, and whose sins are covered. Blessed is the man to whom the Lord will not impute sin."

Who is God going to bless with His forgiveness of sin and imputation of righteousness? Paul says, "Cometh this blessedness, then, on the circumcision only" (v. 9a)? What would the Jewish people answer? They would have to say yes because they thought that no uncircumcised person could ever claim a share of God's covenant. Then Paul says in verse 9b, "For we say that faith was reckoned to Abraham for righteousness." If God blesses those who believe like Abraham, then is that blessing applicable to everybody, or is it applicable only to the circumcised? That is a marvelous argument. Paul is saying, "If you concede that Abraham was justified by faith (and the Jewish people would have to concede that based on Paul's argument in the first eight verses), then is justification for the circumcised or the uncircumcised?" And the Jewish people are going to say, "Even if we concede that Abraham was saved by faith, that could only have occurred if he was already circumcised because no uncircumcised person can ever ever enter into God's covenant."

2. Righteousness reckoned in uncircumcision (v. 10)

Paul was confronting an unbiblical audience with a masterful approach. He asked one key question in verse 9 and asks another beginning in verse 10.

   a) The question (v. 10a)

   "How was it [Abraham's faith] then reckoned? When he was in circumcision, or in uncircumcision?"

   If Abraham was uncircumcised when God imputed righteousness to him, then no one has to be circumcised to be forgiven. So Paul's question is very simple, "Was Abraham circumcised or uncircumcised when righteousness was granted to him?"

   b) The answer (v. 10b)

   "Not in circumcision, but in uncircumcision."

   Abraham was uncircumcised when he was justified. That's tantamount to saying that ceremonies and rituals didn't justify him. You say, "How do you know that?"

   (1) Chronological proof

      Abraham was ninety-nine years old when he was cir-

163

cumcised. On the same day that Abraham was circumcised, Ishmael was also circumcised (Gen. 17:24-25). On that day Ishmael was thirteen years old. When God made His covenant with Abraham in Genesis 15, Ishmael had not yet been born. So, it was at least fourteen years after Abraham was declared righteous that he was circumcised.

(2) Covenantal proof

Circumcision had nothing to do with Abraham's righteousness. He was made righteous and was inside the covenant before he was circumcised. Ishmael was circumcised but was never in the covenant. Circumcision is not even an issue in a covenantal relationship. Therefore, no religious rite or ceremony can ever confer righteousness on anybody. Righteousness can only be received by grace through faith.

B. The Sign of Abraham's Faith (vv. 11-12)

A question immediately comes up, Why have circumcision? What is it for? Paul answers that question in verse 11.

1. The purpose of circumcision (v. 11a)

"And he [Abraham] received the sign of circumcision, a seal of the righteousness of the faith which he had yet being uncircumcised."

If circumcision didn't confer righteousness, then why did God make such an issue out of it? Why did He make it a binding law in Genesis 17:9-14? The "sign of circumcision" is not a reality; it is merely a sign. There is a difference between a sign and the substance of a sign. If you were driving to Los Angeles and saw a sign that said "Los Angeles" with an arrow underneath, and you wouldn't crawl on the sign and say, "We're here!" The sign reflects another reality—it symbolizes something. It is not to be confused with what it is directing you towards. What was circumcision a sign of?

a) The mark of God's physical people

Circumcision was a racial identification. It was the way that the Jewish people in those days could be identified as children of Abraham. And that was a wonderful identification. In Acts 16:1-3, Paul had Timothy circumcised because it would help give them access into Jewish quarters since Timothy would be racially identified with the Jewish people.

b) The mark of God's covenant

In the Old Testament, circumcision identified the Jewish people as God's separated people, and identified the Lord as their God. Joshua 5:2-5 says, "The Lord said unto Joshua, Make thee sharp knives, and circumcise again the children of Israel the second time. And Joshua made him sharp knives, and circumcised the children of Israel at the hill of the foreskins. And this is the reason why Joshua did circumcise: all the people who came out of Egypt, who were males, even all the men of war, died in the wilderness. . . . Now all the people who came out were circumcised." They were circumcised so God could mark them as the people He would fulfill His promises to. So circumcision signified a racial identification and a covenantal relationship.

c) The mark of righteousness

Circumcision is a spiritual sign and a seal of Abraham's uncircumcised faith. Every time people witnessed a circumcision, they should have been reminded that God justified Abraham by faith. You say, "How would circumcision remind them of that?" Physical circumcision was to be a symbol of what God wanted to do on the inside. He wanted to cut away the sinful covering—to purge sin. What was the point of circumcision? It was a racial and covenantal identification, but far more than that, it was a seal.

(1) Authenticated by God

There is a shade of difference between a sign and a seal. A sign points to something; a seal guarantees it. When something had a seal stamped, it was guaranteed. Circumcision was the authentication that God's promises would be fulfilled. Circumcision pointed to the fact that God wanted to circumcise the outside and the inside. Every male child was circumcised so he would be reminded that God wanted to cut away the foreskin of his heart. Circumcision reminded succeeding generations that God was prepared to circumcise their hearts.

(2) Affirmed in the Old Testament

You say, "How were the Jewish people supposed to know that circumcision was only a sign of what God wanted to do to the heart if Paul had to tell them?" They should have known that from the teaching of the Old Testament.

(a) Deuteronomy 30:6—"And the Lord thy God will circumcise thine heart, and the heart of thy seed, to love the Lord thy God with all thine heart, and with all thy soul, that thou mayest live." God had always wanted to circumcise the heart—cut away the skin that crowded the heart with sin. The Israelites could have read that in their own Bible. That had always been God's plan, and every circumcised child was to be a reminder of that plan.

(b) Jeremiah 4:3-4—"For thus saith the Lord to the men of Judah and Jerusalem, Break up your fallow ground, and sow not among thorns. Circumcise yourselves to the Lord, and take away the foreskins of your heart, ye men of Judah and inhabitants of Jerusalem."

(c) Jeremiah 9:24-26—"But let him that glorieth glory in this, that he understandeth and knoweth me, that I am the Lord who exerciseth loving-kindness, justice, and righteousness, in the earth; for in these things I delight, saith the Lord. Behold, the days come, saith the Lord, that I will punish all them who are circumcised with the uncircumcised: Egypt, and Judah, and Edom, and the children of Ammon, and Moab, and all that are in the utmost corners, that dwell in the wilderness; for all these nations are uncircumcised, and all the house of Israel is uncircumcised in the heart." Every child of Israel was a living testimony that the heart needed to be circumcised.

The Signs of the Church Age

1. Communion

Today, when Christians come before the Lord's Table to take communion, are they saved by that act? No, communion demonstrates the Lord's death. It doesn't save us, but it does show that God wants to save us. It also demonstrates that we must be saved. When we take the bread and the cup, we are symbolizing Christ's redemptive act and proclaiming that men needs to be saved. If you think that taking the cup and the bread saves you, then you believe what the Jewish people believed about circumcision.

2. Baptism

If you treat baptism in that same manner, then you have made the same mistake. Baptism proclaims the death of Christ and His resurrection when the believer is immersed in the water, and then comes out. It does not save people; it demonstrates the reality that people must be saved. Baptism is an outward demonstration of an inward reality. Communion is an outward demonstration of an inward salvation.

Just like baptism is a sign that proclaims our union with Christ in His death and resurrection, and communion is a sign that proclaims our participation in His death on our behalf, so circumcision was a sign that proclaimed that God was eager to purge the heart through faith and impute His righteousness by grace. Tragically, the Jewish people abandoned that reality and were left with nothing but a disconnected symbol.

(3) Analyzed by Paul

In Romans 2:25 Paul says, "For circumcision verily profiteth, if thou keep the law." If you are going to keep the law to gain salvation, then you have to keep the whole law. Verse 25 continues, "But if thou be a breaker of the law, thy circumcision is made uncircumcision." Then Paul says, "For he is not a Jew who is one outwardly; neither is that circumcision which is outward in the flesh; but he is a Jew who is one inwardly; and circumcision is that of the heart" (vv. 28-29a). That isn't new teaching; it is the teaching of Jeremiah and Moses. God is after the heart.

Abraham's circumcision was nothing more than an outward symbol of the righteousness he received by faith. But that symbol was perpetuated in the following generations as the method of salvation. To make infant baptism a redeeming act is to perpetuate the same error. That's not what the Scripture teaches. You can't make a saving act out of a symbol. You can't make a saving act out of baptism, communion, and circumcision. They are only symbols.

Interesting Parallels

When the Israelites kept the Passover meal, did that save them? No. It reminded them that they had a God who would save them. Circumcision didn't save them either, but it reminded them that God would purify their hearts.

The Passover was collective—the people celebrated it together. Circumcision was very individual. The church has communion—that's collective—and baptism—that's individual. Collectively and individually, we have testimonies that God saves people. The Passover and the Lord's Table symbolize the saving act, and circumcision and baptism symbolize the cleansing of the individual.

2. The paternity of Abraham (vv. 11b-12)

a) The uncircumcised (v. 11b)

"[Abraham received the sign of circumcision] that he might be the father of all them that believe, though they be not circumcised, that righteousness might be imputed unto them also."

Abraham is not just the father of the Jewish nation; he is the father of all who have been made righteous by faith. He is the father of all who believe, even those who are not circumcised. The concept of "father" refers to the leader of a certain class of people. Since uncircumcised believers were justified in the same manner that Abraham was, he is their father. We all have the same salvation that Abraham had.

b) The circumcised (v. 12)

"[Abraham is] the father of circumcision to them who are not of the circumcision only, but who also walk in the steps of that faith of our father, Abraham, which he had being yet uncircumcised."

Abraham is the father of everybody who believes. Paul is saying, "I don't want you to think I'm prejudiced; it's OK to be circumcised. It's a marvelous symbol and a great reminder."

A circumcised Jewish person who doesn't believe God and doesn't think that righteousness comes by faith can't claim Abraham as his father. That's why Jesus said, "Ye are of your father the devil" (John 8:44*a*) when the Jewish leaders said that Abraham was their father. So Paul says that Abraham is the father of the circumcision if they "walk in the steps of that faith of our father, Abraham" (Rom. 4:12*b*). The Greek literally means "to march in single file." If you step in his footprints, you come to God the way he came.

We are saved by grace through faith. You say, "Can I get to heaven if I haven't been baptized?" Yes. But you should be baptized because baptism is an act of obedience. If you have confessed Jesus as Lord, you will obey Him. Baptism becomes the basis of your testimony. It is a sign that you are saved.

Abraham is the father of everybody who believes by faith. Philippians 3:3 says, "For we are the circumcision, who worship God in the spirit, and rejoice in Christ Jesus, and have no confidence in the flesh." We are not interested in fleshly activity; our confidence is in Christ and His Spirit.

Focusing on the Facts

1. Why does God save people? How has He always saved people? Give some examples (see p. 156).

2. If Abraham had to deny lawkeeping as a way to be right with God, and had to be saved by grace, then what must be true of all men (see p. 157)?

3. The concept that Abraham was not saved by works left important questions in the Jewish mind. What were they? Explain them (see Rom. 3:1; p. 157).

4. Why was circumcision a major issue for the Jewish people (see p. 157)?

5. What did the rabbis teach about circumcision (see pp. 157-58)?

6. What was the major issue of the Jerusalem Council? Explain the controversy (see Acts 15:1; p. 158).

7. Explain Paul's warning to the Philippians and Galatians regarding cir-

cumcision. What results when a person believes he is saved by circumcision (see pp. 158-59)?

8. What relevance does the issue of circumcision have for the church today (see p. 160)?

9. Whom did the Jewish people believe that God's blessing would be given to? Since Abraham was proven to be justified by faith, what part did the Jewish people believe his circumcision played in his justification (see p. 163)?

10. Was Abraham circumcised or uncircumcised when he was granted righteousness? Prove your answer (see pp. 163-64).

11. What was the purpose of circumcision (see Rom. 4:11; p. 164)?

12. What is the difference between a sign and the substance of a sign? What was circumcision a sign of (see p. 164)?

13. In what way was circumcision a sign of what God wanted to do with sin (see p. 165)?

14. What is the difference between a sign and a seal? How was circumcision both a sign and a seal (see p. 165)?

15. What did the Old Testament teach about God's desire to circumcise the heart (see p. 165)?

16. What are signs that exist in the church age? What do they point to (see p. 166)?

17. Fill in the blanks: "Baptism is an outward _____ of an inward _____. Communion is an outward _____ of an inward _____ (see p. 166).

18. What is Paul's definition of a Jew (see Rom. 2:28-29a; p. 167)?

19. According to Romans 4:12, what do the circumcised need to do to show that Abraham is their father (see p. 167)?

Pondering the Principles

1. Read Acts 15:1-21. The issue of circumcision needed to be dealt with before the gospel could spread. What did the Pharisees say was necessary for Gentile Christians to do (see v. 5)? What was Peter's response in verses 7-11? What was James's decision in verses 14-21? What could have happened to Christianity if that problem had not been dealt with?

2. Ceremonies and rituals are basic to religions based on human achievement. What facts could you use to support that faith alone is necessary for salvation? How is circumcision a good representative of any ritual? Formulate a method for witnessing to people who believe that rituals and ceremonies are necessary for salvation.

11
Abraham—Justified by Grace—Part 2

Outline

Review
I. Abraham Was Not Justified by Circumcision

Lesson
II. Abraham Was Not Justified by Keeping the Law
  A. The Promise of God
    1. The description of the promise
      a) Abraham as heir of the world
        (1) The land of Canaan
        (2) The nations of people
        (3) The blessedness of the world
        (4) The Redeemer
          (*a*) Galatians 3:16
          (*b*) Galatians 3:29
          (*c*) Galatians 3:8-9
      b) Christians as heirs of the world
        (1) Romans 8:17
        (2) 1 Corinthians 3:21-23
    2. The deliverance of the promise
      a) Not through law
        (1) God's demonstration of the covenant
        (2) Paul's directions to the Galatians
          (*a*) The curse of the law
          (*b*) The confirmation of the covenant
      b) Through the righteousness received by faith
  B. The Purpose of the Law
    1. The insufficiency of law
    2. The inciting of wrath
      a) Romans 7:7, 9-12
      b) Galatians 3:24
  C. The Provision of Salvation
    1. The people of the law
    2. The people of the faith of Abraham
  D. The Prototype of Faith
    1. Abraham's classification
    2. God's characteristics

a) His power
b) His sovereignty

Review

In Romans 3:21—5:21, Paul shows that salvation, forgiveness of sin, and heaven are not available to men through ritual, ceremony, self-sacrifice, or religious works but only by grace through faith in the person and work of the Lord Jesus Christ. There is no other way. You say, "But aren't the people who trust in their religious works sincere?" Yes, they are probably sincere but will be damned to hell forever if they continue in their error. Salvation comes only by grace through faith in the Lord Jesus Christ.

In Romans 3:21-31 Paul gives us the statement of justification by faith. In Romans 4 he gives us an illustration of that statement. The illustration is Abraham—the model of justification by grace through faith. However, to the Jewish people, Abraham was the model of justication by works. They thought that Abraham was justified because he was circumcised and kept the works of the law, so they believed in personal self-righteousness. Paul says, "Contrary to what you have believed about Abraham, he was justified by grace through faith." Justification by faith is the heart and soul of the Christian faith. It is the blueprint of salvation.

Paul approaches the illustration of Abraham from three perspectives: First, Abraham was justified by faith, not by works (vv. 1-8); second, by grace, not law (vv. 9-17); and third, by divine power, not human effort (vv. 18-25). Those are the three basic themes of Romans 4. We have already looked at verses 1-8 and have seen that Abraham was justified by faith, not works. Verse 3 sums up that thought, "Abraham believed God, and it was counted unto him for righteousness."

We are now looking at the second section in verses 9-17. The key to that section is in verse 16: "Therefore, it is of faith, that it might be by grace." Salvation cannot be earned. If salvation is simply a matter of believing, then it has to be a gift of God's grace. What is grace? It is free favor from God that is given to an undeserving sinner. Abraham was made right with God because he believed Him. And God was gracious to him because He gave him a promise. Verse 16 says, "Therefore, it [the promise] is of faith, that it might be by grace, to the end the promise might be sure to all the seed." Salvation is not earned; it is offered by God as an act of His free favor to an undeserving sinner, and it is received through faith.

In order to show that salvation comes by grace, not law, the first thing the apostle Paul points to is:

I. ABRAHAM WAS NOT JUSTIFIED BY CIRCUMCISION (vv. 9-12; see pp. 162-68)

The Jewish people believed that Abraham was justified by circumcision. But Paul shows that Abraham was declared right with God fourteen years *before* he was circumcised. Circumcision was only a symbol of what God wanted to do in the heart. Every time a father performed a circumcision, he was symbolizing what God wanted to do on the inside—cut away the flesh.

The fact that Abraham was not justified by circumcision went against everything the Jewish people believed. They believed that circumcision saved people, much like others today believe that infant baptism saves people. But circumcision and baptism are only outward symbols of what God wants to do in the heart.

Lesson

II. ABRAHAM WAS NOT JUSTIFIED BY KEEPING THE LAW (vv. 13-17)

The Jewish people believed that a person was saved by circumcision, which was the first act of keeping the law. They believed that Abraham was justified because he was circumcised and kept the law. In verses 13-17 Paul says that Abraham was not made right with God by circumcision because he was circumcised fourteen years after he had been made right with God. He also says that Abraham was not made right with God by keeping the law because the law came four hundred and thirty years after Abraham was made right with God. That is a devastating argument! The Jewish people believed that circumcision and keeping the law brought people into a right relationship with God. Acts 15:5 says, "There rose up certain of the sect of the Pharisees, who believed, saying that it was needful to circumcise them, and to command them to keep the law of Moses."

Paul is saying that a person does not come into a right relationship to God by observing laws and ceremonies. When Abraham was declared right with God, he was not circumcised and had kept no law because the Mosaic law had not yet been given. Then how was he made right with God? Verse 13 says that God gave him a promise, and he believed in it. Abraham was justified by believing God's promise. That makes salvation a grace gift. It is as if God said, "Here's My promise: If you will believe in the Lord Jesus Christ, I will take away your sins, redeem you, and grant you eternal life," and you said, "By faith I receive that gift." Justification is by faith and is born in the grace of God.

A. The Promise of God (v. 13)

"For the promise that he should be the heir of the world was not to Abraham, or to his seed, through the law, but through the righteousness of faith."

The promise that Paul is talking about is the Abrahamic covenant. It was given to Abraham in Genesis 12, and then repeated in Genesis 15, 18, and 22. God said to Abraham, "I want you to leave the land of Ur of the Chaldees and go to a land that I've planned to give you. I am going to make of you a great nation. Whoever blesses you will be blessed and whoever curses you will be cursed" (Gen. 12:1-3). God also said, "I'm going to give you seed like the sand of the sea, and they will be numbered as the stars of the heaven" (Gen. 22:17).

But Abraham saw beyond the physical posterity. He saw beyond Isaac and Isaac's sons. He saw beyond being a father of many nations. He knew that there was a spiritual reality in the promise because God said, "In thee shall all families of the earth be blessed" (Gen. 12:3*b*). That is why Hebrews 11:10 says, "For he looked for a city which hath foundations, whose builder and maker is God." He saw the physical element of the promise, but he knew that spiritual fulfillment would come from the physical seed.

1. The description of the promise (v. 13*a*)

"For the promise that he should be the heir of the world."

a) Abraham as heir of the world

What are the elements of that incredible promise?

(1) The land of Canaan

Genesis 15:18-21 talks about the boundaries of the land of God's covenant, "The Lord made a covenant with Abram, saying, Unto thy seed have I given this land, from the river of Egypt unto the great river, the river Euphrates: the Kenites, and the Kenizzites, and the Kadmonites, and the Hittites, and the Perizzites, and the Rephaim, and the Amorites, and the Canaanites, and the Girgashites, and the Jebusites." The book of Joshua tells the story of Abraham's descendants taking possession of that land under the direction of Joshua.

(2) The nations of people

Out of Abraham came Israel and the Arab nations. Genesis 13:16 says, "And I will make thy seed as the dust of the earth, so that if a man can number the dust of the earth, then shall thy seed also be numbered." Exodus shows us the realization of the seed—the birth and early history of the Semitic peoples.

(3) The blessedness of the world

Genesis 12:3 says, "In thee shall all families of the earth be blessed."

So the promise included the land of Canaan, the people of Israel (the covenant people), and the statement that the entire world would be blessed. Abraham is even called "a father of many nations" (Rom. 4:17). How could he be the father of many nations? How could he be the heir of the world? The answer comes in what I think is the fourth element of the covenant.

(4) The Redeemer

I am convinced that Abraham saw beyond Isaac to a Redeemer. Our Lord Jesus confirms that in John 8:56, "Your father, Abraham, rejoiced to see my day; and he saw it, and was glad." I don't know how much he knew, but he saw the day of the Redeemer. He might have seen the reality of the Redeemer from the typology of the ram that was provided by God when Abraham was ready to take the life of Isaac (Gen. 22:13).

The reason that Abraham could bless the world, inherit it, and be the father of its people is that a Redeemer would come out of his loins and redeem people of all nations by faith. All the sons of faith would be the sons of Abraham.

(*a*) Galatians 3:16—"Now to Abraham and his seed were the promises made. He saith not, And to seeds, as of many; but as of one, And to thy seed, which is Christ." When God made the promise to Abraham, He said that ultimately, there was one promised seed. That seed in Abraham was Christ, and it is only through Christ that blessing is made available to the world.

(*b*) Galatians 3:29—"And if ye be Christ's, then are ye Abraham's seed, and heirs according to the promise." God's promise was that all the world would be blessed in Abraham. That could only be true if out of the loins of Abraham came the seed—Christ. All who put their faith in Christ become one with Him. First Corinthians 6:17 says, "He that is joined unto the Lord is one spirit." Christians are one with Christ, and by faith become the spiritual seed of Abraham.

(*c*) Galatians 3:8-9—"And the scripture, foreseeing that God would justify the Gentiles through faith, preached before the gospel unto Abraham, saying, In thee shall all nations be blessed. So, then, they who are of faith are blessed with faithful Abraham." In other words, when God says, "In thee shall all families of the earth be blessed" (Gen. 12:3*b*), God means that when anyone puts his faith in Christ, who is the seed of Abraham, he becomes a child of faith—a spiritual son of Abraham, who is the model of faith for all the world.

b) Christians as heirs of the world

When you put your faith in Christ, you are identified with Him as the seed of Abraham; you inherit the world along with Abraham. Christians are the heirs of the world. All of us who are in Christ are one with Christ, and therefore are the seed of Abraham by faith. We are part of the fulfillment of God's promise to Abraham to inherit the world.

(1) Romans 8:17—The Lord says that we are "heirs of God, and joint heirs with Christ." As heirs of God, we inherit what God grants to us; as joint heirs with Christ, we inherit what God grants to Christ. In Christ we inherit the world.

(2) 1 Corinthians 3:21-23—Paul says, "Therefore, let no man glory in men. For all things are yours, whether Paul, or Apollos, or Cephas, or the world, or life, or death, or things present, or things to come; all are yours, and ye are Christ's, and Christ is God's." Everything belongs to God and Christ, so everything belongs to you. Don't think that you are a pauper; you have inherited everything that God possesses. That is all a result of coming to Jesus Christ in faith and becoming one with the seed of Abraham.

2. The deliverance of the promise (v. 13b-c)

   a) Not through law (v. 13b)

   "For the promise . . . was not to Abraham, or to his seed, through the law."

   The Abrahamic covenant wasn't conditional. In the Greek, the word "the" is missing before "law." That is an anarthrous construction. The promise didn't come to Abraham through law, the principle of works. It didn't come to him through ceremony either; it came to him as a promise. God said, "Abraham, leave your town to go to the place I am sending you, and I'll do many things for you."

   (1) God's demonstration of the covenant

   When God made His covenant with Abraham, He demonstrated the uniqueness of it. In Genesis 15:12 God put Abraham to sleep. But before He did, He had instructed Abraham to collect a series of animals: a heifer, a female goat, a ram, a turtledove, and a pigeon (v. 9). Abraham cut the large animals in half and put each half opposite the other half, but he didn't cut the birds in half (v. 10). While Abraham was asleep, a burning lamp and a smoking furnace descended and passed between the pieces (v. 17). In those days, when a covenant was made with someone, the covenant was sealed by splitting an animal in half, and the two principals passed between the pieces. They were making an agreement that said, "If I break my covenant, so do to me as we have done to this animal." Now that's a binding covenant! But when God made His covenant with Abraham, He didn't allow Abraham to pass between the pieces because the covenant was never between God and Abraham; it was between God and God. He was saying, "Here is My prom-

175

ise. It doesn't depend on anything you do. What matters is that you believe it." Therefore, faith is not a meritorious work; it is only the instrument that receives the promise.

Abraham was not made the heir of the world because he had earned it. God didn't look at him and say, "Abraham is so righteous that I'm going to give him the world." The promise didn't come through the law; it came through the righteousness of faith.

(2) Paul's directions to the Galatians

(a) The curse of the law

Galatians 3:10 says, "For as many as are of the works of the law are under the curse." If someone wants to think he can get to God by good works, he is under a curse, not a promise. Why? Verse 10 continues, "For it is written, Cursed is everyone that continueth not in all things which are written in the book of the law, to do them." If someone wants to come to God by the law, then he has to keep every element of it or he is cursed. That's why Paul says, "No man is justified by the law in the sight of God, it is evident; for, The just shall live by faith. And the law is not of faith" (vv. 11-12a). In other words, the two are mutually exclusive. Verse 12 continues, "The man that doeth them shall live in them." If someone is going to try to come to God by keeping the law, he must keep it perfectly. But verses 13-14 say, "Christ hath redeemed us from the curse of the law . . . that the blessing of Abraham might come on the Gentiles through Jesus Christ, that we might receive the promise of the Spirit through faith."

(b) The confirmation of the covenant

Galatians 3:17 says, "And this I say, that the covenant that was confirmed before by God in Christ, the law, which was four hundred and thirty years after, cannot annul, that it should make the promise of no effect." The Mosaic law came four hundred and thirty years after the last statement of the promise recorded in Genesis. Galatians 2:21 says, "I do not make void the grace of God; for if righteousness come by the law, then Christ is dead in vain." Galatians 3:1 says, "O foolish Galatians, who hath bewitched you, that ye should not obey the truth?" In verse 2 Paul says, "Received ye the Spirit by the works of the law?" He is saying, "What are you doing fooling around with the law?" Then in verse 17 Paul says that the law was given four hundred and thirty years after the final statement of the covenant. In verse 18 he says, "For if the inheritance be of the law, it is no more of promise; but God gave it to Abraham by promise." The word "gave" is *kecharistai* in the Greek. It means, "to give something permanently." It is used in the perfect tense in Galatians 3:18. God gave Abraham an inheritance, and it stays given.

That truth hasn't changed. God gives us the promise of salvation, and it is to be received by faith. Paul tried very hard to be saved by the law. He said he was "circumcised the eighth day, of the stock of Israel, of the tribe of Benjamin, an Hebrew of the Hebrews; as touching the law, a Pharisee; concerning zeal, persecuting the church; touching the righteousness which is in the law, blameless" (Phil. 3:5-6). But his conclusion was, "[I] do count them but refuse [manure], that I may win Christ, and be found in him, not having mine own righteousness, which is of the law, but that which is through the faith of Christ" (Phil. 3:8b-9a).

b) Through the righteousness received by faith (v. 13c)

"But through the righteousness of faith."

God's promise to Abraham came through righteousness received by faith.

B. The Purpose of the Law (vv. 14-15)

1. The insufficiency of law (v. 14)

"For if they who are of the law be heirs, faith is made void, and the promise made of no effect."

In other words, if you have to keep God's law to be an heir, then faith is nullified and the promise is of no effect. If the original condition of the promise is to keep the law, then faith is void and the promise is useless. The Pharisees believed that righteousness hinged on the law. They were the people of the law—the legalists. If they are the heirs, then the entire promise collapses.

Why can't the law save people? Many think that if you try to keep the Ten Commandments, you will be saved. They believe that obedience to the law will get them into heaven. But that is not true.

2. The inciting of wrath (v. 15)

"Because the law worketh wrath; for where no law is, there is no transgression."

The law incites wrath. It brings death, not life. The law shows you how bad you are. When Paul says, "Where no law is, there is no transgression," he means that if there are no rules, they can't be broken. The law manifests transgression and leads to

177

God's wrath. As soon as God gives a law, it reveals the evil of the human heart.

a) Romans 7:7, 9-12—"I had not known sin but by the law; for I had not known coveting, except the law had said, "Thou shalt not covet. . . . For I was alive apart from the law once; but when the commandment came, sin revived, and I died. And the commandment, which was ordained to life, I found to be unto death. For sin, taking occasion by the commandment, deceived me, and by it slew me. Wherefore, the law is holy, and the commandment holy, and just, and good." Paul is saying, "The problem is that as soon as the law is revealed to me, I see my inability to keep it." As a result, the law puts people under the condemnation of God.

b) Galatians 3:24—"The law was our schoolmaster to bring us unto Christ, that we might be justified by faith." In other words, the purpose of the law was to discipline us, show us how evil we were, and bring us under wrath. If we were afraid of God's wrath, we would repent and come to the Savior in faith.

C. The Provision of Salvation (v. 16)

"Therefore, it [the promise] is of faith, that is might be by grace, to the end the promise might be sure to all the seed; not to that only which is of the law, but to that also which is of the faith of Abraham, who is the father of us all."

That is the goal of all that Paul has said up to this point in Romans 4. If you are not saved by circumcision or some other ritual, and if you are not saved by keeping some law, then salvation is by faith through grace and God receives the glory. In verse 16 Paul says that the promise is "by grace, to the end the promise might be sure to all the seed." He is saying, "If salvation is by grace through faith, then the promise is available to everyone who will constitute the redeemed seed. If salvation is available only to those who keep the law, then it is available to nobody." If the promise is of faith and grace, the result is that it is available to everyone because no one is disqualified by their sin. Then Paul divides the recipients into two categories.

1. The people of the law

The Jews were the people of the law. The phrase "of the law" refers to the Jewish people as did the phrase "the circumcision" in Romans 4:12. The Jewish people are identified with the keeping of the law.

2. The people of the faith of Abraham

Believing Gentiles are the people of the faith of Abraham. You say, "Is the faith of Abraham Gentile faith?" Yes. "Wasn't Abraham a Jew?" Basically he was a Chaldean Gentile. He had no Mosaic orientation. He lived and died before that came to pass. Since Abraham came to God by faith, he is an example of a believing Gentile.

Paul says, "If salvation is by faith and grace, then it is available to everybody whether they are of the law or of the faith of Abraham." He becomes the father for all by his faith. We are all children of Abraham by faith. Now Abraham does have a physical seed in Israel, but Paul's message has to do with his spiritual seed.

D. The Prototype of Faith (v. 17)

1. Abraham's classification (v. 17a)

"(As it is written, I have made thee a father of many nations)."

God intended that Abraham would be the father of many nations. It was a spiritual promise that many people all over the world throughout history would come to God through faith in His Messiah. In addition, those people would become the spiritual children of Abraham, who is the model of faith that we follow. God's eternal purpose was that Abraham be the spiritual prototype of all who come to God by faith. Abraham heard God's promise and received it by faith. He was an unworthy, ungodly sinner who was given a promise by grace that he believed.

2. God's characteristics (v. 17b)

"Before him whom he believed, even God, who giveth life to the dead, and calleth those things which are not, as though they were."

Abraham believed in God. All of us who believe in God, like Abraham, become one with Abraham's spiritual seed, who is Christ. Paul cites two characteristics of God.

a) His power

Paul says that God "giveth life to the dead." No one knew that better than Abraham because Sarah had been barren, and he was willing to sacrifice the child the Lord gave them because he believed in his heart that God was able to raise him from the dead (Heb. 11:19). Abraham believed in God, who raises the dead. That speaks of the power of God.

b) His sovereignty

Paul also says that God "calleth those things which are not, as though they were." That speaks of God's creative power. He brings things into existence. But I think that verse speaks more pointedly to God's ability to create history and chart the course of the world. He is the sovereign who calls people, places, and events into existence. The *calling* that Paul refers to is an effectual, divine determination. He is the God who gives life to the dead and calls things that are not as though they were. What an example of His absolute, ultimate sovereignty! The all powerful, sovereign God is the

179

God Abraham believed in.

Believers have a great promise. God says "I'll give you the world." Jesus said to the disciples, "I'll give you the kingdom. You will sit in My throne with Me. I'll give you heaven and eternity. You will inherit everything." You say, "How?" God gives you a promise. It is offered to you by grace, and you must receive it by faith and abandon working for your salvation.

The Holy War

There is a beautiful allegory contained in *The Holy War* by John Bunyan. The following story is worthy of our thought. (The prince Emmanuel is Christ. The town of Mansoul symbolizes the heart of an individual.)

The Prince ordered a delegation of prisoners to be sent from the town of Mansoul under the guard of Captain Boanerges and Captain Conviction. They were brought into the presence of the Prince in mourning robes, with ropes around their necks, smiting upon their breasts, and "durst not so much as lift their eyes up to heaven." Nor could they hold their peace, but they cried, "O wretched men of Mansoul! O unhappy men!" Then they fell prostrate upon their faces before the Prince. He ascended the throne and ordered the representatives to stand up before him. He asked them if "they were servants of Shaddai, or had they suffered themselves to be corrupted and defiled by the abominable Diaboluo? Would they have been content to have lived under such slavery and tyranny forever? And even when he came himself, against the town of Mansoul, did they not wish that he might gain a victory over them?" To all these questions they replied, "Yes, we have done worse, we deserve punishment, and even death, we have nothing to say, Lord; Thou art just, for we have sinned." "Then the Prince commanded that an herald should be called, and he should go throughout the camp of Emmanuel and proclaim, with the sound of a trumpet, that the Prince had, in his Father's name and for his Father's glory, gotten a perfect conquest and victory over Mansoul, and that the prisoners should follow and say Amen." Then there was a great rejoicing everywhere among the soldiers and captains of Prince Emmanuel's army, but in the hearts of the men of Mansoul this great joy was wanting. But the Prince called them to him again, and said to them, "The sins, trespasses, iniquities, that you, with the whole town of Mansoul, have from time to time committed against my Father and me, I have power and commandment from my Father to forgive to the town of Mansoul, and do forgive you accordingly." Having said this, he gave them a written parchment and sealed with several seals, a large and general pardon, to be proclaimed throughout the whole town of Mansoul at the rising of the sun the next day. The mourning weeds were stripped from them, and he gave them "beauty for ashes, the oil of joy for mourning, and the garments of praise for the spirit of heaviness." He gave to them each jewels of gold and precious stones, and took away their ropes, and put chains of gold about their necks, and earrings in their ears. Then were their fetters broken into pieces before their faces, and cast into the air. So overjoyed were they, their pardon being so sudden and glorious, they almost fainted; but the Prince put his everlasting arms under them, embraced them and kissed them, and bade them be of good cheer. Then he sent them away to their homes with pipe and tabor. Joyful was the meeting of those that had gone down prisoners, with friends on their return. And when they heard the wonderful news of the wisdom and grace of Prince Emmanuel their joy knew no bounds. There was pardon for every one in Mansoul, each one was mentioned by name. Emmanuel came with royal retinue, and took up his abode in the town. He made them a great feast at the palace. He gave them luxuries from his Father's court. Man did eat angels' food and had honey given him out of the rock.

I think Bunyan captures the gospel message. Prince Emmanuel offers you the same forgiveness and freedom from your chains. It is an act of faith that receives the promise of forgiveness in Christ.

Focusing on the Facts

1. Define grace. How was God gracious to Abraham (see Rom. 4:10; p. 171)?

2. What were two things that Abraham did that Jewish people thought justified him? Why was it impossible for those things to justify him (see p. 172)?

3. How was Abraham justified before God (see p. 172)?

4. What is the promise that Paul refers to in Romans 4:13? Give an explanation of it (see pp. 172-73).

5. What are the four elements of the promise given to Abraham? Explain each one (see pp. 173-74).

6. What was Jesus confirming when He said, "Your father, Abraham, rejoiced to see my day; and he saw it, and was glad" (John 8:56; see p. 174)?

7. How was it possible for Abraham to bless the world (see p. 174)?

8. How do Christians become the spiritual seed of Abraham (see Gal. 3:29; p. 174)?

9. How do Christians become heirs of the world (see pp. 174-75)?

10. Explain this statement: The Abrahamic covenant wasn't conditional (see p. 175).

11. Explain how God demonstrated the uniqueness of His covenant with Abraham (see p. 175).

12. What people does the curse of the law fall on? Why are they cursed? What is the only way to avoid the curse (see Gal. 3:10-14; p. 176)?

13. Why can't the law annul God's promise (see Gal. 3:17; p. 176)?

14. How did God's promise come to Abraham (see Rom. 4:13c; p. 177)?

15. Fill in the blanks: If the original condition of the promise is to keep the law, then faith is _____ and the promise is _____ (see p. 177).

16. Why can't the law save people? Explain (see Rom. 4:15; pp. 177-78)?

17. What was Paul's testimony to the effect of the law in his life (see Rom. 7:7, 9:12; p. 178)?

18. What verse describes the goal of Paul's teaching in Romans 4? Explain (see p. 178).

19. To whom is God's promise available (see p. 178)?

20. What characteristics of God does Paul cite in Romans 4:17? Explain each one (see p. 179).

Pondering the Principles

1. As a Christian, you are an heir according to God's promises. Look up the following verses: Romans 8:14-17; Galatians 3:29; 4:5-7; Titus 3:7; James 2:5. What do those verses teach about believers as heirs? According to Romans 8:14, what is a condition for being an heir? According to Titus 3:7, how were you made an heir? According to Romans 8:15-16, what had to happen before you became an heir? Does the pattern of your life reveal that you are a child of God and a joint heir with Christ? In what ways does your life need to change in order to reveal those truths to the world?

2. In Romans 4:17, Paul discusses God's power and sovereignty. When Abraham was going to sacrifice Isaac, he believed in God's power to raise Isaac from the dead. When you are faced with a trial, do you rely on God's power or on your ability to see yourself through the test? What happened when you relied on yourself? on God? What have you learned from those situations? In the future, how will you respond to trials? In the daily decisions of life, do you seek God's will or your own? Since God is able to call people, places, and events into existence, how should you respond to His leading in your life? Do you trust Him to make the right decisions for your life? Does your life manifest that trust? If not, you are probably trusting in yourself. Begin today to trust God's sovereignty.

12
Salvation by Divine Power—
Not Human Effort

Outline

Introduction
A. The Prerequisite to the Promise
B. The Product of the Promise
  1. An incomprehensible promise
    a) Producing a response
    b) Prevailing in trials
  2. An incongruous name
    a) Abraham's embarrassing situation
    b) Sarah's ill-conceived solution
      (1) The contrast between divine power and human effort
        (*a*) The son of natural virility
        (*b*) The son of supernatural power
      (2) The allegory of divine power and human effort

Lesson
I. The Analysis of Faith
  A. Hoped Against Hope
    1. The difference between faith and hope
    2. The demonstration of Abraham's faith
  B. Was Not Weak in Faith
    1. The essence of Abraham's confidence
    2. The example of Abraham's confidence
    a) Affirming the promise
    b) Acting on the promise
  C. Was Not Discouraged by His Natural Weakness
  D. Was Not Doubtful Due to External Circumstances
  E. Did Not Vacillate in Doubt
    1. The struggle of Abraham's faith
    a) Rejecting the promise
    b) Reiterating the promise
    2. The strengthening of Abraham's faith
  F. Gave Glory to God
    1. Illuminating God's trustworthiness
    2. Illustrating God's trustworthiness
  G. Was fully persuaded of God's Power and Promise

II. The Answer to Faith
III. The Application of Faith
  A. The Accessibility of God's Righteousness
    1. The purpose of Scripture
      a) Psalm 78:5-7
      b) Romans 15:4
      c) 1 Corinthians 10:11
    2. The performance of faith
      a) The confidence in God
      b) The condition for salvation
  B. The Affirmation of Christ's Atonement

Introduction

In Romans 4, the apostle Paul presents Abraham (the father of the nation of Israel) as the model, prototype, and supreme example of salvation by faith. The Bible teaches that a man is made right with God by faith. That is not a result of something we do but something we believe. Righteousness is given to the believer and he is made right with God. The great illustration of righteousness by faith is Abraham. In order to understand what Paul is teaching in Romans 4, it is necessary to understand the story of Abraham.

A. The Prerequisite to the Promise

Abraham was sovereignly chosen by God. He responded to that sovereign choice by believing God. That's the basic story of salvation. God sovereignly calls a person, and that person responds by accepting His call. In that simple response, Abraham is defined as the father of our faith.

B. The Product of the Promise

When God called Abraham, He told him that he would produce a seed—that he would produce offspring. His descendants would ultimately number as the sand of the sea and the stars of the heaven (Gen. 22:17).

1. An incomprehensible promise

Abraham was told he would produce multitudes of people when he was the father of nobody. He had no seed and no land; all he had was a promise. He was looking for a son and for a land, so he moved out in faith. Why? Because he believed God.

a) Producing a response

You say, "How did God convince Abraham that He was to be believed?" The Bible doesn't tell us. But somehow God convinced him. When God wants to do something, He can do whatever He chooses. When God called Abraham, He produced in him the response. The call was convincing enough to make Abraham believe even when there was no reason to believe and the odds were stacked against him.

Abraham was the father of nobody on the way to nowhere.

All he knew was what God told him. He believed that God would fulfill His promise. God planted within his heart that confidence to believe.

b) Prevailing in trials

When he was seventy-five, Abraham finally left Haran to go to Canaan (the place God sent him). He was immediately faced with some severe tests of his faith: a famine (Gen. 12:10), Pharaoh (Gen. 12:11-20), a fight with his nephew (Gen. 13:5-9), fear (Gen. 15:1), and foolishness (Gen. 16:1-4). But through all of that difficulty, he held on to God's promise. That is a supernatural response.

2. An incongruous name

a) Abraham's embarrassing situation

Dr. Barnhouse points out some of the difficulty of Abraham's situation in the first volume of his commentary on Romans. "Now Abram was an Oriental. He was used to the palaver of the Orientals. Furthermore, he was strategically located athwart the roads of the camel caravans that carried the commerce of the ancient world between Egypt and the North and the East. He owned the wells, and his flocks and herds were great. The Scripture says that 'Abram was very rich in cattle, in silver, and in gold' (Gen. 13:2). When the caravans of the rich merchants came into the land, either from the north or from the south, they stopped at Abram's wells. The servants of Abram took good care of the needs of the camels and the servants of the traders. Food was sold to the travellers. And in the evening time the merchants would have come to Abram's tent to pay their respects. The questions would have followed a set pattern. How old are you? Who are you? How long have you been here? When the trader had introduced himself, Abram would be forced to name himself: Abram, father of many.

"It must have happened a hundred times, a thousand times, and each time more galling than the time before. 'Oh, Father of many! Congratulations! And how many sons do you have?' And the answer was so humiliating to Abram: 'None.' And, many a time there must have been the half concealed snort of humor at the incongruity of the name and the fact that there were no children to back up such a name. Abram must have steeled himself for the question and the reply, and have hated the situation with great bitterness."

Barnhouse adds, "It was a world of cloth and goat skins, where all lived in tents, and where there was little privacy from the eyes and none in the realm of the ears. There must have been many conversations on the subject—who was sterile, Abram or Sarah? Was he really a full man? Oh, he was the patriarch; his word was law; he had the multitude of

185

cattle and the many servants, but—he had no children, and his name was 'father of many' " ([Grand Rapids: Eerdmans, 1977], pp. 311-12). That gives us some insight into what it must have been like for Abram.

b) Sarah's ill-conceived solution

The pressure on Abraham caused Sarah to come up with an idea.

(1) The contrast between divine power and human effort

    (*a*) The son of natural virility

Sarah decided that Abram needed to live up to his name, so she offered him Hagar, her servant girl. She said, "Let Hagar conceive a son for you. That will demonstrate that you are virile enough to produce offspring." Abraham agreed. Of course, word must have spread rapidly that Abram, in desperation, tried to gain the promised seed by a union with a servant.

It worked. Hagar became pregnant. But Sarah felt despised and hated Hagar. Yet Abram had his heir. So when the next caravan came through, and the traders said, "What is your name?" Abram could say, "Abram." When the traders said, "Oh, father of many. How many?" at least he could say, "One." Finally, at the age of eighty-six he had a son.

I believe that Abram wanted Ishmael to be the fulfillment of God's promise. In Genesis 17:18, he says to God, "Oh, that Ishmael might live before thee!" Abraham is saying, "Oh that Ishmael might be the one You receive." He had produced a son of his own virility.

    (*b*) The son of supernatural power

Thirteen years later when Abraham was ninety-nine and his son was thirteen, God came to him and said, "Abram, Ishmael wasn't my choice. He is the son of your natural virility, not of My supernatural power. He is the son of your flesh. But I'm going to give you another son—a son of promise that you could never produce." Then God told him that his name would be *abrāhām,* which means, "father of multitudes." The year between the time that his name was changed and the promise fulfilled must have been a painful year because now he had to say that he was the father of multitudes when he had one son.

The fact that Abram used the name *Abraham* was indicative of his faith. He happily referred to himself as Abraham because he believed God. Ishmael was the son of natural generation, and Isaac became the son of supernatural generation when Abraham was one hundred years old. Abram begot Ishmael in human strength; Abraham begot Isaac in the power of God.

(2) The allergory of divine power and human effort

Galatians 4:21-23 is one of the most difficult portions of the New Testament to interpret. In it there is one basic connection that I want to point out. Galatians 4:21 says, "Tell me ye that desire to be under the law, do ye not hear the law?" In other words, do you desire to accomplish God's goals by the flesh? Verse 22 says, "For it is written that Abraham had two sons, the one by a bondmaid, the other by a freewoman." Hagar was the bondmaid; Sarah was the freewoman. Verse 23 says, "But he [Ishmael] who was of the bondwoman was born after the flesh [the natural power of Abraham]; but he [Isaac] of the freewoman was by promise." There is the divine connection. Ishmael and Isaac are illustrations in Galatians 4:21-31. Ishmael illustrates the principle of living by the flesh; Isaac illustrates the principle of living by the promise of God. That is the only allegory so stated in all of Scripture (Gal. 4:24).

Ishmael is a son born in the usual way and becomes a living representative of all those who believe they can accomplish God's will through their human effort. Isaac is a son born of faith by a supernatural miracle and becomes an illustration of all who receive spiritual birth. That is the contrast between human effort and divine power. God would never tolerate Ishmael as the son of His promise because he was a child produced by Abraham. He would only tolerate Isaac as the son of His promise because he was supernaturally conceived. Abraham accepted that and waited for Isaac to be born.

In Romans 4:18-25, Paul records that as Abraham waited for the birth of Isaac, he "against hope believed in hope, that he might become the father of many nations, according to that which was spoken, So shall thy seed be. And being not weak in faith, he considered not his own body now dead, when he was about a hundred years old, neither yet the deadness of Sarah's womb. He staggered not at the promise of God through unbelief, but was strong in faith, giving glory to God, and being fully persuaded that, what he had promised, he was able also to perform. And therefore it was imputed to him for righteousness. Now it was not written for his sake alone, that it was imputed to him, but for us also, to whom it shall be imputed, if we believe on him that raised up Jesus, our Lord, from the dead; who was delivered for our offenses, and was raised again for our justification."

Romans 4:1-8 shows that salvation comes by faith, not works. Then verses 9-17 show that salvation comes by grace, not law. Now verses 18-25 show that salvation comes through divine power, not human effort. All of those truths are demonstrated in the life of Abraham. There are three realities to notice in this last section: The Analysis of Faith, The Answer to Faith, and The Application of Faith.

Lesson

I. THE ANALYSIS OF FAITH (vv. 18-21)

Beginning in verse 18 and ending with verse 21, Paul strings together a series of phrases that describe the faith of Abraham. Those phrases interlock; each one is unique to itself, yet includes the meaning of the rest. It is important for us to analyze Abraham's faith because we are also saved by faith. By understanding the kind of faith that saved Abraham, we can understand the faith that saves us.

A. Hoped Against Hope (v. 18)

1. The difference between faith and hope (v. 18*a*)

"Who against hope believed in hope."

That is a figure of speech called an *oxymoron*. It uses opposite ideas to convey a thought. An example of an oxymoron is, "The silence was deafening." Paul uses that figure of speech in verse 18: Abraham hoped when there was no hope. Against all human capacity, Abraham believed God.

Hope and faith are different. Hope is the desire for something to happen. Faith is the confidence that it will happen. It didn't make any sense for Abraham to hope when he did. God told him that he would be the father of many nations, and Abraham believed Him.

2. The demonstration of Abraham's faith (v. 18*b*)

"That he might become the father of many nations, according to that which was spoken, So shall thy seed be."

Abraham would have a multitude come from his loins, even when that seemed impossible since he was ninety-nine years old. Genesis 15:5 says that God "brought him [Abraham] forth abroad, and said, Look now toward heaven, and count the stars, if thou be able to number them: and he said unto him, So shall thy seed be." Then Genesis 15:6 says, "And he believed in the Lord."

Abraham hoped against hope. He wanted something to happen, and he believed that it would. And it was twenty-five years of hoping and waiting from the time that he received the original promise of a son until that son came.

B. Was Not Weak in Faith (vv. 19*a*, 20*b*)

"And being not weak in faith. . . . but was strong in faith."

Paul gives us two perspectives, one negative and one positive. Abraham was not weak in faith. The word "weak" means "without strength." It can also mean, "to doubt or hesitate." But Abraham was strong in faith. That wasn't easy for him since he was so old and God had waited twenty-five years to fulfill the promise.

1. The essence of Abraham's confidence

You say, "How could Abraham possibly maintain any faith?" There are some people who have been praying for something in their lives for two or three months, and some for a few years, and they have lost hope that it will ever happen. But Abraham was strong in faith for twenty-five years. That is hard to understand unless you look at God, "whom he believed . . . who giveth life to the dead, and calleth those things which are not, as though they were" (Rom. 4:17). Abraham never lost hope because he believed two things about God: One, that He could create something that didn't exist; and two, that He could revive something that had existed and ceased to exist. He could raise the dead and create out of nothing. When you believe in a God who can do those things, you can be confident that he will do what He says. Abraham had confidence. He believed in the God of creation and resurrection. Those are the two greatest obstacles to man. If God promises you something that didn't exist, or something that had gone out of existence, but you believed that God could bring into existence what doesn't exist and revive what used to exist, then you won't have a problem believing that God will fulfill His promises.

2. The example of Abraham's confidence

a) Affirming the promise

Genesis 17:4-8 says, "As for me, behold, my covenant is with thee, and thou shalt be a father of many nations. Neither shall thy name any more be called Abram, but thy name shall be Abraham; for a father of many nations have I made thee. And I will make thee exceedingly fruitful, and I will make nations of thee, and kings shall come out of thee. And I will establish my covenant between me and thee and thy seed after thee in their generations for an everlasting covenant, to be a God unto thee, and to thy seed after thee. And I will give unto thee, and to thy seed after thee, the land wherein thou are a sojourner, all the land of Canaan, for an everlasting possession; and I will be their God." Abraham trusted in God's marvelous promise and His ability to create out of nothing. It was no problem for God to make him a son.

b) Acting on the promise

Long after Isaac had been born, when God asked Abraham

189

to offer that promised son as a burnt offering, Abraham obeyed. He marched Isaac up the mountain in Moriah with a bundle of sticks on his back that would kindle the fire. When they reached the top, Abraham laid Isaac on the altar, lifted up the knife, and was ready to plunge it into Isaac's heart. You say, "How could he do that?" Abraham believed in the God who could make things out of nothing. God gave Abraham a son when it was not possible. But Abraham was also confident that if Isaac were to die, then he would be raised from the dead. Hebrews 11:17 says, "By faith Abraham, when he was tested, offered up Isaac." Why? Verse 19 says, "Accounting that God was able to raise him up, even from the dead." Abraham's faith was based upon the character of God, who could create something out of nothing and bring back into existence what had ceased to exist.

C. Was Not Discouraged by His Natural Weakness (v. 19b)

"He considered not his own body now dead, when he was about a hundred years old."

Abraham knew he could make no contribution to God's promise, he knew his procreative power had died, and he knew that Sarah was unable to bear children. But he was not discouraged. The word "considered" is *katanoeō* in the Greek, which means, "to fix your mind on, or think about." Abraham thought about the fact that he was "now dead" in respect to producing children. That is a perfect participle in the Greek and it means that he was in a state of deadness. So, Abraham fixed his mind on the reality that he would never be able to produce his son himself. He was impotent.

He could have reasoned like many would when faced with a situation like that and said, "That's it. God blew it. There was a time when I could have fathered a child, but now I'm old and impotent. The promise can't be fulfilled." But that was not a problem for Abraham because he knew his God could make something out of nothing.

There is a fourth phrase that helps us understand Abraham's faith.

D. Was Not Doubtful Due to External Circumstances (v. 19c)

"Neither yet the deadness of Sarah's womb."

Genesis 18:11 says that Sarah was unable to produce a child. Abraham couldn't produce the seed and Sarah couldn't carry a fertilized egg. There seemed to be no hope. But that didn't rob Abraham of his confidence because his faith was fixed.

E. Did Not Vacillate in Doubt (v. 20a)

"He staggered not at the promise of God through unbelief, but was strong in faith."

The word "staggered" is the Greek work *diakrinō,* which means, "to judge between two things." Abraham didn't waver between two opinions; he was strong in faith. Like the psalmist, he could say, "My heart is fixed, O God, my heart is fixed" (Ps. 57:7*a*). Abraham's eyes were filled with the vision of God, who could bring something out of nothing and raise the dead. His own impotence and the deadness of Sarah's womb were not problems.

1. The struggle of Abraham's Faith

At this point you might ask, "Is Abraham human? He doesn't appear to be like us. If that is the kind of faith that saves, who can measure up to that? Who can say that he never wavers in faith against all human inability?" I certainly can't say that, and neither can you. But I don't think that Paul intended us to believe that Abraham never wavered in faith.

a) Rejecting the promise

Genesis 17:15-17 says, "And God said unto Abraham, As for Sarai, thy wife, thou shalt not call her name Sarai, but Sarah [princess] shall her name be. And I will bless her, and give thee a son also of her: yea, I will bless her, and she shall be a mother of nations; kings of people shall be of her. Then Abraham fell upon his face, and laughed, and said in his heart, Shall a child be born unto him that is an hundred years old? And shall Sarah, that is ninety years old, bear?" He knew Sarah had never produced an offspring. So Abraham says, "God, Ishmael is Your only option" (v. 18). I would say that his faith was wavering at that point. It isn't as strong as we would like to think.

b) Reiterating the Promise

You say, "Why did the apostle Paul say that he staggered not at the promise of God?" Genesis 17:19 says, "And God said, Sarah, thy wife, shall bear thee a son indeed; and thou shalt call his name Isaac: and I will establish my covenant with him for an everlasting covenant, and with his seed after him." God reiterated the promise.

2. The strengthening of Abraham's faith

Abraham's faith was wavering, but all faith works through a struggle. The kind of faith that saves is confident. The ultimate end of Abraham's struggle was that he remained confident. There were times when he had to deal with different options, but when he had to have faith, he exercised firm faith. I think the struggle strengthened his faith.

John Calvin said that we are "never so enlightened that there are no remains of ignorance, nor the heart so established that there are no misgivings. With these evils of our nature, faith maintains a perpetual conflict, in which it is often sorely shaken and put to great stress; but still it conquers." Abraham's faith was battered, but in the end it did not waver. James says, "The trial of your faith ultimately brings perfection" (James 1:4). Ultimately, you stop wavering. Abraham worked through the difficulties. He even worked through the folly of thinking that he and Sarah could bring a child into the world without God's help. When the struggles were over, he was unwavering and strong in faith.

F. Gave Glory to God (v. 20c)

"Giving glory to God."

1. Illuminating God's trustworthiness

Faith glorifies God. How? God told Abraham that He would give him a son. If Abraham believes that, then he is affirming that God is trustworthy. God is glorified when you believe Him. If God says, "I'm going to give you a son," but you say, "I don't believe You. I don't think You always keep Your word," then you are not honoring God. That is the significance of 1 John 5:10, "He that believeth not God hath made him a liar." When you make God a liar by not believing Him, that doesn't bring Him glory because He is the God of truth and cannot lie.

2. Illustrating God's trustworthiness

The three Hebrew young men who were with Daniel in Babylonia were called Mishael, Hananiah, and Azariah. They were better known by their Babylonian names: Meshach, Shadrach, and Abednego. In Daniel 3:13, they were brought before the king, who said, "If you don't cease your identification with your God, I will throw you in a fiery furnace" (v. 15). They said, "Our God, whom we serve, is able to deliver us" (v. 17). You say amen to that, but you're not standing in the flames. That furnace was so hot that the men who threw the others in were burned to death (v. 22). But the three Hebrew young men glorified God for His deliverance and power.

Abraham believed God to the point of being ready to drive a knife into the heart of Isaac.

G. Was Fully Persuaded of God's Power and Promise (v. 21)

"And being fully persuaded that, what he had promised, he was able also to perform."

That speaks of the certainty of Abraham's heart. He was fully convinced of God's power. He had complete hope in God, not human resources.

That is the analysis of Abraham's faith. He hoped against hope, he wasn't weak, he wasn't discouraged by his or someone else's impotence, he wasn't wavering, he glorified God, and he lived in full confidence.

II. THE ANSWER TO FAITH (v. 22)

"And therefore it was imputed to him for righteousness."

Abraham did not possess righteousness—only God does. But because of his faith, God gave Abraham righteousness. That is how the transaction works. We believe God and in doing so receive the gift He offers. God gave Abraham righteousness. The ground of his justification was his faith. He believed God, therefore he was made right with God. A person becomes right with God not by performing spiritual activities but by believing what He says and obeying Him.

Abraham, the sinner, was accepted by God and given divine righteousness, which he received through faith. What a great truth! Verse 22 is the heart of Romans 4. How are you made right with God? Through the kind of faith Abraham had.

III. THE APPLICATION OF FAITH (vv. 23-25)

A. The Accessibility of God's Righteousness (vv. 23-24)

"Now it was not written for his sake alone, that it was imputed to him, but for us also, to whom it shall be imputed, if we believe on him that raised up Jesus, our Lord, from the dead."

1. The purpose of Scripture

What does the account of Abraham mean for us? The Bible records things for all of us, not just for those about whom it is recorded. That is one of the purposes of Scripture. Scripture itself tells us that it was not just for the people that lived during the time in which it was written but for the people of all time.

a) Psalm 78:5-7—"For he established a testimony in Jacob, and appointed a law in Israel, which he commanded our fathers, that they should make them known to their children; that the generation to come might know them, even the children who should be born, who should arise and declare them to their children; that they might set their hope in God, and not forget the works of God, but keep his commandments." The commandments are for everybody who ever lived after they were given.

b) Romans 15:4—"For whatever things were written in earlier times were written for our learning, that we, through patience and comfort of the scriptures, might have hope."

c) 1 Corinthians 10:11—"Now all these things happened unto them [the Israelites] for examples, and they are written for our [everyone's] admonition."

We must be vitally concerned with the story of Abraham because it was written so we would know about him and apply what he learned.

2. The performance of faith

   a) The confidence in God

   Romans 4:24 says, "For us also . . . [righteousness] shall be imputed." We will receive righteousness if we believe in the same God that Abraham believed in—the God who is able to raise the dead. But we are not like Abraham, having never seen that power in action; we have seen it in action because we believe in the God who raised up Jesus our Lord from the dead. Our faith is like Abraham's because we too must believe in a God who can make something out of nothing and raise the dead.

   Abraham is the living evidence that the just shall live by faith in the God who raised Jesus Christ from the dead. I believe that Abraham was given a glimpse of the future and saw ahead to the resurrection of Jesus Christ. In John 8:56 Jesus said, "Your father, Abraham, rejoiced to see my day; and he saw it, and was glad." Salvation comes by faith in the God who raised Jesus Christ from the dead.

   b) The condition for salvation

   Romans 4:24 gives a condition: "If we believe on him." That's the condition for salvation. In Romans, there are some sixty references to faith or unbelief. We are saved because we believe in the God of resurrection. And He proved Himself to be just when He raised up Jesus our Lord from the dead.

B. The Affirmation of Christ's Atonement (v. 25)

"[Jesus] was delivered [a judicial term meaning, 'to give someone over to prison, or to trial and punishment'] for our offenses [Gk., *paraptoma,* "sin"], and was raised again for our justification."

If Jesus had never been raised from the dead, we could never have been justified, because God could not have accepted His sacrifice. God raised Jesus from the dead to show that sin had been conquered. It also demonstrated that God was pleased with what Christ did. God raised Him from the dead, lifted Him to His right hand, exalted Him, and said, "You have accomplished salvation." Jesus was raised into the very presence of God as an affirmation that His atoning death had done its work.

The great theologian Charles Hodge said, "With a dead Saviour, a Saviour over whom death had triumphed and held captive, our justification had been for ever impossible. As it was necessary that the high priest, under the old economy, should not only slay the victim at the altar, but carry the blood into the most holy place, and sprinkle it upon the mercy-seat; so it was necessary not only that our great High Priest should suffer in the outer court, but that He should pass into heaven to present His righteousness before God for our justification. Both, therefore, as the evidence of the acceptance of His satisfaction on our behalf, and as a necessary step to secure the application of the merits of His sacrifice, the resurrection of Christ was absolutely essential, even for our justification" (*Commentary on the Epistle to the Romans* [Grand Rapids: Eerdmans, 1886], p. 129). Christ went to the cross, died for our sins, and rose again. We believe in Him who died for us, and was raised from the dead for our justification.

What is the significance of Romans 4 for you? What kind of faith appropriates Christ and brings righteousness? You need hopeful faith, the kind that hopes against hope. You need the kind of faith that says, "I am out of options. I have nothing in myself. My body is dead. I cannot redeem myself; neither can anyone else. I am impotent. Those around me are impotent." Hopeful and humble faith is the kind of faith that says, "I have nothing to offer." That is the kind of faith that was imputed to Abraham as righteousness.

Saving faith is in the right object—the Creator God who raised Christ from the dead. It is an unwavering faith—the faith that fights through the struggle and says, "I believe. I'm convinced." It is not the kind that says, "I believe" but soon disappears when Jesus says something that is not received well. Saving faith is strong. It is also submissive and demonstrates patience. It allows God to be God. And it is selfless and obedient. Abraham left everything and hoped against hope because he believed God. Saving faith is hopeful, humble, strong, confident, submissive, and obedient. We have every reason to put that kind of faith in God because He raised Jesus from the dead. The payment for our sin was made. We are righteous in Christ if we believe in Him.

Focusing on the Facts

1. When God called Abraham, what did He tell him that he would produce? What were Abraham's circumstances at the time (see p. 184)?

2. How was Abraham able to believe God in spite of his circumstances (see p. 184)?

3. What were some of the tests that Abraham faced when he arrived in Canaan (see p. 185)?

4. What was the problem that Abraham faced because of the meaning of his name (see p. 185)?

5. What was Sarah's solution to Abraham's problem? What resulted (see p. 186)?

6. Explain how Ishmael and Isaac represent the contrast between divine power and human effort (see p. 186).

7. What is the difference between faith and hope (see p. 188)?

8. What two things did Abraham believe about God? Why did those things give Abraham confidence in God (see Rom. 4:17; pp. 189-90)?

9. Why was Abraham willing to kill Isaac, even though he knew he would be killing the fulfillment of God's promise (see p. 190)?

10. What did Abraham realize about his own ability to contribute to the fulfillment of God's promise (see p. 190)?

11. What does Paul mean when he says that Abraham "staggered not" (see Rom. 4:20a; p. 191)?

12. Give an example of a situation when Abraham's faith wavered. What was God's response (see Gen. 17:15-19; pp. 191-92)?

13. What strengthened Abraham's faith (see p. 191)?

14. What does believing in God's promises say about God Himself (see p. 192)?

15. How did Shadrach, Meshach, and Abednego give glory to God (see Dan. 3:15; p. 192)?

16. Why did God give Abraham righteousness (see p. 193)?

17. What is one of the purposes of Scripture according to Romans 4:23-24? Support your answer with other verses (see p. 193).

18. How is our faith like the faith of Abraham (see p. 194)?

19. What is the condition for salvation, according to Romans 4:24 (see p. 194)?

20. Why did God raise Jesus from the dead (see pp. 194-95)?

Pondering the Principles

1. Isaac and Ishmael provide a perfect illustration of the contrast between divine power and human effort. How much of your life is spent in performing activities by your own effort rather than by God's power? Give some examples of activities you have performed by your own effort and those you have performed by God's power. What were the results? Read Galatians 4:21-31. What was Paul's conclusion in verse 31? Read Galatians 5:1, 13-26. According to Paul, how is the Christian to live? According to verse 16, what should a Christian do so that he will not live by his own effort? According to verse 17, what is happening in your life when you are trying to live under your own power? What is the fruit of the Spirit? That fruit is the result of living a life under the divine power of God. Make the commitment today to allow God to have control of your daily activities.

2. Romans 4:18 says that Abraham "against hope believed in hope."

What was he hoping for? What did he base his hope on? What are some of the things you are hoping for? Is your hope based on the Bible or your own feelings? Abraham had a reason to hope because God gave him a promise. Based on 1 John 3:1-3, what are you hoping for? How long have you been waiting? Abraham waited for twenty-five years to see his son Isaac, and he was only the beginning of the fulfillment of God's promise. According to verse 3, what is the result of your hoping? Thank God that He will one day fulfill all His promises to you.

3. Since you became a Christian, how has your faith grown? What made it grow? Abraham struggled with his faith on many occasions, but it became stronger. What are some of the things that have strengthened your faith? Read James 1:2-8. What kind of attitude should you have when you are faced with struggles? Why? What will be the result as you patiently endure through those struggles? If you don't know how to respond during a trial, what should you do? By following the instruction of James, you will become even stronger in your faith.

4. How has your faith glorified God in the past? How is your faith glorifying God right now? Have there been times in your life when your lack of faith has caused others to think evil of God? Name some. Is there a present situation you are not trusting God in? Why are you showing a lack of faith? How is that affecting those around you? Read 1 Corinthians 10:31-33. What is the purpose of your life? What benefit does Paul say is a result of glorifying God? If you are not glorifying God in some activity, you are being disobedient. Confess your sin, repent of it, and begin to fulfill God's design for your life.

Scripture Index

Genesis
3:15   74, 141
6:8   106, 156
11:27   127
11:31-32   128
12:1, 4   119-20, 127
12:1-3   127, 172-73
12:3   173-74
12:4, 5   128, 129
12:6-7   128
12:8   128
12:10   185
12:10-20   129
12:11-20   185
13:2   185
13:5-9   185
15:1   185
15:5, 6   188
15:6   119
15:9, 10, 12, 17 175
15:18-21   173
16:1-16   129
17:4-8   189
17:5   140
17:9-14   157-58, 164
17:15-17, 18 191
17:18   186
17:19   191
17:24-25   164
18:11   190
19:26   129
22:13   174
22:17   140, 173, 184
23:4   130
23:6   129
26:5   115

Exodus
3:16   126

19:8   108
23:7   77
33:12   106
34:6-7   152
34:7   76

Leviticus
16:21-22   149

Deuteronomy
6:4   103
30:6   165
32:4   77

Joshua
1:8   85
5:2-5   164-65
7:19   67
24:2   127

Ruth
1:16   104
4:6-13   51

I Kings
8:46-53   43-44
18:36   126

2 Chronicles
20:7   126

Job
9:2   25, 41
9:3-20   25-26
9:20   146
25:4   42
27:10   89
33:26   122

Psalm
32:1-2, 3, 4 147
42:1   85
42:1-3   85-86
49:7-8   78

51:1-4	86
51:17	88
57:7	191
73:25	85
78:5-7	193
78:38	65
84:1-4	148
89:14	77
103:12	149
115:1	57
119:126	107
119:142	31
130:3	43
130:3-4	151-52
143:2	43

Proverbs

28:13	86

Isaiah

41:8	115, 126
42:8	143
45:5, 21-23	57
45:5-6	103
45:8	30
45:22	103
53:4 5	121
53:5, 10	151
55:1	50
61:10	47
64:6	30, 43, 143

Jeremiah

4:3-4	166
8:8	107
9:24-26	166
42:2-6	44
42:7	44
42:20-22	44

Daniel

3:13, 15, 17, 22	192
9:7	31
9:24	122

Hosea

3:1-2	156

Joel

2:32	10

Amos

5:21-23	34

Jonah

4:2	104

Micah

6:6-7	29, 42, 122
7:18	65

Habakkuk

1:13	65, 76
2:4	106, 116
2:19-20	103

Malachi

2:17	65

Matthew

5:3-4, 6-7	87
5:17	108
5:20	31, 108
5:48	108, 144
6:33	58
7:16	84
7:22-23	83
7:23	85
9:12	146
10:29	148
10:37	85
12:44	12
12:45	12
13:1-8	81
13:5, 7	36
13:8	84, 90
13:20, 22	36
16:24	88
19:16	42, 81
19:16-22	81-82
20:1-16	145
23:27	81
24:45	99
25:1-13	82-83
27:24	17

Mark

4:26-29	90
8:31	77
9:12	77
12:30	85
16:15	105

Luke

2:32	30
3:10	42

9:22	77	20:21	12
10:25	42	24:25	83
12:6	148		
15:11-32	87	**Romans**	
15:14	49	1:5	11, 37, 60
17:25	77	1:16, 17	29
18:10-14	79	1:17	116
John		1:18	27, 77
1:9	30	1:21	82
1:11-13	134	2:2-3	27
1:12	99	2:4	64
1:29	149	2:11-12	27-28
3:3, 6	99	2:12	157
6:28	42	2:17-20, 24	82
6:37	48	2:25	167
6:56, 66	45	2:28-29	167
6:66	14	3:1	157
8:12	30	3:9	27
3:30-32	36	3:10-20	28
8:31	14, 134	3:12	143
8:37, 40	83	3:19	45, 106
8:44	168	3:20	34, 43, 45, 108, 143
8:56	141, 174, 194	3:20-21	29
14:5	42	3:21	29, 33, 45, 122
14:6	105	3:21-25	25, 27, 41, 61
14:28	74	3:21-31	72, 115
14:29-30	75	3:22	38
14:31	75	3:22-23	47-48
15:24	82	3:22-24	8
16:8	83	3:22, 25, 26, 28	81
17:4	61	3:23	49
19:19	17	3:24	49-51
19:30	46	3:24-25	62, 73
20:28	10	3:25	51, 61-63, 78
		3:26	66
Acts		3:27	78-79, 131
2:36	10	3:28	9, 33, 80-81
2:37	41	3:29-30	104
4:12	105	3:31	9, 107
9:6	42	4:1	118
9:16	77	4:1-8	117
13:39	47-48	4:2	79, 118
14:14-18	64	4:2-3	35
15:1	158	4:3	106, 120, 137, 156, 171
15:5	172	4:4	142-44
16:1-3	164	4:5	32, 35, 80, 146
16:16, 17	42	4:6	33
16:30	41		
17:30-31	64		

4:6-8	147, 163	3:21-23	175
4:7-8	35, 148	6:17	100
4:9	163	8:5	104
4:10	163-64	10:11	193
4:11	47, 98, 164-67	10:31	58
4:12	168, 178	12:3	10-11
4:13	122, 172	15:1-2	133
4:14	177	15:3-8	133
4:15	33, 177-78	15:10	81
4:16	156, 171		
4:17	173, 179, 188	**2 Corinthians**	
4:18	188	4:4	30
4:18-25	188	5:17	13, 101, 132
4:19, 20	188-91	5:18	74
4:20-22	36	5:21	52, 77, 98
4:21	192-93	7:9, 10	86-87
4:22	193		
4:23-24	193	**Galatians**	
4:24	194	1:8	134
4:25	194-95	2:16	48, 80
5:1	36, 80	2:16, 21	33
5:6	146	2:20	101
5:8-10	74	2:21	50
5:17	98	3:1, 2, 17, 18	176-77
5:19	99	3:6-9	119, 140
6:17	37	3:7	114
6:23	51, 76	3:8, 11	80
7:7	28	3:8-9	174
7:7, 9-12	178	3:9	127
7:13	108	3:10-11	33
7:15	86	3:10-14	176
7:17	102	3:16	141, 174
8:2	102	3:17	176
8:3	80	3:24	99, 108, 178
8:3-4	108-9	3:26	99, 119
8:7	85	3:27	100
8:17	175	3:28-29	100
10:9	10, 80	3:29	174
10:9-10	46-47	4:4	30
10:17	47	4:5-6, 7	100-101
11:6	142	4:6	88-89
11:36	144	4:9	18
14:17	18	4:10-11	18
15:4	193	4:21-23, 24	187
		5:1	18
1 Corinthians		5:1-4, 6-7	159
1:26-31	78	6:12-13	159
2:12	90		
2:14	16	**Ephesians**	
		1:3	100

1:14	144
2:1-3	13
2:4, 8-9	13
2:4-5	32
2:8	33, 47
2:8-9	36, 79, 156
2:8-10	33
2:10	13
4:5-6	106
4:13	90

Philippians

1:6	91
1:20	88
1:29	52
2:5-11	60
2:9-11	78
3:2	152
3:3	168
3:4-5	158
3:5-6	49, 177
3:7	131
3:7-9	102
3:8-9	34, 177

Colossians

1:13	74
1:16	57, 144
1:20	14
1:21-22	14
1:23	14
2:3	15
2:8	15
2:9	16
2:10	14, 21
2:11	17
2:12	17, 52
2:14	17
2:14-15	17
2:16	17-18
2:16-17	17-18
2:18	18-19
2:18-19	19
2:20-21	20
2:21-23	20-21

1 Thessalonians

1:9	135
1:10	73
5:8	136

2 Thessalonians

2:13-16	136

1 Timothy

1:9	146
1:12-15	146
1:15	49
2:5-6	105
2:6	51

2 Timothy

1:8-10	33
2:12	10

Titus

2:11-13	11
2:13-14	74
2:14	11
3:4-5	34
3:5	132

Hebrews

1:3	78
9:1-9	150
9:5	51
9:6-8	52
9:11-12	52
9:11-15	150
9:12	31
9:24-26	151
10:1	151
10:4	34, 77
10:12	78
10:14	31
11:1	130
11:8	119
11:9, 10	120
11:10	130, 173
11:13	129
11:17, 19	190
11:17-18, 19	120
11:19	179
12:1	47, 107
12:2	47

James

1:4	192
1:17, 18	132
2:10	108
2:14-26	107
2:17	36

203

2:23	126	2:12	149
4:4	90	2:12-13	91
4:6	88	2:15	90
		3:1	99
1 Peter		3:2	102
1:18-19	51	3:10	14
1:23	90, 99	3:14	89
2:25	135	4:7-8	89
4:18	146	5:4-5	90
2 Peter		2 John	
1:1	122	10-11	134
1:4	101	Jude	
2:5	146	14-15	146-47
2:15	83	Revelation	
1 John		16:9, 11, 21	84
1:8-10	87	19:10	20
2:3-5	91	22:9	20

Moody Press, a ministry of the Moody Bible Institute, is designed for education, evangelization, and edification. If we may assist you in knowing more about Christ and the Christian life, please write us without obligation: Moody Press, c/o MLM, Chicago, Illinois 60610.